# SUETONIUS

## GALBA, OTHO, VITELLIUS

*Edited with Introduction and Notes by*

**Charles L. Murison**

University of Western Ontario

**Published by Bristol Classical Press**

General Editor: John H. Betts

# For Kenneth Wellesley

First published in 1992 by
Bristol Classical Press
an imprint of
Gerald Duckworth & Co. Ltd
The Old Piano Factory
48 Hoxton Square, London N1 6PB

A catalogue record for this book is available from the British Library

ISBN 1-85399-120-1

Printed in Great Britain by
Billing and Sons Ltd, Worcester

# Contents

# *Preface*

The primary purpose of this Commentary is to enable anglophone students of Latin in the upper forms of schools and in colleges and universities to understand the value of Suetonius as an historical source for the turbulent sequence of events which occurred between the spring of A.D. 68, when C. Iulius Vindex began in Gaul a rebellion against Nero, and the latter part of December, 69, when supporters of Vespasian captured Rome and killed Vitellius, thus bringing about the fourth imperial accession in the space of just over one year. References are also given to the other major sources for this period, especially the *Histories* of Tacitus, Plutarch's *Lives* of Galba and Otho, and the surviving epitomes and fragments of Dio Cassius (an English translation is supplied for actual quotations from Plutarch and Dio). The aim is to provide a coherent and reasonable explanation for the policies and strategies of the participants in these events.

The Commentary is *mainly* historical, though major textual cruces are considered briefly, as are points of especial syntactical difficulty. Although a basic Bibliography is attached to the Introduction, my aim in the Commentary has been to make references to modern works intelligible where they occur – to avoid obliging the reader to flip back and forth to and from a master list of 'works cited'. The emphasis is inevitably on works in English (and, to a lesser extent, French); however, references are provided to major works in other languages, especially German.

I should like to acknowledge the debt of gratitude I owe to my Canadian colleagues Douglas Gerber and Ivars Avotins for countless items of advice and assistance; to my students Patricia Wilson and Todd Pedersen for acting as 'guinea-pigs' and also for comment and eagle-eyed proof reading; to Kit Hargin-Reilly for producing a splendid typescript; to Geoffrey Lewis, for treating my wilder theories with an appropriate but humane scepticism; but most of all to Kenneth Wellesley, who first inspired my interest in this period: as a small thank-offering for over thirty years of teaching, advice and friendship, this book is respectfully dedicated to him.

Londonii Canadensium,                                                C.L.M.
Id. Mart. MCMLXXXIX

# Introduction

Suetonius is a popular author today and always has been: in the Introduction to his Teubner edition of 1908, M. Ihm mentions the calculation of J. von Gruber (1834) that between the years 1470 and 1829 there had been over two hundred editions of the *Lives of the Caesars*; and there does not seem to have been much falling-off in scholarly interest in the latter part of the nineteenth century. However, in the twentieth century things have been rather different – especially among English-speaking scholars – until very recently.

Although there has been, in the years since the Second World War, a steady trickle of monographs on various aspects of Suetonius' life and work from continental scholars (see, for example, the studies by Steidle, della Corte, D'Anna, Mouchová, Gugel and, most recently, de Coninck and Gascou listed in the bibliography attached to this Introduction), it was as recently as 1983 that the first full-length study in English devoted to Suetonius made its appearance. By an odd but not unparalleled coincidence *two* books appeared in that year, B. Baldwin's *Suetonius* and A. Wallace-Hadrill's *Suetonius – The Scholar and his Caesars*; and in 1987 yet another study in English was published, R.C. Lounsbury's *The Arts of Suetonius – An Introduction*. Beyond this, of course, there have been shorter essays of importance; and since the publication in 1952 by Marec and Pflaum of an inscription from Hippo Regius in N. Africa bearing on the career of Suetonius (*CRAI* [1952] 76-85) there has been prolonged and lively, though ultimately inconclusive, debate about the details of his life and the administrative posts which he occupied. Given all this scholarly activity and the heightened interest in Suetonius in the English-speaking world, K.R. Bradley was fully justified in giving to a recent article the title 'The Rediscovery of Suetonius' (*CP* 80 [1985] 254-65).

Of course, beyond the world of scholarship, popular enthusiasm for Suetonius has always remained at a high level and is particularly lively at present. Television series, films and novels dealing especially with the Julio-Claudian period have created a picture of the Roman Principate which probably owes more to Suetonius than to any other source. And it is at the level of this *National Enquirer* approach to ancient history that much of Suetonius' popular appeal undoubtedly operates.

While this element of human interest is undeniable, this was certainly *not* Suetonius' principal reason for undertaking the imperial biographies. The fact that the *Divus Iulius* and the *Augustus* are by far the longest of the *Lives* has given rise to elaborate theories connected with the presumed course of Suetonius' own life, about which we know almost nothing concrete: specifically, his dismissal from the post of imperial secretary (*ab epistulis*) in A.D. 122 is thought to have involved an end to his access to the state archives, so that the *Lives* of emperors who ruled after Augustus do not show as much detail nor, especially, do they quote *verbatim* from documents such as the emperors' correspondence (except for quotations from the letters of Augustus, which had, presumably, been examined earlier while Suetonius still had access to the archives). In addition, it has been suggested that he began to grow weary of the project, so that the later *Lives* are brief and even perfunctory; on this see, for example, G.B. Townend in T.A. Dorey (ed.), *Latin Biography* 90-1.

What has emerged most clearly from the scholarship of the last decade or so is that Suetonius had a clear and definite idea of what the Principate was about and of the talents which an emperor should possess (oratorical and literary skill, for example), and of how he should behave with regard to various social groups, military affairs, the provision of largesse, games, spectacles and public works, and the administration of justice. A major part, therefore, of Suetonius' task was to illustrate the extent to which each individual emperor conformed, or failed to conform, to the imperial ideal; see especially A. Wallace-Hadrill, *Suetonius – The Scholar and his Caesars*, chapters 5-8; J. Gascou, *Suétone Historien* 717-73; K.R. Bradley, 'Imperial Virtues in Suetonius' *Caesares*', *JIES* 4 (1976) 245-53; 'The Significance of the *spectacula* in Suetonius' *Caesares*', *RSA* 11 (1981) 129-37; F. Millar, *The Emperor in the Roman World* 203-72.

Since the seizure of supreme power and its consolidation in the form of the Principate represented the work and the achievement of Julius Caesar and Augustus, it naturally follows that these are the longest, the most carefully researched and the most elaborate of the *Lives*. The subsequent *Lives* are, inevitably, less detailed; as K.R. Bradley puts it: 'Suetonius is a selective, not a comprehensive reporter, and it must follow that in all the *Lives* Suetonius included no more, and no less, than what he considered appropriate for the purpose at hand. Once adherence to or deviation from the ideal had been exemplified in each *Life*, with the necessary information all set in the framework dictated by genre, that purpose had been served and embellishment was unnecessary' (*CP* 80 [1985] 263). Furthermore, the question of access to the archives now seems less important than it did a few years ago: letters of Augustus appear to have been generally available to scholars (cf. A. Wallace-Hadrill, *Suetonius* 91-6; B. Baldwin, *Suetonius* 47-9) and Suetonius' use of archive material appears somewhat haphazard anyway (cf. L. de Coninck, *Suetonius en de Archivalia* 213-15; 218-19), so that Suetonius' dismissal from the post of *ab epistulis* may well have no bearing at all on the length of, or detail contained within, any specific *Life*. Indeed, there is now no compelling reason to doubt that, when we are told that Suetonius dedicated his imperial biographies to the praetorian prefect C. Septicius Clarus (Lyd. *De Mag.* 2.6), an event which clearly happened before they both fell from grace (SHA *Hadr.* 11.3), the reference is to all the *Lives* and not just those of, say, Julius Caesar and Augustus (cf. G. Alföldy, *ZPE* 36 [1979] 233-53, espec. 251-3). On the other hand, Sir Ronald Syme has recently suggested that the first chapter of the *Life* of Galba was the concluding paragraph of Nero's biography: the *Lives* from Julius Caesar to Nero were the original design (and were dedicated to Septicius Clarus). *Galba* to *Domitian* represent a sequel, composed after Suetonius' enforced retirement (*Hermes* 109 [1981] 105-17, espec. 115-17).

If there has, then, been recent scholarly progress on the question of Suetonius' aims in the *Caesares,* there is little, if any, agreement on his merits as a literary artist. Indeed, since the latter part of the nineteenth century at least, the majority of writers on Latin literature have tended to regard the words 'Suetonian style' as an oxymoron! 'Sueton schreibt farblos' (Norden); 'Ma un vero scrittore non è. È uno studioso' (Funaioli; cf. Wallace-Hadrill: 'It is the business-like style of the ancient scholar'). Even more deadly is the idea that in the *Caesares* Suetonius is no more than a scissor-and-paste man and that his 'style' is no more than the style of his various sources ('succubo delle fonti' – G. D'Anna). Furthermore, from the idea that 'the style is the man' a picture has emerged of Suetonius as a dry-as-dust, shy, retiring, scholarly (?) bureaucrat – in the memorable phrase of R.C. Lounsbury, 'a...dim, dull, pallid, papyrus-pushing Bob Cratchit' (*CJ* 82 [1987] 160; for the quotations above, see Lounsbury's *The Arts of Suetonius* chapter 1 and nn.). And even those scholars who do admire

Suetonius' narrative technique tend to have negative things to say about his style: for example, G.B. Townend analyses sensitively and sympathetically Suetonius' account of Nero's death (*Nero* 47.3-49.1), but in the same essay he says: '...the disjointed and staccato language of Suetonius is often displeasing and sometimes actually incomprehensible to the reader, when so much of an anecdote has been pared away that the point is lost' (T.A. Dorey [ed.], *Latin Biography* 93-6; cf. 92; see also the comments of F.R.D. Goodyear in E.J. Kenney and W.V. Clausen [eds], *The Cambridge History of Classical Literature* II, 662-3).

In general, modern readers must approach with extreme caution ancient writers who use the 'plain style'; in fact, it is easy to fall into the error of supposing that such authors have no style at all! Caesar (in whom Suetonius was deeply interested) is perhaps the outstanding example of this style in Latin and he is wholly insidious. In the *de bello Gallico*, for example, very rarely can Caesar be convicted of misrepresentation of *fact*; however, by means of subtle changes of emphasis, omission of apparently minor details and slight re-arrangement of material, he manages to control the impression created in the reader's mind. (On this aspect of Caesar, see M.L.W. Laistner, *The Greater Roman Historians* 36-44.) We should always remember that it was to this 'artless' Suetonius that Pliny, in urging him to publish something, said: *perfectum opus absolutumque est, nec iam splendescit lima sed atteritur* (*Ep.* 5.10.3). A writer using the 'plain style' does not dash off his work; he writes, revises and writes again: the hard part is to make it all look easy (for which the Latin is, of course, *ars est celare artem*). A useful and often enlightening exercise is to take almost any sentence where Suetonius is describing the actions of an emperor, or a policy or an event, and analyse its content *word by word*, considering not only the information conveyed, but also the precise choice of expression (why this word and not that word?), the relative emphasis produced by position and by word-order generally and, finally, the *emotional* content of adjectives and adverbs (for an example, see below *G.* 14.3, n. on *quosdam... condemnavit*).

The more one attempts to fathom Suetonius, the more elusive he becomes. Readers nowadays are thoroughly conditioned to divide literature into various genres; and so Suetonius' *Caesares* are automatically dumped into a pigeon-hole labelled 'biography'. This gives hostile modern critics the opportunity to castigate Suetonius further for his 'failure' to conform to the various norms of ancient (i.e.,

Hellenistic, overtly moralising) biography. We must therefore ask what it was, exactly, that Suetonius was producing in the *Caesares*. Wallace-Hadrill's recent answer is perhaps surprising: 'Negatively Suetonius wrote not-history; positively he wrote scholarship' (*Suetonius* 10; see further, 8-25). R.G. Lewis, in an important essay entitled 'Suetonius' *Caesares* and their literary antecedents' (forthcoming in *ANRW* II 33,5), argues that there were Latin rather than Greek models for the major divisions into which the *Lives* naturally fall (birth, family background, life up till accession; conduct as Emperor; last days, death, general description) and that, in fact, 'no traditional genre or concept of "biography" had fully emerged by Suetonius' day to which he might otherwise have been constrained to conform'.

If, then, even the genre is not clear, what is it that the modern reader wants from Suetonius? In other words, why do we read him today? This is a thoroughly pertinent question to raise in the introduction to a commentary on the *Lives* of Galba, Otho and Vitellius, when we have the very much fuller *Histories* of Tacitus (for A.D. 69, with flashbacks to major events in 68) and also Plutarch's *Lives* of Galba and Otho, which are considerably longer than those of Suetonius.

One answer, less important perhaps than the others, lies in a personal reaction to the sort of criticism which attacks Suetonius because he is a biographer and not a historian, because he is fond of anecdotes and is less restrained in the telling of them than others and because his focus is kept rigidly upon the subject of his biography, and which then proceeds to denigrate the actual historical information which he does provide. See, for example, V.M. Scramuzza, *The Emperor Claudius* (Cambridge, Mass., 1940) 26: 'It is difficult to say whether Suetonius wrote the *Lives of the Caesars* as serious history, or light biography, or with some other end in view. A rhetor by profession and instinct, he is always ready to sacrifice historical accuracy to stylistic virtuosity. Constantly striving after effect he creates figures that are vivid and colorful, but like no human being ever seen.' Criticism such as this (and there is much more in like vein) is best countered by a detailed examination of what Suetonius actually says. If he is as sloppy and inaccurate as Scramuzza alleges, his failings should show up particularly clearly in the *Lives* of Galba and Otho, and, to a lesser extent, of Vitellius, because of the important surviving parallel accounts mentioned above. In general, an examination of these sources makes it hard to justify this sort of attack on Suetonius: in places he is certainly guilty of extreme compression (as in his account of the disturbance caused by Otho's Praetorian Guard, where he pares away 'unnecessary' detail and eliminates altogether the banquet which Otho gave for eighty senators and their wives; see pp. 112-15); again, in some places he seems prepared to quote his sources from memory, especially where the topic is of less interest to him (e.g. the details of Vitellius' arrangement of his forces for the invasion of Italy; see p. 151) and this can lead him into inaccuracy; and certainly he has his prejudices and perhaps even psychological quirks (cf. T.F. Carney, *PACA* 11 [1968] 7-24). On the other hand, there is no difficulty in seeing the subjects of these *Lives* as consistent and integrated personalities. Galba is not very sympathetically handled (cf. *G.* 14.1 nn.), but the picture we get of the aged *vir militaris* – hopelessly out of touch with the realities of his position in January, 69, reacting to events rather as would the modern stereotype of a retired Indian Army colonel and yet facing his final ordeal like a true soldier – ultimately arouses our pity and certainly rings true. The picture of Otho, ostensibly the greatest villain of the three emperors, is heightened not only by the nobility of his end but also by an apparent admiration which Suetonius has some difficulty in suppressing (see pp. 122-3): his character was obviously the most complex of the three and for ancient theories of a fixed personality it was almost impossible to explain (for Suetonius' difficulties, see *O.* 12.1, nn.). And even Vitellius, the least complicated and interesting of the emperors of 69, in spite of being *vel praecipue luxuriae saevitiaeque deditus* (*Vit.* 13.1), is still possessed of a certain crude geniality and even has a sense of humour (cf. espec. *Vit.* 13.2). These emperors, then, emerge as individuals and certainly not as mere 'types'.

Another reason for using Suetonius as a vehicle for the study of the period 68-9 is the difference of viewpoint which he affords. The great bulk of the work on this period done in recent years (and since the mid-nineteenth century generally) has concentrated on Tacitus and the *Histories* – justifiably so, since Tacitus is by far the most important single source and even a commentary on Suetonius must make constant reference to the *Histories*. The result of this, however, is a 'Tacitean' view of the period: what Tacitus says comes to be regarded as the norm and any information in our other sources which differs from what he says is a variation or even a 'deviation' from this norm. Methodologically, of course, for the historian such a method of proceeding is highly suspect: Tacitus is probably the most reliable of our sources, but he too has his prejudices and hobby horses (e.g., military indiscipline, senatorial dislike of the Principate, social snobbery) and he is not above suppressing material on grounds of taste (e.g., the detail about Galba's head; see *G.* 20.2 nn.) or even in order to give his narrative artistic shape (e.g., the question of the three [?] attempted abdications by Vitellius; see *Vit.* 15.2-4 nn.). Suetonius was, of course, an *eques* – a civil servant and a scholar. He is not jaundiced about the Principate and his attitude towards it is certainly different from that of the senatorial historian. This does not, however, imply wholesale acceptance of the idea of a doggedly 'equestrian viewpoint', seen at every turn by F. della Corte in *Svetonio, Eques Romanus* [Milano/Varese, 1958], especially 173-201; for criticisms of this view, see G.B. Townend, *JRS* 49 [1959] 202-3; B. Mouchová *ZJKF* 8 [1966] 5-8. For instance, we may see examples of bureaucratic precision in Suetonius' figure for the size of the equestrian commission established by Galba to recover most of Nero's excessively large gifts (*G.* 15.1 nn.) and for Vitellius' consular designations *in decem annos* (*Vit.* 11.2 n.); his legal interest can be seen in his remarks on Galba's treatment of the jury panels (*G.* 14.3), and in his careful use of correct legal terminology concerning Otho's divorce (*O.* 3.2), Otho's land transactions when appointed an *arbiter* (*O.* 4.2) and in Vitellius' threat of action for *calumnia* and his *formula iniuriarum* (*Vit.* 7.2).

Finally, in approaching the crisis of 68-9 through Suetonius' *Lives* of Galba, Otho and Vitellius, we can avoid the possible pitfall of seeing this period in isolation from the earlier history of the Principate. It is all too easy to read the *Histories* of Tacitus (and Plutarch's *Galba* and *Otho* too, since these are not complete *Lives* but sections of a continuous narrative) as a complete and independent unit, since Tacitus himself, starting on 1st January, 69, gives us all the background we need to follow the action. However, with the *Life* of Galba Suetonius takes us back not only to the beginnings of the Principate (*G.* 1) but even further, to the Republic and the rôle of the Sulpicii Galbae in the turbulent history of the second and first centuries B.C. With the *Lives* of Otho and Vitellius we are made aware of the great changes which came about in Roman society and government as a result of the Augustan revolution, and in the background history of the families of Otho and Vitellius we see the emergence of the new 'nobility' of the Julio-Claudian period. By the time we reach 68 in each *Life*, then, we are aware of the types of issue which came together to form the crisis of 68-9 (e.g., the arbitrary nature of the Principate, the characters of the emperors, the rôles of favourites and freedmen, the feelings of desperation among 'opposition groups', the dissatisfaction of the various armies and their commanders) and we are prepared for the part which each of the three emperors was to play in its dénouement.

Regarding the sources for this period, there were major works, now lost, by Cluvius Rufus, Fabius Rusticus and Pliny the Elder which underlie our extant accounts. My view is that Pliny the Elder's *Historiae a fine Aufidi Bassi was* probably the so-called 'common source' for this period. (On this highly controversial topic, see the masterly discussion of R. Syme, *Tacitus* 176-90 and App. 29, 32, 76, 77.) Beyond that, however, the greatest caution is necessary. I do not accept the proposition that our extant authors used only one or two sources in writing their accounts and that all variations or alternatives to be found in their works are copied *holus bolus* from earlier accounts now lost: this is, as W.W. Tarn put it (*Alexander the Great II* 306-7), '...the well-known belief that no writer we possess can ever have done any work himself, but always had it done for him by some unknown predecessor who has perished without trace.' Also, although we know of monographs by Herennius Senecio (on Helvidius Priscus), Ti. Claudius Pollio (on L. Annius Bassus), Julius Secundus (on Otho), Pompeius Planta (on the Bedriacum campaign?) and memoirs by Vespasian, Mucianus, Marius Celsus (probably: see Syme, *Tacitus* 683) and perhaps also by Suetonius Paulinus and Vestricius Spurinna (and memoirs, especially, are likely to have been thoroughly self-serving), any or all of which an intelligent and perceptive student such as Pliny the Elder, or Tacitus, or Suetonius, may have used, we should never exclude from our consideration of sources information acquired by our extant authorities directly (or indirectly) from the personal recollections of acquaintances and friends. For example, Pliny the Younger was a friend of Tacitus (*Ep.* 6.16 and 20 provide the latter with information on the eruption of Vesuvius in 79 for the *Histories*) and a patron of Suetonius: through him both Tacitus and Suetonius may have met or obtained information about 68-69 from Verginius Rufus and Vestricius Spurinna. Suetonius certainly had information also from his father (see *O*. 10.1) and Plutarch visited the north of Italy in the company of his patron L. Mestrius Florus (*O.* 14.2-3). Sources of this type are usually undetectable and make nonsense of any attempt to expound in detail the origin of each and every variant in our extant accounts (for probable traces of such material see, for example, pp. 81, 98-9, 104, 122, 126, 160, 166-7).

We should also consider the possibility that Suetonius used (or had at least read, and may have remembered details of) Plutarch's *Lives of the Caesars* and Tacitus' *Histories*. Plutarch probably wrote these *Lives* soon after the death of Domitian (see R. Syme, *MH* 37 [1980] 106-8); Suetonius himself wrote works in Greek (cf. Schanz-Hosius-Krüger *III*[3] [1922] 58, 61) and there is no reason to assume that he would not have examined carefully a series of *Lives* which covered much of his area of biographical interest. (C.P. Jones, *Plutarch and Rome* 62, even suggests that he may have got the idea of writing a series of imperial biographies from Plutarch.) As for the *Histories*, the likelihood that Suetonius had at least read them seems all the greater: as a protégé of Pliny the Younger, the friend of Tacitus, it is hard to imagine Suetonius being unaware of this work. However, it is quite impossible to *prove* that at any point in these *Lives* Suetonius is actually correcting what Tacitus had said in the *Histories*, though we may occasionally suspect it (e.g., pp. 70, 124-5, 126, 158).

Finally, with regard to the non-literary material surviving from the period 68-9, a similar note of caution is necessary. Coins, especially, were issued in this period *mainly* for purposes of propaganda, and although a representative selection of these issues certainly survives, the *interpretation* of them (especially the anonymous issues from Spain and Gaul) is extremely difficult and is almost always, unfortunately, subjective rather than objective (on this topic, see further C.H.V. Sutherland, *JRS* 49 [1959] 46-55). The survival of inscriptions is probably much more haphazard than that of coins and there is nothing to suggest that what we have from the period is anything more than a random sample. Again, similar caution is necessary if the inscription is an official document of any sort and with regard to private funerary inscriptions we should always remember Dr Johnson's dictum that 'In lapidary inscriptions a man is not upon his oath.' The most important series of inscriptions from this period is the *Acta Fratrum Arvalium*, but these not only reflect 'official truth' (see, most fatuously, the entry for 14th March, 69), but are frequently very fragmentary: more than one reconstruction is therefore possible and here too caution is necessary. Lastly, papyri. In many ways these are subject to the same drawbacks as inscriptions, with the added difficulty that they are all from the Nile valley. However, there are few of importance for the study of this period.

In the preparation of my commentary, I have frequently referred to those of P. Venini (1977), G.W. Mooney (1930), C. Hofstee (1898) and G. Baumgarten-Crusius (Turin ed., 1824). The text is based on that of M. Ihm's Teubner edition of 1908, with considerable changes in orthography, punctuation and paragraphing. The texts of other ancient authors cited are as follows: Tacitus (Teubner, ed. Koestermann); Plutarch's *Lives* (Teubner, rev. ed. by Ziegler); Josephus, Philostratus, Dio (LCL); Aurelius Victor (Teubner, ed. Pichlmayr; Eutropius: Teubner, ed. Dietsch; Orosius: ed. Zangemeister [1967 repr. of 1882 edn., Wien]). The most readily available English translations of the *Lives* of Galba, Otho and Vitellius are those by J.C. Rolfe in the Loeb series and by Robert Graves in the Penguin Classics.

# Basic Bibliography

## Suetonius

Alföldy, G., 'Marcius Turbo, Septicius Clarus und die Historia Augusta', *ZPE* 36 (1979) 233-53

Anna, G. d', *Le idee letterarie di Suetonio*, Firenze, 1954

Baldwin, B., 'Suetonius, birth, disgrace and death', *AClass* 18 (1975) 61-70

Baldwin, B., 'Was Suetonius disgraced?', *EMC* 19 (1975) 22-6

Baldwin, B., *Suetonius*, Amsterdam, 1983

Bowersock, G.W., 'Suetonius and Trajan', *Hommages à M. Renard, I* 119-25

Bradley, K.R., 'The Composition of Suetonius' *Caesares* again', *JIES* 1 (1973) 257-63

Bradley, K.R., 'Imperial virtues in Suetonius' *Caesares*', *JIES* 4 (1976) 245-53

Bradley, K.R., 'The significance of the *spectacula* in Suetonius' *Caesares*', *RSA* 11 (1981) 129-37

Bradley, K.R., 'The Rediscovery of Suetonius', *CP* 80 (1985) 254-65

Carney, T.F., 'How Suetonius' Lives reflect on Hadrian', *PACA* 11 (1968) 7-24

Cizek, E., *Structures et idéologie dans 'les Vies des Douze Césars' de Suétone*, Paris, 1977

Coninck, L. de, *Suetonius en de archivalia*, Brussel, 1983

Corte, F. della, *Svetonio eques Romanus*, Milano/Varese 1958; 2nd ed. Firenze, 1967

Ektor, J., 'L'impassibilité et l'objectivité de Suétone', *LEC* 48 (1980) 317-26

Flach, D., 'Zum Quellenwert der Kaiserbiographien Suetons', *Gymnasium* 79 (1972) 273-89

Flach, D., 'Die Überlieferungslage zur Geschichte des Vierkaiserjahres', *AncSoc* 4 (1973) 157-76

Funaioli, G., 'Suetonius' no. 3, *RE IV* A (1931) 591-640

Gascou, J., *Suétone historien*, Rome, 1984

Gugel, H. *Studien zur biographischen Technik Suetons*, Wien, 1977 (Wiener Studien, Beiheft 7)

Hardy, E.G., 'Plutarch, Tacitus, and Suetonius, on Galba and Otho', *Studies in Roman History*, London, 1906, 295-334

Krauss, F.B., *An interpretation of the omens, portents and prodigies recorded by Livy, Tacitus and Suetonius*, Philadelphia, 1930

Lambrecht, U., *Herrscherbild und Principatsidee in Suetons Kaiserbiographien*, Bonn, 1984

Lewis, R.G., 'Suetonius' *Caesares* and their literary antecedents', *ANRW* II 33,5 (forthcoming)

Lounsbury, R.C., *The Arts of Suetonius – An Introduction*, New York, 1987

Macé, A., *Essai sur Suétone*, Paris, 1900

Marec, E., & H.G. Pflaum, 'Nouvelle Inscription sur la carrière de Suétone, l'historien,' *CRAI* (1952) 76-85

Mouchová, B., 'Ausgewählte Parallelen aus der Lebensbeschreibung Kaisers Otho bei Sueton und den Historien des Tacitus', *LF* 89 (1966) 257-61

Mouchová, B., *Studie zu Kaiserbiographien Suetons*, Praha, 1968

Paratore, E., 'Claude et Néron chez Suétone', *RCCM* 1 (1959) 326-41

Sage, P., 'L' expression narrative des XII Césars de Suétone; analyse d'une structure de phrase,' *Latomus* 38 (1979) 499-524

Sage, P., 'Quelques aspects de l'expression narrative dans les *XII Césars* de Suétone', *RBPh* 57 (1979) 18-50

Steidle, W., *Sueton und die antike Biographie*, München, 1951

Syme, R., 'Biographers of the Caesars', *MH* 37 (1980) 104-28

Syme, R., 'The Travels of Suetonius Tranquillus', *Hermes* 109 (1981) 105-17

Townend, G.B., 'The date of composition of Suetonius' *Caesares*', *CQ* 9 (1959) 285-93

Townend, G.B., 'The Hippo Inscription and the Career of Suetonius', *Historia* 10 (1961) 99-109

Townend, G.B., 'Suetonius and his Influence', *Latin Biography* (ed. T.A. Dorey) 79-111

Venini, P., 'Sulle vite svetoniane di Galba, Otone e Vitellio', *RIL* 108 (1974) 991-1014.

Wallace-Hadrill, A., *Suetonius – The Scholar and his Caesars*, London, 1983

The following sections list fundamental works frequently consulted during the preparation of the commentary; however, to avoid excessive repetition they are infrequently cited below.

## Historical Background of A.D. 68-69

Dessau, H., *Geschichte der römischen Kaiserzeit II.1* Berlin, 1926 277-373

Feliciani, N., 'L'Anno dei quatro Imperatori', *RSA* 11 (1907) 3-33; 378-409

Fuhrmann, M., 'Das Vierkaiserjahr bei Tacitus' *Philologus* 104 (1960) 250-78

Gerstenecker, J., *Der Krieg des Otho und Vitellius in Italien im J. 69*, München, 1882

Grassl, H., *Untersuchungen zum Vierkaiserjahr 68/69 n.Chr. Ein Beitrag zur Ideologie und Sozialstruktur des frühen Prinzipats*, (Diss. Graz, 23), Wien, 1973

Greenhalgh, P.A.L., *The Year of the Four Emperors*, London, 1975

Grenzheuser, B., *Kaiser und Senat in der Zeit von Nero bis Nerva*, Diss. Münster, 1964

Hallermann, B., *Untersuchungen zu den Truppenbewegungen in den Jahren 68/69 n.Chr.*, Diss. Würzburg, 1963

Manfrè, G., *La crisi politica dell'anno 68-69 d.C.*, Bologna, 1947

Manni, E., 'Lotta politica e guerra civile nel 68-69 d.C.', *RFC* 24 (1946) 122-56

Martin, P.H., *Die anonymen Münzen des Jahres 68 nach Christus*, Mainz, 1974

Puhl, M., *De Othone et Vitellio Imperatoribus Quaestiones*, Diss. Hallé, 1883

Stevenson, G.H., 'The Year of the Four Emperors', *CAH X* 808-39, Cambridge, 1934

Wellesley, K., *The Long Year A.D. 69*, London, 1975; 2nd ed. Bristol, 1989

Zancan, P., *La crisi del principato nell'anno 69 d.C.*, Padova, 1939

## Galba

Fabbricotti, E., *Galba*, Roma, 1976

Fluss, M. (?), 'Sulpicius' no. 63, *RE IV* A (1931) 772-801

Kraay, C.M., *The Aes Coinage of Galba*, New York, 1956

Raoss, M., 'La rivolta di Vindice ed il successo di Galba,' *Epigraphica* 20 (1958) 46-120 & 22 (1960) 37-151

Sancery, J., *Galba ou l'armée face au pouvoir*, Paris, 1983

Sievers, G.R., 'Nero und Galba', *Studien zur Geschichte der römischen Kaiser* Berlin, 1870, 108-70

## Otho

Drexler, H., 'Zur Geschichte Kaiser Othos bei Tacitus und Plutarch', *Klio* 37 (1959) 153-78

Klingner, F., 'Die Geschichte Kaiser Othos bei Tacitus', *Berichte Verh. Sächsischen Ak. (phil.-hist. Kl.)* 92 (1940) 3-27

Krauss, L., *De Vitarum Imperatoris Othonis Fide Quaestiones*, Progr. Zweibrücken, 1889

Nagl, A. (?), 'Salvius' no. 21 *RE I* A (1920) 2035-55

Paul, L., 'Kaiser Marcus Salvius Otho', *RhM* 57 (1902) 76-136

## Vitellius

Coale, Jr, A.J., *Vitellius Imperator: A Study in the Literary and Numismatic Sources for the Rebellion and Rule of the Emperor Vitellius, A.D. 69*, Diss. Michigan, 1971

Engel, R., 'Das Charakterbild des Kaisers A. Vitellius bei Tacitus und sein historischer Kern', *Athenaeum* 55 (1977) 345-68

Hanslik, R., 'Vitellius' no. 7(b) *RE* Suppl. *IX* (1962) 1706-33

Momigliano, A., 'Vitellio', *SIFC* 9 (1931) 117-61; 163-87

# Abbreviations

Abbreviations are generally as in the *Oxford Classical Dictionary* (2nd ed., 1970) and in J. Marouzeau, *L'Année Philologique* (slightly anglicised – e.g. *AJP* instead of *AJPh*). The following are peculiar to this commentary:

| | |
|---|---|
| *AFA* | *Acta Fratrum Arvalium* (see also Henzen) |
| *ANRW* | *Aufstieg und Niedergang der Römischen Welt* ( = *Festschrift J. Vogt*) ed. H. Temporini, Berlin, 1972- (in progress) |
| *BMC Imp.* | *Coins of the Roman Empire in the British Museum*, Vols *I* and *II* ed. H. Mattingly, London, 1923 and 1930 |
| *BMC Rep.* | *Coins of the Roman Republic in the British Museum* ed. H.A. Grueber, 3 Vols, London, 1910 (repr. 1970) |
| Buckland, *Textbook*[3] | W.W. Buckland, *A Text-book of Roman Law*, 3rd ed., rev. by P. Stein, Cambridge, 1963 |
| EJ | V. Ehrenberg and A.H.M. Jones, *Documents Illustrating the Reigns of Augustus and Tiberius*, 2nd ed., Oxford, 1955 |
| Friedländer-Wissowa, *Sittengeschichte* | L. Friedländer, *Darstellungen aus der Sittengeschichte Roms*, 4 Vols, 10th ed., rev. by G. Wissowa, Leipzig, 1922 |
| Friedländer, *RLM* | 7th ed., translated as *Roman Life and Manners under the Early Empire*, London, 1908-13 |
| Henzen | G. Henzen, *Acta Fratrum Arvalium*, Berlin, 1874 (repr. 1967) |
| LCL | Loeb Classical Library |

| | |
|---|---|
| L-S | C.T. Lewis and C. Short, *Latin Dictionary*, Oxford, 1879 |
| Magie, *Roman Rule* | D. Magie, *Roman Rule in Asia Minor, to the third century after Christ*, 2 Vols, Princeton, 1950 |
| Marquardt, *Privatleben*[2] | J. Marquardt, *Das Privatleben der Römer*, 2nd ed., rev. A. Mau, Leipzig, 1886 |
| *MRR* | T.R.S. Broughton, *The Magistrates of the Roman Republic*, 2 Vols with Suppl., Cleveland, 1951, 1952, 1960 |
| MW | M. McCrum and A.G. Woodhead, *Select Documents of the Principates of the Flavian Emperors, A.D. 68-96*, Cambridge, 1961 |
| Nash | E. Nash, *Pictorial Dictionary of Ancient Rome*, 2 Vols, 2nd ed., London, 1968 |
| *OLD* | *Oxford Latin Dictionary*, Oxford, 1968-1982 |
| Smallwood | E.M. Smallwood, *Documents Illustrating the Principates of Gaius Claudius and Nero*, Cambridge, 1967; repr. Bristol, 1984 |
| Syme, *RR* | R. Syme, *The Roman Revolution*, Oxford, 1939 |
| Syme, *Tacitus* | R. Syme, *Tacitus*, 2 Vols, Oxford, 1958 |
| *TLL* | *Thesaurus Linguae Latinae* |
| Thomasson, *Die Statthalter... Nordafrikas* | B.E. Thomasson, *Die Statthalter der römischen Provinzen Nordafrikas von Augustus bis Diocletianus*, 2 Vols, Lund, 1960 |

## C. SVETONI TRANQVILLI
## DE VITA CAESARVM
## LIBER VII
## GALBA OTHO VITELLIVS


### Galba

**1.1** Progenies Caesarum in Nerone defecit: quod futurum compluribus quidem signis, sed vel evidentissimis duobus apparuit. Liviae
olim post Augusti statim nuptias Veientanum suum revisenti
praetervolans aquila gallinam albam ramulum lauri rostro tenentem,
ita ut rapuerat, demisit in gremium; cumque nutriri alitem, pangi
ramulum placuisset, tanta pullorum suboles provenit, ut hodieque ea
villa 'ad Gallinas' vocetur, tale vero lauretum, ut triumphaturi
Caesares inde laureas decerperent; fuitque mos triumphantibus, alias
confestim eodem loco pangere; et observatum est sub cuiusque
obitum arborem ab ipso institutam elanguisse. ergo novissimo
Neronis anno et silva omnis exaruit radicitus, et quidquid ibi
gallinarum erat interiit. ac subinde tacta de caelo Caesarum aede
capita omnibus simul statuis deciderunt, Augusti etiam sceptrum e
manibus excussum est.

**2.1** Neroni Galba successit nullo gradu contingens Caesarum domum,
sed haud dubie nobilissimus magnaque et vetere prosapia, ut qui
statuarum titulis pronepotem se Quinti Catuli Capitolini semper
ascripserit, imperator vero etiam stemma in atrio proposuerit, quo
paternam originem ad Iovem, maternam ad Pasiphaam Minonis
uxorem referret.

**3.1** imagines et elogia universi generis exequi longum est, familiae
breviter attingam. qui primus Sulpiciorum cognomen Galbae tulit cur
aut unde traxerit, ambigitur. quidam putant, quod oppidum
Hispaniae frustra diu oppugnatum inlitis demum galbano facibus
succenderit; alii, quod in diuturna valitudine galbeo, id est remediis
lana involutis, assidue uteretur; nonnulli, quod praepinguis fuerit

1

visus, quem galbam Galli vocent; vel contra, quod tam exilis, quam sunt animalia quae in aesculis nascuntur appellanturque galbae. **3.2** familiam illustravit Servius Galba consularis, temporum suorum †et eloquentissimus, quem tradunt Hispaniam ex praetura optinentem, triginta Lusitanorum milibus perfidia trucidatis, Viriatini belli causam extitisse. eius nepos ob repulsam consulatus infensus Iulio Caesari, cuius legatus in Gallia fuerat, conspiravit cum Cassio et Bruto, propter quod Pedia lege damnatus est. **3.3** ab hoc sunt imperatoris Galbae avus ac pater: avus clarior studiis quam dignitate – non enim egressus praeturae gradum – multiplicem nec incuriosam historiam edidit; pater consulatu functus, quanquam brevi corpore atque etiam gibber modicaeque in dicendo facultatis, causas industrie actitavit. **3.4** uxores habuit Mummiam Achaicam, neptem Catuli proneptemque L. Mummi, qui Corinthum excidit; item Liviam Ocellinam ditem admodum et pulchram, a qua tamen nobilitatis causa appetitus ultro existimatur et aliquanto enixius, postquam subinde instanti vitium corporis secreto posita veste detexit, ne quasi ignaram fallere videretur. ex Achaica liberos Gaium et Servium procreavit, quorum maior Gaius attritis facultatibus urbe cessit prohibitusque a Tiberio sortiri anno suo proconsulatum voluntaria morte obiit.

**4.1** Ser. Galba imperator M. Valerio Messala Cn. Lentulo cons. natus est VIIII. Kal. Ian. in villa colli superposita prope Tarracinam sinistrorsus Fundos petentibus, adoptatusque a noverca sua Livia nomen et Ocellare cognomen assumpsit mutato praenomine; nam Lucium mox pro Servio usque ad tempus imperii usurpavit. constat Augustum puero adhuc, salutanti se inter aequales, apprehensa buccula dixisse 'καὶ σὺ τέκνον τῆς ἀρχῆς ἡμῶν παρατρώξῃ' sed et Tiberius, cum comperisset imperaturum eum, verum in senecta, 'vivat sane,' ait, 'quando id ad nos nihil pertinet'. **4.2** avo quoque eius fulgur procuranti, cum exta de manibus aquila rapuisset et in frugiferam quercum contulisset, responsum est summum sed serum imperium portendi familiae; et ille irridens, 'sane', inquit, 'cum mula pepererit'. nihil aeque postea Galbam temptantem res novas confirmavit quam mulae partus, ceterisque ut obscaenum ostentum abhorrentibus, solus pro laetissimo accepit memor sacrificii dictique avi.
**4.3** sumpta virili toga somniavit Fortunam dicentem, stare se ante fores defessam et nisi ocius reciperetur, cuicumque obvio praedae futuram. utque evigilavit, aperto atrio simulacrum aeneum deae

cubitali maius iuxta limen invenit idque gremio suo Tusculum, ubi aestivare consueverat, avexit et in parte aedium consecratum menstruis deinceps supplicationibus et pervigilio anniversario coluit. **4.4** quanquam autem nondum aetate constanti veterem civitatis exoletumque morem ac tantum in domo sua haerentem obstinatissime retinuit, ut liberti servique bis die frequentes adessent ac mane salvere, vesperi valere sibi singuli dicerent. **5.1** inter liberales disciplinas attendit et iuri. dedit et matrimonio operam; verum amissa uxore Lepida duobusque ex ea filiis remansit in caelibatu neque sollicitari ulla condicione amplius potuit, ne Agrippinae quidem, quae, viduata morte Domiti, maritum quoque adhuc necdum caelibem Galbam adeo omnibus sollicitaverat modis, ut in conventu matronarum correpta iurgio atque etiam manu pulsata sit a matre Lepidae.

**5.2** observavit ante omnis Liviam Augustam, cuius et vivae gratia plurimum valuit et mortuae testamento paene ditatus est; sestertium namque quingenties praecipuum inter legatarios habuit, sed quia notata, non perscripta erat summa, herede Tiberio legatum ad quingenta revocante, ne haec quidem accepit.

**6.1** honoribus ante legitimum tempus initis praetor commissione ludorum Floralium novum spectaculi genus elephantos funambulos edidit; exim provinciae Aquitaniae anno fere praefuit; mox consulatum per sex menses ordinarium gessit, evenitque ut in eo ipse †L. Domitio patri Neronis, ipsi Salvius Otho pater Othonis succederet, velut praesagium insequentis casus, quo medius inter utriusque filios extitit imperator.

**6.2** a Gaio Caesare < ...... in locum Gaetu > lici substitutus, postridie quam ad legiones venit, sollemni forte spectaculo plaudentes inhibuit data tessera, ut manus paenula continerent; statimque per castra iactatum est:

disce miles militare: Galba est, non Gaetulicus.

**6.3** pari severitate interdixit commeatus peti. veteranum ac tironem militem opere assiduo corroboravit matureque barbaris, qui iam in Galliam usque proruperant, coercitis, praesenti quoque Gaio talem et se et exercitum approbavit, ut inter innumeras contractasque ex omnibus provinciis copias neque testimonium neque praemia ampliora ulli perciperent; ipse maxime insignis, quod campestrem decursionem scuto moderatus, etiam ad essedum imperatoris per viginti passuum milia cucurrit.

**7.1** caede Gai nuntiata multis ad occasionem stimulantibus quietem praetulit. per hoc gratissimus Claudio receptusque in cohortem amicorum tantae dignationis est habitus, ut cum subita ei valitudo nec adeo gravis incidisset, dilatus sit expeditionis Britannicae dies. Africam pro consule biennio optinuit extra sortem electus ad ordinandam provinciam et intestina dissensione et barbarorum tumultu inquietam; ordinavitque magna severitatis ac iustitiae cura etiam in parvulis rebus. **7.2** militi, qui per expeditionem artissima annona residuum cibariorum tritici modium centum denariis vendidisse arguebatur, vetuit, simul atque indigere cibo coepisset, a quoquam opem ferri; et is fame extabuit. at in iure dicendo cum de proprietate iumenti quaereretur, levibus utrimque argumentis et testibus ideoque difficili coniectura veritatis, ita decrevit ut ad lacum, ubi adaquari solebat, duceretur capite involuto atque ibidem revelato eius esset, ad quem sponte se a potu recepisset.

**8.1** ob res et tunc in Africa et olim in Germania gestas ornamenta triumphalia accepit et sacerdotium triplex, inter quindecimviros sodalesque Titios item Augustales cooptatus; atque ex eo tempore prope ad medium Neronis principatum in secessu plurimum vixit, ne ad gestandum quidem umquam iter ingressus quam ut secum vehiculo proximo decies sestertium in auro efferret, donec in oppido Fundis moranti Hispania Tarraconensis oblata est. **8.2** acciditque, ut cum provinciam ingressus sacrificaret, intra aedem publicam puero e ministris acerram tenenti capillus repente toto capite canesceret, nec defuerunt qui interpretarentur significari rerum mutationem successurumque iuveni senem, hoc est ipsum Neroni. non multo post in Cantabriae lacum fulmen decidit repertaeque sunt duodecim secures, haud ambiguum summae imperii signum.

**9.1** per octo annos varie et inaequabiliter provinciam rexit, primo acer et vehemens et in coercendis quidem delictis vel immodicus. nam et nummulario non ex fide versanti pecunias manus amputavit mensaeque eius adfixit, et tutorem, quod pupillum, cui substitutus heres erat, veneno necasset, cruce adfecit; implorantique leges et civem Romanum se testificanti, quasi solacio et honore aliquo poenam levaturus, mutari multoque praeter ceteras altiorem et dealbatam statui crucem iussit. paulatim in desidiam segnitiamque conversus est, ne quid materiae praeberet Neroni et, ut dicere solebat, quod nemo rationem otii sui reddere cogeretur.

**9.2** Carthagine nova conventum agens tumultuari Gallias comperit legato Aquitaniae auxilia implorante; supervenerunt et Vindicis litterae hortantis, ut humano generi assertorem ducemque se accommodaret. nec diu cunctatus condicionem partim metu partim spe recepit; nam et mandata Neronis de nece sua ad procuratores clam missa deprenderat et confirmabatur cum secundissimis auspiciis et ominibus virginis honestae vaticinatione, tanto magis quod eadem illa carmina sacerdos Iovis Cluniae ex penetrali somnio monitus eruerat ante ducentos annos similiter a fatidica puella pronuntiata. quorum carminum sententia erat oriturum quandoque ex Hispania principem dominumque rerum.

**10.1** igitur cum quasi manumissioni vacaturus conscendisset tribunal, propositis ante se damnatorum occisorumque a Nerone quam plurimis imaginibus et astante nobili puero, quem exulantem e proxima Baliari insula ob id ipsum acciverat, deploravit temporum statum consalutatusque imperator legatum se senatus ac populi R. professus est. **10.2** dein iustitio indicto, e plebe quidem provinciae legiones et auxilia conscripsit super exercitum veterem legionis unius duarumque alarum et cohortium trium; at e primoribus prudentia atque aetate praestantibus vel instar senatus, ad quos de maiore re quotiens opus esset referretur, instituit. **10.3** delegit et equestris ordinis iuvenes, qui manente anulorum aureorum usu evocati appellarentur excubiasque circa cubiculum suum vice militum agerent. etiam per provincias edicta dimisit, auctor in singulis universisque conspirandi simul et ut qua posset quisque opera communem causam iuvarent.

**10.4** per idem fere tempus in munitione oppidi, quod sedem bello delegerat, repertus est anulus opere antiquo, scalptura gemmae Victoriam cum tropaeo exprimente; ac subinde Alexandrina navis Dertosam appulit armis onusta, sine gubernatore, sine nauta aut vectore ullo, ut nemini dubium esset iustum piumque et faventibus diis bellum suscipi: cum repente ex inopinato prope cuncta turbata sunt. **10.5** alarum altera castris appropinquantem paenitentia mutati sacramenti destituere conata est aegreque retenta in officio, et servi, quos a liberto Neronis ad fraudem praeparatos muneri acceperat, per angiportum in balneas transeuntem paene interemerunt, nisi cohortantibus in vicem ne occasionem omitterent, interrogatisque de qua occasione loquerentur, expressa cruciatu confessio esset. **11.1** accessit ad tanta discrimina mors Vindicis, qua maxime consternatus destitutoque similis non multum afuit quin vitae renuntiaret.

sed supervenientibus ab urbe nuntiis ut occisum Neronem cunctosque in verba sua iurasse cognovit, deposita legati suscepit Caesaris appellationem iterque ingressus est paludatus ac dependente a cervicibus pugione ante pectus; nec prius usum togae reciperavit quam oppressis qui novas res moliebantur, praefecto praetori Nymphidio Sabino Romae, in Germania Fonteio Capitone, in Africa Clodio Macro legatis.

**12.1** praecesserat de eo fama saevitiae simul atque avaritiae, quod civitates Hispaniarum Galliarumque, quae cunctantius sibi accesserant, gravioribus tributis, quasdam etiam murorum destructione punisset et praepositos procuratoresque supplicio capitis adfecisset cum coniugibus ac liberis; quodque oblatam a Tarraconensibus e vetere templo Iovis coronam auream librarum quindecim conflasset ac tres uncias, quae ponderi deerant, iussisset exigi. **12.2** ea fama et confirmata et aucta est, ut primum urbem introiit. nam cum classiarios, quos Nero ex remigibus iustos milites fecerat, redire ad pristinum statum cogeret, recusantis atque insuper aquilam et signa pertinacius flagitantis non modo inmisso equite disiecit, sed decimavit etiam. item Germanorum cohortem a Caesaribus olim ad custodiam corporis institutam multisque experimentis fidelissimam dissolvit ac sine commodo ullo remisit in patriam, quasi Cn. Dolabellae, iuxta cuius hortos tendebat, proniorem. **12.3** illa quoque verene an falso per ludibrium iactabantur, adposita lautiore cena ingemuisse eum, et ordinario quidem dispensatori breviarium rationum offerenti paropsidem leguminis pro sedulitate ac diligentia porrexisse, Cano autem choraulae mire placenti denarios quinque donasse prolatos manu sua e peculiaribus loculis suis.

**13.1** quare adventus eius non perinde gratus fuit, idque proximo spectaculo apparuit, siquidem Atellanis notissimum canticum exorsis:

venit Onesimus a villa

cuncti simul spectatores consentiente voce reliquam partem rettulerunt ac saepius versu repetito egerunt. **14.1** maiore adeo et favore et auctoritate adeptus est quam gessit imperium, quanquam multa documenta egregii principis daret; sed nequaquam tam grata erant, quam invisa quae secus fierent.

**14.2** regebatur trium arbitrio, quos una et intra Palatium habitantis nec umquam non adhaerentis paedagogos vulgo vocabant. ii erant T. Vinius legatus eius in Hispania, cupiditatis immensae; Cornelius Laco ex assessore praefectus praetorii, arrogantia socordiaque intolerabilis; libertus Icelus, paulo ante anulis aureis et Marciani cognomine ornatus ac iam summae equestris gradus candidatus. his diverso vitiorum genere grassantibus adeo se abutendum permisit et tradidit, ut vix sibi ipse constaret, modo acerbior parciorque, modo remissior ac neglegentior quam conveniret principi electo atque illud aetatis.

**14.3** quosdam claros ex utroque ordine viros suspicione minima inauditos condemnavit. civitates R. raro dedit, iura trium liberorum vix uni atque alteri ac ne is quidem nisi ad certum praefinitumque tempus. iudicibus sextam decuriam adici precantibus non modo negavit, sed et concessum a Claudio beneficium, ne hieme initioque anni ad iudicandum evocarentur, eripuit. **15.1** existimabatur etiam senatoria et equestria officia bienni spatio determinaturus nec daturus nisi invitis ac recusantibus. liberalitates Neronis non plus decimis concessis per quinquaginta equites R. ea condicione revocandas curavit exigendasque, ut et si quid scaenici ac xystici donatum olim vendidissent, auferretur emptoribus, quando illi pretio absumpto solvere nequirent.

**15.2** at contra nihil non per comites atque libertos pretio addici aut donari gratia passus est, vectigalia immunitates, poenas innocentium impunitates noxiorum. quin etiam populo R. deposcente supplicium Haloti et Tigillini solos ex omnibus Neronis emissariis vel maleficentissimos incolumes praestitit atque insuper Halotum procuratione amplissima ornavit, pro Tigillino etiam saevitiae populum edicto increpuit.

**16.1** per haec prope universis ordinibus offensis vel praecipua flagrabat invidia apud milites. nam cum in verba eius absentis iurantibus donativum grandius solito praepositi pronuntiassent, neque ratam rem habuit et subinde iactavit legere se militem, non emere consuesse; atque eo quidem nomine omnis, qui ubique erant, exacerbavit. ceterum praetorianos etiam metu et indignitate commovit, removens subinde plerosque ut suspectos et Nymphidi socios. **16.2** sed maxime fremebat superioris Germaniae exercitus fraudari se praemis navatae adversus Gallos et Vindicem operae. ergo primi obsequium rumpere ausi Kal. Ian. adigi sacramento nisi in nomen senatus recusarunt statimque legationem ad praetorianos cum mandatis destinaverunt: displicere imperatorem in Hispania factum; eligerent ipsi quem cuncti exercitus comprobarent. **17.**1 quod ut nuntiatum est, despectui esse non tam senectam suam quam orbitatem ratus, Pisonem Frugi Licinianum nobilem egregiumque iuvenem ac sibi olim probatissimum testamentoque semper in bona et nomen adscitum repente e media salutantium turba adprehendit filiumque appellans perduxit in castra ac pro contione adoptavit, ne tunc quidem donativi ulla mentione facta. quo faciliorem occasionem M. Salvio Othoni praebuit perficiendi conata intra sextum adoptionis diem.

**18.**1 magna et assidua monstra iam inde a principio exitum ei, qualis evenit, portenderant. cum per omne iter dextra sinistraque oppidatim victimae caederentur, taurus securis ictu consternatus rupto vinculo essedum eius invasit elatisque pedibus totum cruore perfudit; ac descendentem speculator impulsu turbae lancea prope vulneravit. urbem quoque et deinde Palatium ingressum excepit terrae tremor et assimilis quidam mugitui sonus. **18.**2 secuta sunt aliquanto manifestiora. monile margaritis gemmisque consertum ad ornandam Fortunam suam Tusculanam ex omni gaza secreverat; id repente quasi augustiore dignius loco Capitolinae Veneri dedicavit, ac proxima nocte somniavit speciem Fortunae querentis fraudatam se dono destinato, minantisque erepturam et ipsam quae dedisset. cumque exterritus luce prima ad expiandum somnium, praemissis qui rem divinam apparrent, Tusculum excucurrisset, nihil invenit praeter tepidam in ara favillam atratumque iuxta senem in catino vitreo tus tenentem et in calice fictili merum. **18.**3 observatum etiam est Kal. Ian. sacrificanti coronam de capite excidisse, auspicanti pullos avolasse; adoptionis die neque milites adlocuturo castrensem sellam de more positam pro tribunali oblitis ministris et in senatu curulem perverse collocatam. **19.**1 prius vero quam occideretur sacrificantem mane haruspex identidem monuit, caveret periculum, non longe percussores abesse.

haud multo post cognoscit teneri castra ab Othone, ac plerisque ut eodem quam primum pergeret suadentibus – posse enim auctoritate et praesentia praevalere – nihil amplius quam continere se statuit et legionariorum firmare praesidiis, qui multifariam diverseque tendebant. loricam tamen induit linteam, quanquam haud dissimulans parum adversus tot mucrones profuturam. **19.**2 sed extractus rumoribus falsis, quos conspirati, ut eum in publicum elicerent, de industria dissiparant, paucis temere affirmantibus transactum negotium, oppressos, qui tumultuarentur. advenire frequentis ceteros gratulabundos et in omne obsequium paratos, iis ut occurreret prodiit tanta fiducia, ut militi cuidam occisum a se Othonem glorianti, 'quo auctore?' responderit, atque in forum usque processit. ibi equites, quibus mandata caedes erat, cum per publicum dimota paganorum turba equos adegissent, viso procul eo parumper restiterunt; dein rursum incitati desertum a suis contrucidarunt.

**20.1** sunt qui tradant, ad primum tumultum proclamasse eum: 'quid agitis commilitones? ego vester sum et vos mei,' donativum etiam pollicitum. plures autem prodiderunt optulisse ultro iugulum et ut hoc agerent ac ferirent, quando ita videretur, hortatum. illud mirum admodum fuerit, neque praesentium quemquam opem imperatori ferre conatum et omnes qui arcesserentur sprevisse nuntium excepta Germanicianorum vexillatione. ii ob recens meritum, quod se aegros et invalidos magno opere fovisset, in auxilium advolaverunt, sed serius itinere devio per ignorantiam locorum retardati.

**20.2** iugulatus est ad lacum Curti ac relictus ita uti erat, donec gregarius miles a frumentatione rediens abiecto onere caput ei amputavit; et quoniam capillo arripere non poterat, in gremium abdidit, mox inserto per os pollice ad Othonem detulit. ille lixis calonibusque donavit, qui hasta suffixum non sine ludibrio circum castra portarunt adclamantes identidem, 'Galba Cupido, fruaris aetate tua,' maxime irritati ad talem iocorum petulantiam, quod ante paucos dies exierat in vulgus, laudanti cuidam formam suam ut adhuc floridam et vegetam respondisse eum:

$$\text{ἔτι μοι μένος ἔμπεδόν ἐστιν.}$$

ab is Patrobii Neroniani libertus centum aureis redemptum eo loco, ubi iussu Galbae animadversum in patronum suum fuerat, abiecit. sero tandem dispensator Argivus et hoc et ceterum truncum in privatis eius hortis Aurelia via sepulturae dedit.

**21.1** statura fuit iusta, capite praecalvo, oculis caeruleis, adunco naso, manibus pedibusque articulari morbo distortissimis, ut neque calceum perpeti neque libellos evolvere aut tenere omnino valeret. excreverat etiam in dexteriore latere eius caro praependebatque adeo ut aegre fascia substringeretur.

**22.1** cibi plurimi traditur, quem tempore hiberno etiam ante lucem capere consuerat, inter cenam vero usque eo abundanti < s >, ut congestas super manus reliquias circumferri iuberet spargique ad pedes stantibus. libidinis in mares pronior et eos non nisi praeduros exoletosque; ferebant in Hispania Icelum e veteribus concubinis de Neronis exitu nuntiantem non modo artissimis osculis palam exceptum ab eo, sed ut sine mora velleretur oratum atque seductum.

**23.1** periit tertio et septuagesimo aetatis anno, imperii mense septimo. senatus, ut primum licitum est, statuam ei decreverat rostratae columnae superstantem in parte fori, qua trucidatus est; sed decretum Vespasianus abolevit, percussores sibi ex Hispania in Iudaeam submisisse opinatus.

# Otho

**1.1** Maiores Othonis orti sunt oppido Ferentio, familia vetere et honorata atque ex principibus Etruriae. avus M. Salvius Otho, patre equite R., matre humili incertum an ingenua, per gratiam Liviae Augustae, in cuius domo creverat, senator est factus nec praeturae gradum excessit.

**1.2** pater L. Otho, materno genere praeclaro multarumque et magnarum propinquitatium, tam carus tamque non absimilis facie Tiberio principi fuit, ut plerique procreatum ex eo crederent. urbanos honores, proconsulatum Africae et extraordinaria imperia severissime administravit. ausus etiam est in Illyrico milites quosdam, quod motu Camilli ex paenitentia praepositos suos quasi defectionis adversus Claudium auctores occiderant, capite punire et quidem ante principia se coram, quamvis ob id ipsum promotos in ampliorem gradum a Claudio sciret. **1.3** quo facto sicut gloriam auxit, ita gratiam minuit; quam tamen mature reciperavit detecta equitis R. fraude, quem prodentibus servis necem Claudio parare compererat. namque et senatus honore rarissimo, statua in Palatio posita, prosecutus est eum et Claudius adlectum inter patricios conlaudans amplissimis verbis hoc quoque adiecit: 'vir, quo meliores liberos habere ne opto quidem.' ex Albia Terentia splendida femina duos filios tulit, L. Titianum et minorem M. cognominem sibi; tulit et filiam, quam vixdum nubilem Druso Germanici filio despondit.

**2.1** Otho imperator IIII. Kal. Mai. natus est Camillo Arruntio Domitio Ahenobarbo cons. a prima adulescentia prodigus ac procax, adeo ut saepe flagris obiurgaretur a patre, ferebatur et vagari noctibus solitus atque invalidum quemque obviorum vel potulentum corripere ac distento sago impositum in sublime iactare. **2.2** post patris deinde mortem libertinam aulicam gratiosam, quo efficacius coleret, etiam diligere simulavit quamvis anum ac paene decrepitam; per hanc insinuatus Neroni facile summum inter amicos locum tenuit congruentia morum, ut vero quidam tradunt, et consuetudine mutui stupri. ac tantum potentia valuit, ut damnatum repetundis consularem virum, ingens praemium pactus, prius quam plane restitutionem ei impetrasset, non dubitaret in senatum ad agendas gratias introducere. **3.1** omnium autem consiliorum secretorumque particeps die, quem necandae matri Nero destinarat, ad avertendas suspiciones cenam utrique exquisitissimae comitatis dedit; item Poppaeam Sabinam tunc adhuc amicam eius, abductam marito demandatamque interim sibi, nuptiarum specie recepit nec corrupisse contentus adeo dilexit, ut ne rivalem quidem Neronem aequo tulerit animo. **3.2** creditur certe non modo missos ad arcessendam non recepisse, sed ipsum etiam exclusisse quondam pro foribus astantem miscentemque frustra minas et preces ac depositum reposcentem. quare diducto matrimonio sepositus est per causam legationis in Lusitaniam. et satis visum, ne poena acrior mimum omnem divulgaret, qui tamen sic quoque hoc disticho enotuit:

> cur Otho mentito sit, quaeritis, exul honore?
> uxoris moechus coeperat esse suae.

provinciam administravit quaestorius per decem annos, moderatione atque abstinentia singulari. **4.1** ut tandem occasio ultionis data est, conatibus Galbae primus accessit; eodemque momento et ipse spem imperii cepit magnam quidem et ex condicione temporum, sed aliquanto maiorem ex affirmatione Seleuci mathematici. qui cum eum olim superstitem Neroni fore spopondisset, tunc ultro inopinatus advenerat imperaturum quoque brevi repromittens. **4.2** nullo igitur officii aut ambitionis in quemquam genere omisso, quotiens cena principem acciperet, aureos excubanti cohorti viritim dividebat, nec minus alium alia via militum demerebatur; cuidam etiam de parte finium cum vicino litiganti adhibitus arbiter totum agrum redemit emancipavitque, ut iam vix ullus esset, qui non et sentiret et praedicaret solum successione imperii dignum. **5.1** speraverat autem fore ut adoptaretur a Galba, idque in dies expectabat. sed postquam Pisone praelato spe decidit, ad vim conversus est instigante super animi dolorem etiam magnitudine aeris alieni. neque enim dissimulabat, nisi principem se stare non posse, nihilque referre ab hoste in acie an in foro sub creditoribus caderet. **5.2** ante paucos dies servo Caesaris pro impetrata dispensatione decies sestertium expresserat; hoc subsidium tanti coepti fuit. ac primo quinque speculatoribus commissa res est, deinde decem aliis, quos singuli binos produxerant; omnibus dena sestertia repraesentata et quinquagena promissa. per hos sollicitati reliqui, nec adeo multi, haud dubia fiducia in ipso negotio pluris adfuturos. **6.1** tulerat animus post adoptionem statim castra occupare cenantemque in Palatio Galbam adgredi, sed obstitit respectus cohortis, quae tunc excubabat, ne oneraretur invidia, quod eiusdem statione et Gaius fuerat occisus et desertus Nero. medium quoque tempus religio et Seleucus exemit.

**6.2** ergo destinata die praemonitis consciis, ut se in foro sub aede Saturni ad miliarium aureum opperirentur, mane Galbam salutavit, utque consueverat osculo exceptus, etiam sacrificanti interfuit audivitque praedicta haruspicis. deinde liberto adesse architectos nuntiante, quod signum convenerat, quasi venalem domum inspecturus abscessit proripuitque se postica parte Palati ad constitutum. alii febrem simulasse aiunt eamque excusationem proximis mandasse, si quaereretur. **6.3** tunc abditus propere muliebri sella in castra contendit ac deficientibus lecticaris cum descendisset cursumque cepisset, laxato calceo restitit, donec omissa mora succollatus et a praesente comitatu imperator consalutatus inter faustas adclamationes strictosque gladios ad principia devenit, obvio quoque non aliter ac si conscius et particeps foret adhaerente. ibi missis qui Galbam et Pisonem trucidarent, ad conciliandos pollicitationibus militum animos nihil magis pro contione testatus est, quam id demum se habiturum, quod sibi illi reliquissent.

**7.1** dein vergente iam die ingressus senatum positaque brevi oratione quasi raptus de publico et suscipere imperium vi coactus gesturusque communi omnium arbitrio, Palatium petit. ac super ceteras gratulantium adulantiumque blanditias ab infima plebe appellatus Nero nullum indicium recusantis dedit, immo, ut quidam tradiderunt, etiam diplomatibus primisque epistulis suis ad quosdam provinciarum praesides Neronis cognomen adiecit. certe et imagines

statuasque eius reponi passus est et procuratores atque libertos ad eadem officia revocavit, nec quicquam prius pro potestate subscripsit quam quingenties sestertium ad peragendam Auream domum.
7.2 dicitur ea nocte per quietem pavefactus gemitus maximos edidisse repertusque a concursantibus humi ante lectum iacens per omnia piaculorum genera Manes Galbae, a quo deturbari expellique se viderat, propitiare temptasse; postridie quoque in augurando tempestate orta graviter prolapsum identidem obmurmurasse:

$$\tau\acute{\iota} \ \gamma\acute{\alpha}\rho \ \mu o\iota \ \kappa\grave{\alpha}\grave{\iota} \ \mu\alpha\kappa\rho o\hat{\iota}\varsigma \ \alpha\mathit{\mathring{v}}\lambda o\hat{\iota}\varsigma;$$

8.1 sub idem vero tempus Germaniciani exercitus in Vitelli verba iurarant. quod ut comperit, auctor senatui fuit mittendae legationis, quae doceret electum iam principem, quietem concordiamque suaderet; et tamen per internuntios ac litteras consortem imperii generumque se Vitellio optulit.

verum haud dubio bello iamque ducibus et copiis, quas Vitellius praemiserat, appropinquantibus animum fidemque erga se praetorianorum paene internecione amplissimi ordinis expertus est.
8.2 [et] placuerat per classiarios arma transferri remittique navibus; ea cum in castris sub noctem promerentur, insidias quidam suspicati tumultum excitaverunt; ac repente omnes nullo certo duce in Palatium cucurrerunt caedem senatus flagitantes, repulsisque tribunorum qui inhibere temptabant, nonnullis et occisis, sic ut erant cruenti, ubinam imperator esset requirentes perruperunt in triclinium usque nec nisi viso destiterunt.
8.3 expeditionem autem inpigre atque etiam praepropere incohavit, nulla ne religionum quidem cura, sed et motis necdum conditis ancilibus, quod antiquitus infaustum habetur, et die, quo cultores deum Matris lamentari et plangere incipiunt, praeterea adversissimis auspiciis. nam et victima Diti patri caesa litavit, cum tali sacrificio contraria exta potiora sint, et primo egressu inundationibus Tiberis retardatus ad vicensimum etiam lapidem ruina aedificiorum praeclusam viam offendit.

9.1 simili temeritate, quamvis dubium nemini esset quin trahi bellum oporteret, quando et fame et angustiis locorum urgeretur hostis, quam primum tamen decertare statuit, sive impatiens longioris sollicitudinis speransque ante Vitelli adventum profligari plurimum posse, sive impar militum ardori pugnam deposcentium. nec ulli pugnae affuit substititque Brixelli. 9.2 et tribus quidem, verum mediocribus proelis apud Alpes circaque Placentiam et ad Castoris, quod loco nomen est, vicit; novissimo maximoque apud Betriacum fraude superatus est, cum spe conloquii facta, quasi ad condicionem pacis militibus eductis, ex inproviso atque in ipsa consalutatione dimicandum fuisset.

**9.3** ac statim moriendi impetum cepit, ut multi nec frustra opinantur, magis pudore, ne tanto rerum hominumque periculo dominationem sibi asserere perseveraret, quam desperatione ulla aut diffidentia copiarum; quippe residuis integrisque etiam nunc quas secum ad secundos casus detinuerat, et supervenientibus aliis e Dalmatia Pannoniaque et Moesia, ne victis quidem adeo afflictis ut non in ultionem ignominiae quidvis discriminis ultro et vel solae subirent.

**10.1** interfuit huic bello pater meus Suetonius Laetus, tertiae decimae legionis tribunus angusticlavius. is mox referre crebro solebat Othonem etiam privatum usque adeo detestatum civilia arma, ut memorante quodam inter epulas de Cassi Brutique exitu cohorruerit; nec concursurum cum Galba fuisse, nisi confideret sine bello rem transigi posse; tunc ad despiciendam vitam exemplo manipularis militis concitatum, qui cum cladem exercitus nuntiaret nec cuiquam fidem faceret ac nunc mendaci nunc timoris, quasi fugisset, ex acie argueretur, gladio ante pedes eius incubuerit. hoc viso proclamasse eum aiebat, non amplius se in periculum talis tamque bene meritos coniecturum.

**10.2** fratrem igitur fratrisque filium et singulos amicorum cohortatus, ut sibi quisque pro facultate consuleret, ab amplexu et osculo suo dimisit omnis, secretoque capto binos codicillos exaravit, ad sororem consolatorios et ad Messalinam Neronis, quam matrimonio destinarat, commendans reliquias suas et memoriam. quicquid deinde epistularum erat, ne cui periculo aut noxae apud victorem forent, concremavit. divisit et pecunias domesticis ex copia praesenti.

**11.1** atque ita paratus intentusque iam morti, tumultu inter moras exorto ut eos, qui discedere et abire coeptabant, corripi quasi desertores detinerique sensit, 'adiciamus,' inquit, 'vitae et hanc noctem,' his ipsis totidemque verbis, vetuitque vim cuiquam fieri; et in serum usque patente cubiculo, si quis adire vellet, potestatem sui praebuit. **11.2** post hoc sedata siti gelidae aquae potione arripuit duos pugiones et explorata utriusque acie, cum alterum pulvino subdidisset, foribus adopertis artissimo somno quievit. et circa lucem demum expergefactus uno se traiecit ictu infra laevam papillam

14

irrumpentibusque ad primum gemitum modo celans modo detegens plagam exanimatus est et celeriter, nam ita praeceperat, funeratus, tricensimo et octavo aetatis anno et nonagensimo et quinto imperii die.

**12.1** tanto Othonis animo nequaquam corpus aut habitus competit. fuisse enim et modicae staturae et male pedatus scambusque traditur, munditiarum vero paene muliebrium, vulso corpore, galericulo capiti propter raritatem capillorum adaptato et adnexo, ut nemo dinosceret; quin et faciem cotidie rasitare ac pane madido linere consuetum, idque instituisse a prima lanugine, ne barbatus umquam esset; sacra etiam Isidis saepe in lintea religiosaque veste propalam celebrasse. **12.2** per quae factum putem, ut mors eius minime congruens vitae maiore miraculo fuerit. multi praesentium militum cum plurimo fletu manus ac pedes iacentis exosculati, fortissimum virum, unicum imperatorem praedicantes, ibidem statim nec procul a rogo vim suae vitae attulerunt; multi et absentium accepto nuntio prae dolore armis inter se ad internecionem concurrerunt. denique magna pars hominum incolumem gravissime detestata mortuum laudibus tulit, ut vulgo iactatum sit etiam, Galbam ab eo non tam dominandi quam rei p. ac libertatis restituendae causa interemptum.

## Vitellius

**1.1** Vitelliorum originem alii aliam et quidem diversissimam tradunt, partim veterem et nobilem, partim vero novam et obscuram atque etiam sordidam; quod ego per adulatores obtrectatoresque imperatoris Vitelli evenisse opinarer, nisi aliquanto prius de familiae condicione variatum esset. **1.2** extat Q. †Elogi ad Quintum Vitellium Divi Augusti quaestorem libellus, quo continetur, Vitellios Fauno Aboriginum rege et Vitellia, quae multis locis pro numine coleretur, ortos toto Latio imperasse; horum residuam stirpem ex Sabinis transisse Romam atque inter patricios adlectam; **1.3** indicia stirpis mansisse diu viam Vitelliam ab Ianiculo ad mare usque, item coloniam eiusdem nominis, quam gentili copia adversus Aequiculos tutandam olim depoposcissent; tempore deinde Samnitici belli praesidio in Apuliam misso quosdam ex Vitellis subsedisse Nuceriae eorumque progeniem longo post intervallo repetisse urbem atque ordinem senatorium. **2.1** contra plures auctorem generis libertinum prodiderunt, Cassius Severus nec minus alii eundem et sutorem veteramentarium, cuius filius sectionibus et cognituris uberius compendium nanctus, ex muliere vulgari, Antiochi cuiusdam furnariam exercentis filia, equitem R. genuerit. sed quod discrepat, sit in medio.

**2.2** ceterum P. Vitellius domo Nuceria sive ille stirpis antiquae sive pudendis parentibus atque avis, eques certe R. et rerum Augusti procurator, quattuor filios amplissimae dignitatis cognomines ac tantum praenominibus distinctos reliquit Aulum, Quintum, Publium, Lucium. Aulus in consulatu obiit, quem cum Domitio Neronis Caesaris patre inierat, praelautus alioqui famosusque cenarum magnificentia. Quintus caruit ordine, cum auctore Tiberio secerni minus idoneos senatores removerique placuisset. **2.3** Publius, Germanici comes, Cn. Pisonem inimicum et interfectorem eius accusavit condemnavitque, ac post praeturae honorem inter Seiani conscios arreptus et in custodiam fratri datus scalpro librario venas sibi incidit, nec tam mortis paenitentia quam suorum obtestatione obligari curarique se passus in eadem custodia morbo periit. **2.4** Lucius ex consulatu Syriae praepositus, Artabanum Parthorum regem summis artibus non modo ad conloquium suum, sed etiam ad veneranda legionum signa pellexit. mox cum Claudio principe duos insuper ordinarios consulatus censuramque gessit. curam quoque imperi sustinuit absente eo expeditione Britannica; vir innocens et industrius, sed amore libertinae perinfamis, cuius etiam salivis melle commixtis, ne clam quidem aut raro sed cotidie ac palam, arterias et fauces pro remedio fovebat. **2.5** idem miri in adulando ingenii primus C. Caesarem adorare ut deum instituit, cum reversus ex Syria non aliter adire ausus esset quam capite velato circumvertensque se, deinde procumbens. Claudium uxoribus libertisque addictum ne qua non arte demereretur, proximo munere a Messalina petit ut sibi pedes praeberet excalciandos; detractumque socculum dextrum inter togam tunicasque gestavit assidue, nonnumquam osculabundus. Narcissi quoque et Pallantis imagines aureas inter Lares coluit. huius et illa vox est, 'saepe facias,' cum saeculares ludos edenti Claudio gratularetur. **3.1** decessit paralysi altero die quam correptus est, duobus filiis superstitibus, quos ex Sestilia probatissima nec ignobili femina editos consules vidit, et quidem eodem ambos totoque anno, cum maiori minor in sex menses successisset. defunctum senatus

publico funere honoravit, item statua pro rostris cum hac inscriptione: PIETATIS IMMOBILIS ERGA PRINCIPEM.
**3.2** A. Vitellius L. filius imperator natus est VIII. Kal. Oct., vel ut quidam VII. Id. Sept., Druso Caesare Norbano Flacco cons. genituram eius praedictam a mathematicis ita parentes exhorruerunt, ut pater magno opere semper contenderit, ne qua ei provincia vivo se committeretur, mater et missum ad legiones et appellatum imperatorem pro afflicto statim lamentata sit. pueritiam primamque adulescentiam Capreis egit inter Tiberiana scorta, et ipse perpetuo spintriae cognomine notatus existimatusque corporis gratia initium et causa incrementorum patri fuisse; **4.1** sequenti quoque aetate omnibus probris contaminatus, praecipuum in aula locum tenuit, Gaio per aurigandi, Claudio per aleae studium familiaris, sed aliquanto Neroni acceptior, cum propter eadem haec, tum peculiari merito, quod praesidens certamini Neroneo cupientem inter citharoedos contendere nec quamvis flagitantibus cunctis promittere audentem ideoque egressum theatro revocaverat, quasi perseverantis populi legatione suscepta, exorandumque praebuerat.

**5.1** trium itaque principum indulgentia non solum honoribus verum et sacerdotiis amplissimis auctus, proconsulatum Africae post haec curamque operum publicorum administravit et voluntate dispari et existimatione. in provincia singularem innocentiam praestitit biennio continuato, cum succedenti fratri legatus substitisset; at in urbano officio dona atque ornamenta templorum subripuisse et commutasse quaedam ferebatur proque auro et argento stagnum et aurichalcum supposuisse.

**6.1** uxorem habuit Petroniam consularis viri filiam et ex ea filium Petronianum captum altero oculo. hunc heredem a matre sub condicione institutum, si de potestate patris exisset, manu emisit brevique, ut creditum est, interemit, insimulatum insuper parricidii et quasi paratum ad scelus venenum ex conscientia hausisset. duxit mox Galeriam Fundanam praetorio patre ac de hac quoque liberos utriusque sexus tulit, sed marem titubantia oris prope mutum et elinguem.

**7.1** a Galba in inferiorem Germaniam contra opinionem missus est. adiutum putant T. Vini suffragio, tunc potentissimi et cui iam pridem per communem factionis Venetae favorem conciliatus esset; nisi quod

Galba prae se tulit nullos minus metuendos quam qui de solo victu cogitarent, ac posse provincialibus copiis profundam gulam eius expleri, ut cuivis evidens sit contemptu magis quam gratia electum. **7.2** satis constat exituro viaticum defuisse, tanta egestate rei familiaris, ut uxore et liberis, quos Romae relinquebat, meritorio cenaculo abditis domum in reliquam partem anni ablocaret utque ex aure matris detractum unionem pigneraverit ad itineris impensas. creditorum quidem praestolantium ac detinentium turbam et in iis Sinuessanos Formianosque, quorum publica vectigalia interverterat, non nisi terrore calumniae amovit, cum libertino cuidam acerbius debitum reposcenti iniuriarum formulam, quasi calce ab eo percussus, intendisset nec aliter quam extortis quinquaginta sestertiis remisisset.

**7.3** advenientem male animatus erga principem exercitus pronusque ad res novas libens ac supinis manibus excepit velut dono deum oblatum, ter consulis filium, aetate integra, facili ac prodigo animo. quam veterem de se persuasionem Vitellius recentibus etiam experimentis auxerat, tota via caligatorum quoque militum obvios exosculans perque stabula ac deversoria mulionibus ac viatoribus praeter modum comis, ut mane singulos iamne iantassent sciscitaretur seque fecisse ructu quoque ostenderet. **8.1** castra vero ingressus nihil cuiquam poscenti negavit atque etiam ultro ignominiosis notas, reis sordes, damnatis supplicia dempsit.

quare vixdum mense transacto, neque diei neque temporis ratione habita, ac iam vespere, subito a militibus e cubiculo raptus, ita ut erat in veste domestica, imperator est consalutatus circumlatusque per cele berrimos vicos, strictum Divi Iuli gladium tenens detractum delubro Martis atque in prima gratulatione porrectum sibi a quodam. **8.2** nec ante in praetorium rediit quam flagrante triclinio ex conceptu camini, cum quidem consternatis et quasi omine adverso anxiis omnibus, 'bono,' inquit, 'animo estote! nobis adluxit,' nullo sermone alio apud milites usus. consentiente deinde etiam superioris provinciae exercitu, qui prior a Galba ad senatum defecerat, cognomen Germanici delatum ab universis cupide recepit, Augusti distulit, Caesaris in perpetuum recusavit.

**9.1** ac subinde caede Galbae adnuntiata, compositis Germanicis rebus, partitus est copias, quas adversus Othonem praemitteret quasque ipse perduceret. praemisso agmine laetum evenit auspicium, siquidem a parte dextra repente aquila advolavit lustratisque signis ingressos viam sensim antecessit. at contra ipso movente statuae equestres, cum plurifariam ei ponerentur, fractis repente cruribus pariter corruerunt, et laurea, quam religiosissime circumdederat, in profluentem excidit; mox Viennae pro tribunali iura reddenti gallinaceus supra umerum ac deinde in capite astitit. quibus ostentis par respondit exitus; nam confirmatum per legatos suos imperium per se retinere non potuit.

**10.**1 de Betriacensi victoria et Othonis exitu, cum adhuc in Gallia esset, audiit nihilque cunctatus, quicquid praetorianarum cohortium fuit, ut pessimi exempli, uno exauctoravit edicto iussas tribunis tradere arma. centum autem atque viginti, quorum libellos Othoni datos invenerat exposcentium praemium ob editam in caede Galbae operam, conquiri et supplicio adfici imperavit, egregie prorsus atque magnifice et ut summi principis spem ostenderet, nisi cetera magis ex natura et priore vita sua quam ex imperii maiestate gessisset. **10.**2 namque itinere incohato per medias civitates ritu triumphantium vectus est perque flumina delicatissimis navigiis et variarum coronarum genere redimitis, inter profusissimos obsoniorum apparatus, nulla familiae aut militis disciplina, rapinas ac petulantiam omnium in iocum vertens, qui non contenti epulo ubique publice praebito, quoscumque libuisset in libertatem asserebant, verbera et plagas, saepe vulnera, nonnumquam necem repraesentantes adversantibus. **10.**3 utque campos, in quibus pugnatum est, adit, abhorrentis quosdam cadaverum tabem detestabili voce confirmare ausus est, optime olere occisum hostem et melius civem. nec eo setius ad leniendam gravitatem odoris plurimum meri propalam hausit passimque divisit. pari vanitate atque insolentia lapidem memoriae Othonis inscriptum intuens dignum eo Mausoleo ait, pugionemque, quo is se occiderat, in Agrippinensem coloniam misit Marti dedicandum. in Appennini quidem iugis etiam pervigilium egit. **11.**1 urbem denique ad classicum introiit paludatus ferroque succinctus, inter signa atque vexilla, sagulatis comitibus ac detectis commilitonum armis.

**11.**2 magis deinde ac magis omni divino humanoque iure neglecto Alliensi die pontificatum maximum cepit, comitia in decem annos ordinavit seque perpetuum consulem. et ne cui dubium foret, quod exemplar regendae rei p. eligeret, medio Martio campo adhibita publicorum sacerdotum frequentia inferias Neroni dedit ac sollemni convivio citharoedum placentem palam admonuit, ut aliquid 'et de dominico' diceret, incohantique Neroniana cantica primus exultans etiam plausit.

**12.1** talibus principiis magnam imperii partem non nisi consilio et arbitrio vilissimi cuiusque histrionum et aurigarum administravit et maxime Asiatici liberti. hunc adulescentulum mutua libidi ͵ constupratum, mox taedio profugum cum Puteolis poscam vendentem reprehendisset, coiecit in compedes statimque solvit et rursus in deliciis habuit; iterum deinde ob nimiam contumaciam et furacitatem gravatus circumforano lanistae vendidit dilatumque ad finem muneris repente subripuit et provincia demum accepta manumisit ac primo imperii die aureis donavit anulis super cenam, cum mane rogantibus pro eo cunctis detestatus esset severissime talem equestris ordinis maculam.

**13.1** sed vel praecipue luxuriae saevitiaeque deditus epulas trifariam semper, interdum quadrifariam dispertiebat, in iantacula et prandia et cenas comisationesque, facile omnibus sufficiens vomitandi consuetudine. indicebat autem aliud alii eadem die, nec cuiquam minus singuli apparatus quadringenis milibus nummum constiterunt. **13.2** famosissima super ceteras fuit cena data ei adventicia a fratre, in qua duo milia lectissimorum piscium, septem avium apposita traduntur. hanc quoque exuperavit ipse dedicatione patinae, quam ob immensam magnitudinem 'clipeum Minervae πολιούχου' dictitabat. in hac scarorum iocinera, phasianarum et pavonum cerebella, linguas phoenicopterum, murenarum lactes a Parthia usque fretoque Hispanico per navarchos ac triremes petitarum commiscuit. **13.3** ut autem homo non profundae modo sed intempestivae quoque ac sordidae gulae, ne in sacrificio quidem umquam aut itinere ullo temperavit, quin inter altaria ibidem statim viscus et farris frusta paene rapta e foco manderet circaque viarum popinas fumantia obsonia vel pridiana atque semesa.

**14.1** pronus vero ad cuiuscumque et quacumque de causa necem atque supplicium nobiles viros, condiscipulos et aequales suos, omnibus blanditiis tantum non ad societatem imperii adlicefactos vario genere fraudis occidit, etiam unum veneno manu sua porrecto in aquae frigidae potione, quam is adfectus febre poposcerat. **14.2** tum faeneratorum et stipulatorum publicanorumque, qui umquam se aut Romae debitum aut in via portorium flagitassent, vix ulli pepercit: ex quibus quendam in ipsa salutatione supplicio traditum statimque revocatum, cunctis clementiam laudantibus, coram interfici iussit, velle se dicens pascere oculos; alterius poenae duos filios adiecit deprecari pro patre conatos. 14.3 sed et equitem R. proclamantem, cum raperetur ad poenam, 'heres meus es,' exhibere testamenti tabulas coegit, utque legit coheredem sibi libertum eius ascriptum, iugulari cum liberto imperavit. quosdam et de plebe ob id ipsum, quod Venetae factioni clare male dixerant, interemit contemptu sui et nova spe id ausos opinatus. 14.4 nullis tamen infensior quam vernaculis et mathematicis, ut quisque deferretur, inauditum capite puniebat exacerbatus, quod post edictum suum, quo iubebat intra Kal. Oct. urbe Italiaque mathematici excederent, statim libellus propositus est, et Chaldaeos dicere, bonum factum, ne Vitellius Germanicus intra eundem Kalendarum diem usquam esset. 14.5 suspectus et in morte matris fuit, quasi aegrae praeberi cibum prohibuisset, vaticinante Chatta muliere, cui velut oraculo adquiescebat, ita demum firmiter ac diutissime imperaturum, si superstes parenti extitisset. alii tradunt ipsam taedio praesentium et imminentium metu venenum a filio impetrasse, haud sane difficulter.

15.1 octavo imperii mense desciverunt ab eo exercitus Moesiarum atque Pannoniae, item ex transmarinis Iudaicus et Syriaticus, ac pars in absentis pars in praesentis Vespasiani verba iurarunt. ad retinendum ergo ceterorum hominum studium ac favorem nihil non publice privatimque nullo adhibito modo largitus est. dilectum quoque ea condicione in urbe egit, ut voluntariis non modo missionem post victoriam, sed etiam veteranorum iustaeque militiae commoda polliceretur. 15.2 urgenti deinde terra marique hosti hinc fratrem cum classe ac tironibus et gladiatorum manu opposuit, hinc Betriacenses copias et duces; atque ubique aut superatus aut proditus salutem sibi et milies sestertium a Flavio Sabino Vespasiani fratre pepigit; statimque pro gradibus Palati apud frequentes milites cedere se imperio quod invitus recepisset professus, cunctis reclamantibus rem distulit ac nocte interposita primo diluculo sordidatus descendit ad rostra multisque cum lacrimis eadem illa, verum e libello, testatus est. 15.3 rursus interpellante milite ac populo et ne deficeret hortante omnemque operam suam certatim pollicente, animum resumpsit Sabinumque et reliquos Flavianos nihil iam metuentis vi subita in

Capitolium compulit succensoque templo Iovis Optimi Maximi oppressit, cum et proelium et incendium e Tiberiana prospiceret domo inter epulas. non multo post paenitens facti et in alios culpam conferens vocata contione iuravit coegitque iurare et ceteros nihil sibi antiquius quiete publica fore. **15.4** tunc solutum a latere pugionem consuli primum, deinde illo recusante magistratibus ac mox senatoribus singulis porrigens, nullo recipiente, quasi in aede Concordiae positurus abscessit. sed quibusdam adclamantibus ipsum esse Concordiam, rediit nec solum retinere se ferrum affirmavit, verum etiam Concordiae recipere cognomen; **16.1** suasitque senatui, ut legatos cum virginibus Vestalibus mitterent pacem aut certe tempus ad consultandum petituros.

postridie responsa opperienti nuntiatum est per exploratorem hostes appropinquare. continuo igitur abstrusus gestatoria sella duobus solis comitibus, pistore et coco, Aventinum et paternam domum clam petit, ut inde in Campaniam fugeret; mox levi rumore et incerto, tamquam pax impetrata esset, referri se in Palatium passus est. ubi cum deserta omnia repperisset, dilabentibus et qui simul erant, zona se aureorum plena circumdedit confugitque in cellulam ianitoris, religato pro foribus cane lectoque et culcita obiectis.

**17.1** irruperant iam agminis antecessores ac nemine obvio rimabantur, ut fit, singula. ab his extractus e latebra, sciscitantes, quis esset – nam ignorabatur – et ubi esse Vitellium sciret, mendacio elusit; deinde agnitus rogare non destitit, quasi quaedam de salute Vespasiani dicturus, ut custodiretur interim vel in carcere, donec religatis post terga manibus, iniecto cervicibus laqueo, veste discissa seminudus in forum tractus est inter magna rerum verborumque ludibria per totum viae Sacrae spatium, reducto coma capite, ceu noxii solent, atque etiam mento mucrone gladii subrecto, ut visendam praeberet faciem neve summitteret; **17.2** quibusdam stercore et caeno incessentibus, aliis incendiarium et patinarium vociferantibus, parte vulgi etiam corporis vitia exprobrante; erat enim in eo enormis proceritas, facies rubida plerumque ex vinulentia, venter obesus, alterum femur subdebile impulsu olim quadrigae, cum auriganti Gaio ministratorem exhiberet. tandem apud Gemonias minutissimis ictibus excarnificatus atque confectus est et inde unco tractus in Tiberim.

**18.1** periit cum fratre et filio anno vitae septimo quinquagesimo; nec fefellit coniectura eorum qui augurio, quod factum ei Viennae ostendimus, non aliud portendi praedixerant quam venturum in alicuius Gallicani hominis potestatem, siquidem ab Antonio Primo adversarum partium duce oppressus est, cui Tolosae nato cognomen in pueritia Becco fuerat: id valet gallinacei rostrum.

# *Commentary*

## Galba

### THE FALL OF THE JULIO-CLAUDIAN HOUSE (1)

The first chapter of the *Life* of Galba serves as an introduction to
Books 7 and 8 of the *Lives of the Caesars*. This is the first major
break-point in the *Lives* and S. feels constrained to indicate its
importance. He does this not by looking forward to the Year of the
Four Emperors or to the Flavian regime but by going back to the point
where the Julii and the Claudii came together with the marriage of
Livia and Octavian and formed the dynasty which established the
Principate and ruled Rome for a century. This chapter could equally
well have served as a postscript to the *Life* of Nero; on this see further
R. Syme, *MH* 37 (1980) 117-18.

**1.1** *Progenies Caesarum in Nerone defecit*: this is the bluntest statement
in our major sources of what was believed to be the main reason for
the civil strife of A.D. 68-70, and it is constantly repeated in later
authors; e.g. Dio 62.18.4 and 63.29.3; Aur. Vict. *Caes*. 5.17; Eutrop.
7.15; Oros. 7.15; even Tacitus has Galba refer in passing to *finita
Iuliorum Claudiorumque domo* (*H* 1.16.1). However, none of these
sources are factually correct: while no males survived Nero, there was
one female, Junia Calvina, a direct descendant of Augustus, who
survived until 79 at least, when Vespasian claimed that the ominous
opening of the Mausoleum of Augustus applied to her (S. *Vesp*. 23.4;
see also *Ann*. 12.4.1, 8.1; 14.12; Sen. *Apocol*. 8).

*compluribus quidem signis*: the context makes it clear that what S. is
talking about is portents that Nero was to be the last of the *progenies
Caesarum*. This therefore excludes the dreams, auspices and omens
listed by him at *Ner*. 46, which were taken to refer simply to Nero's
coming end, without any wider 'Julio-Claudian' significance; cf.

similarly Dio 63.26.5, 27.1.

*Livia olim post Augusti... nuptias*: Livia Drusilla, later named Iulia Augusta after her testamentary adoption by Augustus (which gave rise to the erroneous, but convenient, 'Livia Augusta': cf. *G*. 5.2; *O* 1.1), was the daughter of M. Livius Drusus Claudianus and his wife Alfidia. She was born on 30th January, 58 B.C. and was married, probably in 43 B.C., to her father's kinsman (possibly even nephew) Ti. Claudius Nero, to whom she bore two sons: in 42 B.C. Ti. Claudius Nero (the later Emperor Tiberius) and in 38 Decimus (later Nero) Claudius Drusus. By this time Octavian had met Livia and become enamoured of her: at his request Nero not only divorced her but, on 17th January, 38 B.C., complaisantly gave her away at the marriage ceremony and participated in the subsequent festivities, a mere three days after the birth of Drusus; though it appears that she had been living with Octavian since she was six months pregnant (cf. *Aug*. 69.1; *Ann*. 5.1). In later years, 17th January was especially celebrated: after Augustus' death it became a public holiday and on this date, early in the principate of Claudius, Livia herself was deified. This was the day *par excellence* which brought the Julii and Claudii together (cf. EJ pp. 45, 46).

*statim*: according to Dio (48.52.3), this incident occurred in 37 B.C., which is a year or more after the marriage of Livia and Octavian. On the other hand, Pliny says that it happened *cum pacta esset illa* (*sc. Livia Drusilla*) *Caesari* (*NH* 15.136), which implies late 39 B.C. and which for a portent of this type is much more impressive. It would seem that this story about Livia had no precise time reference, though clearly it belonged somewhere near the beginning of her association with Octavian.

*Veientanum suum*: only S. mentions the famous villa of Livia at Prima Porta, some nine miles from Rome, in connection with this story. The villa was situated on a craggy hill of volcanic tufa overlooking the Tiber valley near the point where the Via Flaminia and Via Tiberina diverge. Excavations in 1863 uncovered two masterpieces: the most famous of all statues of Augustus (now in the Vatican Museum), and the fresco from an underground room which 'shows a garden of somewhat sombre woodland beyond a low garden-paling, and its subtle gradation of blues and greens, with birds here and there amongst the leaves, has something of the melancholy graciousness of the age of Corot' (M. Wheeler, *Roman Art and Architecture* [London, 1964] 183 and fig. 166).

*praetervolans aquila gallinam albam... demisit in gremium*: eagle portents are particularly common in S. and are usually associated with predictions of supreme power, e.g. *Aug.* 94.7; 96.1; cf. 97.1; *Tib.* 14.4; *Claud.* 7; and, concerning the emperors of A.D. 69, *G.* 4.2; *Vit.* 9; *Vesp.* 5.6.

This particular story (cf. Pliny, *NH* 15.136-7 and Dio 48.52.3-4) is reminiscent of the story of 'Lucumo' (Tarquinius Priscus) in Livy (1.34.8-9, on which see R.M. Ogilvie's *Commentary* [Oxford, 1965] on 1.34.8, *s.v.* 'aquila'). Pliny reveals that Livia consulted the augurs, and reared the hen and its offspring and planted the laurel branch at their instruction. S., however, is not really interested in the nuances of interpretation of this event as a prophecy of power for the Julio-Claudian family: for him its significance lies only in the deaths of the trees and the chickens.

*ad Gallinas*: the use of *ad* with the accusative to indicate 'in the vicinity of' or 'near' a place is well-known; S. uses this sort of expression in *Aug.* 5 when giving the location of Augustus' birthplace: r*egione Palati ad Capita Bubula* (cf. *Dom.* 1.1: *regione urbis sexta ad Malum punicum*). This use of *ad* is not vague, nor does it reflect any topographic uncertainty: in an ancient city, where not all streets were named and houses were not numbered, this was simply the method of giving an address.

*triumphaturi Caesares*: this phrase must be interpreted strictly. It refers only to triumphs and not *ovationes* (see next n.).

*laureas decerperent*: the use of laurel was one of the distinctive signs of a triumph. The *currus triumphalis* was decorated with laurel branches and the *triumphator* wore on his head a *corona laurea* (also called the *corona triumphalis*) and held in his right hand a laurel branch. On the other hand, a general granted an *ovatio* wore, during his ceremonial entry into Rome, a wreath of myrtle and the laurel had no part in his *ornatus*. See further, B. Curran and F. Williams, *LCM* 6 (1981) 209-12.

*fuitque mos triumphantibus, alias confestim eodem loco pangere*: cf. Pliny, who is more explicit and somewhat different (*NH* 15.137): *mireque silva ea* (sc. from the branch planted by Livia) *provenit: ex ea triumphans postea Caesar laurum in manu tenuit coronamque capite gessit, ac deinde imperatores Caesares cuncti; traditusque mos est ramos quos tenuerant serendi...* This process of propagation involved is presumably the use of cuttings.

*et observatum est sub cuiusque obitum... interiit*: we may perhaps accept that there was a laurel-grove at Livia's villa at Prima Porta and that a tradition grew up among the members of the Julio-Claudian family of using laurel branches from it for triumphs. Conceivably, too, successive members of the family planted additional trees, and all of this may have been because of some story about Livia, which became increasingly elaborate with the passage of time. However, with the remarks here cited S. enters the realm of fantasy: taken literally, they would mean that all the trees planted subsequent to Livia's original planting were dead by the beginning of A.D. 68 (with the possible exception of 'Nero's tree'!) and that in that year everything else withered up and died. However, Pliny directly contradicts this tale in a casual aside. The passage quoted in the n. immediately above (*NH* 15.137) ends as follows: *... traditusque mos est ramos quos tenuerant serendi et durant silvae nominibus suis discretae*. The total annihilation of the poultry as well is, therefore, wholly predictable.

*Caesarum aede*: S.'s allusion is quite unclear. A *templum divi Augusti* was built by Tiberius and completed, or at any rate dedicated, by Gaius in A.D. 37 (S. *Tib.* 47; cf. *Ann.* 6.45.1; S. *Calig.* 21; Dio 59.7.1; cf. 56.46.3 and 57.10.2; *BMC Imp* I Gaius nos. 41-3, 69 and p. 156 n. 1). Its exact site is unknown, but from *Calig.* 22.4 it would appear to have been somewhere between the Palatine and Capitoline Hills. However, Pliny the Elder (*NH* 12.94) speaks of having seen a huge cinnamon root *in Palatii templo quod fecerat divo Augusto coniunx Augusta...*; this would appear to be another building, perhaps more of a domestic chapel than a large public temple. It would be natural, after Livia's death and deification, that 'her' temple would come to attract not only an image of Livia herself but also cult statues of the other Julio-Claudian *divi* and *divae* (besides Julius Caesar and Augustus, these were Livia, Gaius' sister Drusilla, Claudius, Nero's wife Poppaea and daughter Claudia). This building was, in fact, destroyed by fire, according to Pliny (*NH* 12.94, which must be before 77) – perhaps the origin of the story of lightning.

### GALBA'S BACKGROUND AND CAREER TO APRIL, 68 (2.1-9.1)

**2.1** *nullo gradu contingens Caesarum domum*: in the context of this remark, S. is obviously stressing the magnitude of the break which occurred in A.D. 68. However, he may also be providing, *en passant*, a gentle corrective to Plut. *G.* 3.2.

*pronepotem se Quinti Catuli Capitolini semper ascripserit*: there are, however, no examples of this extant. Q. Lutatius Q.f.Q.n. Catulus (*cos.* 78 B.C.) was one of the leading figures in the clique of *nobiles* who dominated Roman politics from the retirement of Sulla to the establishment of the *amicitia* between Caesar, Pompey and Crassus in 60 B.C. He is referred to as *Capitolinus* because he was, from 78 B.C., responsible for the rebuilding of the great Capitoline temple, destroyed by fire in 83. It was Catulus' temple which burned down in December A.D. 69 (see below, *Vit.* 15.3).

*imperator vero etiam stemma... referret*: this is, of course, an attempt to rival the ultimate ancestry of the *gens Iulia* and we may here see a remnant of Galban propaganda which in A.D. 68 sought to build up the image of the new Emperor by providing him with a line of descent at least as impressive as that of the family which he had replaced.

The *imagines* of distinguished ancestors were kept in *armaria* (display cases? cupboards?) in the *atrium* of a noble Roman's house. The pedigree was indicated by the arrangement of the *imagines* and by painted lines connecting them.

**3.1** *imagines et elogia universi generis exsequi longum est, familiae breviter attingam*: in this case *elogia* seem to refer to the short laudatory inscriptions attached to the *imago* of each distinguished ancestor (see further below, *Vit.* 1.2, n. on *extat Q. †Elogi... libellus*).

Though Galba's long and distinguished ancestry was perhaps the main reason for his being considered *capax imperii* in 68 (while Verginius Rufus, for example, was not; cf. *H* 1.52.4; 2.76.2), we can scarcely blame S. for his reluctance even to attempt to summarize the history and achievements of the *gens Sulpicia*, since the record of the

Sulpicii goes back to the earliest days of the Roman Republic. Prior to the second Punic War, when the Sulpicii Galbae can be distinguished as a separate *stirps*, members of this *gens* had held seventeen consulships and two dictatorships; and there were in addition fifteen *tribuni militum consulari potestate*, five *interreges*, three censors, and one of the *decemviri* of 451 B.C.

However, during the last two centuries of the Republic the Sulpicii Galbae seem to have become the predominant *stirps*. The table appended to this Commentary (Appendix A; p. 174) is derived from the work of Münzer and Fluss (*RE* IV A 753-4, 755-6) and J. H. Oliver (*AJA* 46 [1942] 380-8): down to 31 B.C., the forms of the names are as given by Broughton (*MRR*); in each case the *RE* number is appended to the name.

*qui primus Sulpiciorum cognomen Galbae tulit...ambigitur*: S. is clearly uncertain regarding not only the origin of and reason for the name Galba, but also the identity of the first Galba, as indeed we are today. Since P. Sulpicius Galba Maximus, *cos.* 211 B.C., and Ser. Sulpicius Galba, *aed. cur.* 209 B.C., are almost certainly of the same generation and probably brothers, and both bear the *cognomen* Galba, we can be sure that they are not its originators. The consular *fasti* list Galba Maximus as 'Ser.f.P.n.': the 'Ser.' is unknown, but the grandfather 'P.' may, on an economical hypothesis, reasonably be identified with P. Sulpicius Saverrio, *cos.* 279 B.C. The unknown 'Ser.', father of Galba Maximus, would therefore be the originator of the *cognomen* Galba and he is therefore entered, quite hypothetically, in the stemma as 'Ser. Sulpicius Galba.'

*quidam putant...appellanturque galbae*: of the four etymologies of 'Galba' given by S., the first cannot be correct because the name came into use at about the time of the *first* Punic War; the second is possible though the true meaning of *galbeus* (or *galbea*) is 'armband'. The word was originally written with an initial 'C' and denotes military or triumphal decorations. The change in spelling proves that the word was used in written form prior to the introduction (during the third century B.C.) of 'G' as a means of distinguishing one of the sounds originally represented by 'C'; as a nickname for a family as loaded with honours as the early Sulpicii, it seems entirely appropriate. S.'s third suggestion has some merit too, since in Old German the ending *-kalb* means 'swelling'; cf. English *calf* (of the leg). The fourth suggestion cannot be assessed, since S. is the only source for this grub or insect.

**3.2** *familiam illustravit*: the meaning of this expression is not wholly clear, since *Servius Galba consularis* ( = Ser. Sulpicius Ser.f.P.n. Galba, *cos*. 144 B.C.; see next n.) was not the first consul to bear the name Galba. S. may not, however, have been aware of this since he does not mention Galba Maximus (*cos*. 211, 200; *dict*. 203). On the other hand, the consul of 144 B.C. became so notorious that S.'s use of *illustravit* may be deliberate and ironic.

*Servius Galba consularis*: Servius Sulpicius Galba (*RE* 58), grandson of Galba Maximus, was probably born in the 190s B.C. He provides one of the grimmest examples of greed and cruelty found in the Senate during the middle part of the second century B.C., its period of greatest ascendancy.

In 151-150 B.C. during his praetorship and its prorogation in Further Spain, Galba promised peace to the Lusitani (then at war with Rome) and land to settle on. When they had divided into three separate groups and had laid down their arms, he took 8,000 of them, massacred the majority and then sold the survivors into slavery (App. *Hisp*. 59-60; Val. Max. 8.1.2; 9.6.2; Oros. 4.21.10). On his return to Rome in 149 B.C. he was prosecuted but spoke so movingly in his own defence that all action against him was dropped (Livy, *Per*. 49; Cic. *Brut*. 89-90; Val. Max. 8.1.2; 8.7.1). (Later the same year a *quaestio de rebus repetundis* was established, the first of the *quaestiones perpetuae*.) A few years later, in 144 B.C., in spite of his earlier conduct Galba became consul.

†*et eloquentissimus*: Ihm's text is barely satisfactory; Bentley's *vel* for *et* is a simple and easy emendation, but I. Casaubon's suggestion *ditissimus et eloquentissimus*, based on App. *Hisp*. 60, is perhaps closer to what S. wrote. Cicero is our major source of information about Galba as an orator, and from his general references to him it is clear that, for Cicero, he and C. Laelius were the pre-eminent orators of their day; cf. *de Or*. 1.58.

*Viriatini belli causam extitisse*: Viriatus was a Lusitanian shepherd and one of the few survivors of the group massacred by Galba. About

147 B.C. he was chosen as commander-in-chief of the Lusitani, and he fought with great success against the Romans in subsequent years. Although he was ultimately murdered and Lusitania was subdued by the Romans, Viriatus was remembered by all as a great and brave captain and an inspiration to his people: *vir duxque magnus* (Livy *Per.* 54).

*eius nepos*: that Ser. Sulpicius Galba (*RE* 61), praetor in 54 B.C. was the grandson of the consul of 144 B.C. is highly unlikely, even if not quite impossible. If what S. tells us here is accurate, the *stemma* of the Sulpicii Galbae will have to be emended. The praetor of 54 will then become the son of Ser. Sulpicius Galba, *cos.* 108 B.C.

*ob repulsam consulatus infensus Iulio Caesari*: this story too presents certain superficial difficulties. Galba served in Gaul as Caesar's legate during 58-56 B.C. He subsequently returned to Rome and became praetor in 54. In 50 he stood for the patrician consulship as 'Caesarian' candidate, but was defeated by the 'optimate' L. Lentulus Crus. Subsequently, he became so alienated from Caesar that he joined the conspiracy of Brutus and Cassius, as S. tells us below. (Possibly he had asked Caesar for a consulship after Caesar had become master of Italy and was refused.)

*Pedia lege damnatus est*: on 19th August, 43 B.C., Octavian became consul for the first time, along with his kinsman Q. Pedius. One of his first acts thereafter was to set up a special court to try Caesar's assassins (and certain other enemies as well); all of these were duly condemned (Dio 46.48-49; cf. Livy, *Epit.* 120; App. *BCiv.* 3.95). The law was formally proposed by Q. Pedius (Vell. Pat. 2.69.5) but the initiative certainly came from Octavian (cf. his own words at *RG* 2.1).

**3.3** *avus clarior studiis quam dignitate*: C. Sulpicius Galba is practically unknown apart from the details given here. His *History* apparently covered the period from the foundation of Rome to his own day.

*pater consulatu functus*: he was suffect consul in 5 B.C.

*brevi corpore atque etiam gibber*: cf. Macrob. 2.4.8: *[Augustus] Galbae, cuius informe gibbo erat corpus, agenti apud se causam et frequenter dicenti, 'corrige in me siquid reprehendis,' respondit: 'ego te monere possum, corrigere non possum.'*

*Mummiam Achaicam, neptem Catuli proneptemque L. Mummi*: the Princeps Galba seems to have been especially proud of his descent from Q. Lutatius Catulus, *cos.* 78 B.C. (cf. above *G.* 2 and Plut. *G.* 3.1). His mother Mummia Achaica may have been the daughter of a Lutatia (a daughter of the *cos.* of 78 B.C.), and of the Mummius mentioned by Plutarch (*Crassus* 10.2-4) as legate of M. Licinius Crassus Dives in the expedition against Spartacus in 72 B.C. This Mummius was presumably the grandson of L. Mummius Achaicus, *cos.* 146 B.C. How the marriage of Mummia Achaica with Galba's father ended is unknown: there may have been a divorce or she may have died (perhaps even in childbirth when Galba was born; cf. the closeness of his relationship with his stepmother, who had pursued his father and may have married him soon after the end of the first marriage).

*Liviam Ocellinam*: the background of the Princeps' rich, beautiful and ardent stepmother is not well known. She appears to have been a very distant cousin of Livia Augusta.

**3.4** *quorum Gaius maior... morte obiit*: C. Sulpicius Galba, the elder brother of the Princeps, was *consul ordinarius* in A.D. 22. Under the Principate, the practice developed whereby the governorships of Africa and Asia were awarded each year (more or less) to the two most senior consulars who had not yet held either, with the lot determining who got which province. As the number of suffect consuls rose, it naturally took longer for any individual to reach the position of senior eligible consular, and inevitably some ex-consuls proved unsuitable for such a job or incapable of carrying it out properly or simply did not wish it; equally inevitably, the emperor became involved in the process of deciding who the senior consulars were in any given year and, in effect, the emperor prepared the list of those who would draw lots for the consular provinces (and likewise for the praetorian provinces). Tiberius' refusal to permit C. Sulpicius Galba to participate in the drawing of lots (*anno suo*; i.e., his 'turn' came in A.D. 36, according to *Ann.* 6.40.2) was probably caused by the suspicion that, since he had squandered all his own resources, he would attempt to recoup his losses at the expense of his province.

**4.1** *M. Valerio Messala Cn. Lentulo cons. natus est VIIII Kal. Ian.*: according to this evidence, Galba was born on 24th December, 3 B.C. However, in the final chapter of this *Life* (*G.* 23) S. tells us that Galba died in his 73rd year, i.e. within a month after his 72nd birthday, which presupposes 5 B.C. as his year of birth; likewise, Dio (64.6.5²) says that he lived 72 years and 23 days, which taken with Tacitus' evidence (*H* 1.27.1 – Galba perished on 15th January, A.D. 69) confirms his birthdate of 24th December and also gives his year of birth as 5 B.C. In yet another context, however, S. implies (*Ner.* 40.3) that Galba was *in* his 73rd year when he came to power: this would mean that Galba was in his 74th year by January, 69, which is, in fact, what Tacitus appears to tell us at *H* 1.49.2. Given this sort of confusion in our sources, certainty about the year of Galba's birth is impossible. On balance, however, we should accept what S. gives us here: in this context he is concerned with Galba's actual birthdate (not the length of his life or reign) and he gives it in a clear and intelligible form.

*adoptatusque a noverca sua... usurpavit*: this must be a 'testamentary adoption' (that is, institution as heir with the condition of taking the testator's name) because in classical law a woman, being incapable of *patria potestas*, could not adopt during her lifetime. However, S. is not quite accurate about the form of Galba's name after his stepmother's death: when he was consul in A.D. 33, it was inscribed in the *fasti Ostienses* as 'L. Livius Ocella Sulpicius Galba' (cf. EJ p. 43). On testamentary adoption, see R. Syme, *Tituli* 4 (1982) 397-410.

*Augustum puero adhuc, salutanti se inter aequales*: for the general reception of his friends and clients which the emperor, like any other Roman *patronus*, conducted each morning, see *OCD²* s.v. 'salutatio'; J. Crook, *Consilium Principis* 23; and below *G.* 17, n. on *repente e media salutantium turba adprehendit*. It appears however, that on certain occasions the emperor gave more general receptions (cf. S. *Vesp.* 4.4: *publica salutatione*), to which women and boys and girls were admitted (in addition to this passage, see S. *Claud.* 35.2). The occasion described here by S. appears to be a formal reception by Augustus of children (presumably of upper-class families) who were all of approximately the same age – perhaps it was something like a modern 'debut.'

*constat Augustum puero adhuc...pertinet*: unless we are prepared to credit Augustus and Tiberius with second sight, this story requires explanation. S.'s use of the word *constat* shows that the prophecy story was widely current subsequent to A.D. 68. However, the versions of it given in our sources differ somewhat in importance and details: Tacitus (*Ann*. 6.20) has Tiberius, *graecis verbis*, say, '*Et tu, Galba, quandoque degustabis imperium,*' *seram ac brevem potentiam significans*. Dio (57.19.4) has a similar story, connected with Galba's betrothal; Tiberius' words are, καὶ σύ ποτε τῆς ἡγεμονίας γεύσῃ ['You too will have a taste of sovereignty some day'], and again mention is made of the fact that Galba will reign in his old age. Dio mentions this story again in connection with Tiberius at 64.1.1; see also Jos. *AJ* 18.217. A majority of our sources clearly attach this story to Tiberius, but *when* Tiberius is supposed to have made the prophecy cannot be determined, since Tacitus appears to have worked it into his narrative of the year A.D. 33 simply because Galba was consul then. Townend suggests (*Hermes* 88 [1960] 113-19) that the original source is a work of the Flavian period by the astrologer Balbillus, son of Tiberius' astrologer Thrasyllus, 'on the influence of astrology and other predictions on the imperial succession, with special reference to the successes of Thrasyllus and of Balbillus himself' (*op. cit.* 116). Some such word as 'Caesar' was then misinterpreted to mean 'Augustus' by one source (?Cluvius Rufus) and so S. found two versions, between which he had no means of choosing.

**4.2** *avo quoque eius fulgur procuranti...* '*cum mula pepererit*': the Romans regarded lightning as visible proof of Jupiter's presence among them, and a thunderbolt was usually considered indicative of his displeasure (but not always; cf. S. *Aug*. 94.2). However, lightning was certainly a *prodigium*, and rituals were developed to avert the divine anger and find out what the phenomenon portended; for this the Romans borrowed from the *disciplina Etrusca* and the *haruspices* were the experts who interpreted the results of the expiatory sacrifice. The story of the eagle and the entrails contains many references to power: the eagle is, of course, the symbol of Jupiter; the oak is sacred to him and it bears its acorns *in the autumn*. In this case, too, they were abundant – hence *summum sed serum imperium*. For other portents of Galba's rise to supreme power, see below, 9.2, 10.4 and cf. Dio 64.1.

**4.3** *sumpta virili toga*: the assumption of the *toga virilis* by a Roman youth was one of the most important days in his life, since it was on this occasion that he was formally enrolled as a full citizen and entered in the register of his *tribus*. (A Jewish bar-mitzvah probably provides the closest modern parallel to such an occasion.) The ceremony could happen at any time between the twelfth and nineteenth years of life at the discretion of the *paterfamilias* or guardian, with the commonest limits being the fourteenth and sixteenth years. There was a marked tendency for the age to be lowered as time went on, especially within the Imperial house. Although there was a definite custom (probably early) of assuming the *toga virilis* on 17th March (the *Liberalia*), there are numerous instances known of other dates and, indeed, Galba's date was 1st January, A.D. 14 (Dio 56.29.5-6), shortly after his sixteenth birthday.

*somniavit Fortunam*: this is either a propaganda story put about at the time of Galba's bid for power or it is a tale which arose after his success as an elaboration of the undeniable fact that Galba was indeed an enthusiastic devotee of the goddess Fortuna (cf. Dio 64.1.1 and for her appearance on his coinage, *BMC Imp*. I 'Galba' nos. 38-45, 230-1). During the Principate *Fortuna* was, with *Victoria*, the pre-eminent attribute of the imperial house (dedications to *Fortuna Augusta* are numerous: e.g., CIL VI 180-1, 186-7, 196-7, 3680; X 820-8; XIV 2040) and this deity received offerings or vows from the Arval Brethren also (cf. *AFA* ?70 [= MW 4]; 29th January, 89; 25th March, 101; 6th October, 213).

*aperto atrio*: this phrase means, in effect: 'when the front door of the house was opened.' The *vestibulum*, where clients waited in the morning for the *patronus* to open his front door as a signal that the *salutatio* could begin, lay outside the door of the house proper.

*gremio suo Tusculum... avexit*: Tusculum (near modern Frascati), birthplace of Cato the Censor, was about 15 miles from Rome, occupying an impressive site along the ridge of Mt. Algidus over 2,100 feet above sea-level. Because of its proximity to Rome, its impressive surroundings and the splendid views afforded over the Roman *campagna*, Tusculum became almost a suburb of Rome, and the area was dotted with the villas of the wealthy. See further E.T. Salmon, *Roman Colonization under the Republic* (London, 1969) 49, 50 and 172 n. 59.

**4.4** *veterem civitatis exoletumque morem... obstinatissime retinuit:* S. may be correct when he describes this as a *veterem civitatis exoletumque morem*. All the evidence for it, however, comes from the period of the Principate, and most of it is later than S. (see following n.).

*ut liberti servique bis die frequentes adessent... singuli dicerent:* S. appears to have missed part of the essence of this ceremony. It was the entire household (not just slaves and freedmen) which greeted the *paterfamilias* in the morning (and evening). Offerings were made to the household gods and to the Genius of the *paterfamilias*; (cf. *Otho* 6.2: *mane Galbam salutavit... etiam sacrificanti interfuit...*). This practice *ought* to be archaic, reflecting as it does a simple, unsophisticated, family type of worship. However, this passage and the one at *Otho* 6.2 provide the earliest extant evidence for the family *salutatio* and sacrifice in the morning: it may well have been an ancient custom, but the absence of any earlier mention of it may suggest conscious archaism (see further Fronto *ad M. Caes.* 4.6.1; SHA *Alex. Sev.* 29).

**5.1** *inter liberales disciplinas attendit et iuri:* it would appear that by *liberales disciplinas* S. is not referring to the traditional seven liberal arts of grammar, dialectic (or logic), rhetoric, geometry, arithmetic, astronomy (or astrology) and music. From this passage and others where S. includes among *liberales disciplinae* such diverse topics as *eruditio* (*Calig.* 53.1) and *philosophia* and *cognitio veterum oratorum* (*Ner.* 52.1), we may conclude that a reasonable translation of *disciplinae liberales* would be 'studies in the humanities.'

Legal training was not far advanced by the time of Galba's youth. During the last period of the Republic, certain men, learned in the law, were recognized as *iurisconsulti* or *iurisperiti*, and legal training at this time consisted merely of young men who had lately assumed the *toga virilis* attending the consultations of some famous jurist, as when the young Cicero sat at the feet of Q. Mucius Scaevola 'the Augur' in 89-88 B.C. (Cic. *Brut.* 306 and *Amic.* 1). With the coming of the Principate, this informal system of dispensing legal advice was brought to an end and henceforth jurisconsults were licensed by the state, i.e., were granted the *ius respondendi* by the emperors, beginning with Augustus. The two most influential jurists of the

Augustan age were M. Antistius Labeo and his great rival C. Ateius Capito (*cos.* A.D. 5). See further H.F. Jolowicz and B. Nicholas, *Historical Introduction to the Study of Roman Law*[3] (Cambridge, 1972) 91-7, 359-63, 378-82.

*amissa uxore Lepida*: this paragraph contains all the information which we possess about Galba's wife, and it does not enable us to identify her positively. We may conclude from Dio 57.19.1 & 4 and 57.18.10b that Galba was betrothed some time *after* 10th October, A.D. 19, which serves as a *terminus post quem*. This would appear to conform to the general age-pattern for first marriages among the Roman nobility; cf. R.P. Saller, *CP* 82 (1987) 21-34, esp. 29-30. Tacitus (*Ann.* 3.35.2) mentions a Lepidus who had a *nubilem filiam* in A.D. 21, and an economical hypothesis would make this otherwise unknown lady Galba's wife; cf. R. Syme *JRS* 45 (1955) 22-3 and nn. 74, 88. For possible objections to this view, see below, n. on *correpta iurgio... a matre Lepidae*.

From the information given here we can conclude that Galba's wife died *after* the beginning of Claudius' principate, since Agrippina was in exile when Domitius died and she was restored by Claudius, presumably in 41 (S. *Ner.* 6.4; Dio 60.4.1). It does not, however, follow that Lepida died in or even near this year.

*Agrippinae*: Iulia Agrippina, (?) eldest daughter of Germanicus and Agrippina the Elder, born at Ara Ubiorum (later Colonia Agrippinensis, in her honour; cf. *Ann.* 12.27) on 6th November, probably A.D. 15, married Cn. Domitius Ahenobarbus (see next n.) in 28 and on 15th December, 37, bore him a son, the future Emperor Nero. The accession of her brother Gaius to the Principate a few months earlier brought Agrippina and her sisters Drusilla and Livilla to positions of prominence and influence (S. *Calig.* 15.3; Dio 59.3.4). However, her ambition to enjoy absolute power seems always to have been insatiable and through her brother's infatuation with M. Aemilius Lepidus, she saw her way open: Gaius announced his intention of making Lepidus his successor as Princeps (Dio 59.22.6-7) and Agrippina formed an adulterous liaison with him (cf. *Ann.* 14.2.2: *quae* [*sc.* Agrippina] *puellaribus annis stuprum cum Lepido spe dominationis admiserat*). However, in 39 Lepidus was alleged to have formed a conspiracy against Gaius, in which Agrippina was implicated. Lepidus was executed, and Agrippina was then sent into exile to the Pontian Islands (S. *Calig.* 24.3; cf. 39.1 and 43; Dio 59.22.7-8; cf. 59.21.1-2); see also C.J. Simpson in C. Deroux [Ed.] *Stud. in Lat. Lit. and Rom. Hist.* II (Bruxelles, 1980) 347-66. She was brought back from exile by Claudius after his accession, but since the new Princeps was then married to the dangerous and jealous Messalina, who hated her, she decided to remarry – preferably someone both rich and powerful. Hence her pursuit of Galba. After her failure there, she married C. Sallustius Crispus Passienus (*cos. suff.* A.D. 27, *cos II ord.* A.D. 44), witty, elegant and, above all, extremely wealthy, probably before the middle of 42. This marriage proved fatal for Passienus: with the fall of Messalina in 48, Agrippina saw her chance to marry Claudius. Passienus conveniently died, allegedly poisoned by his wife (Suet. *Vita Passieni Crispi*). For the death of Agrippina herself, see below *O.* 3.1, n. on *die, quem necandae matri Nero destinaret.*

*morte Domiti*: Domitius died of dropsy at Pyrgi, probably in December 40. He seems to have possessed a personality as repellent as any to be found during the early Principate (cf. *Ner.* 5.1: *omni parte vitae detestabilem*); and he perhaps deserves to be best remembered for his cynical and prophetic remark about his son. He denied *quicquam ex se et Agrippina nisi detestabile et malo publico nasci potuisse* (S. *Ner.* 6.2; cf. Dio 61.2.3).

*in conventu matronarum*: this does not refer to some kind of upper-class 'coffee morning'. There was apparently in Rome a formal body of aristocratic married women: no doubt it had originally come into being for some religious purpose, though the scanty 'evidence' for its existence during the Republic is highly ambiguous (Livy 5.25.8 and 27.37.9) and this passage in S. is the only mention of it in the first century A.D. Its organization, composition and functions are therefore unknown (cf. Friedländer-Wissowa, *Sittengeschichte I*[10] 282 and n. 6; see also J. Straub, *Bonner Hist.-Aug.-Colloqu.* 1964-5, 221-40, esp. 227-8).

*correpta iurgio atque etiam manu pulsata sit a matre Lepidae*: as we have seen, this must have happened in 41-2, between the time of Agrippina's restoration and her marriage to Passienus Crispus. The fascinating question arises: which Roman matron would have the temerity to slap Agrippina at what was almost a public function? If Galba's wife Lepida was the daughter of M. Aemilius Lepidus (cos. A.D. 6), as is generally asserted, her mother, given this action, ought to have been a member of the Julio-Claudian house, and an important member at that. However, it is exceedingly difficult, if not impossible, to find a suitable candidate. It is just conceivable, though not likely, that Galba's wife was the much-married Domitia Lepida, Nero's father's sister, the daughter of Antonia the Elder. If this were correct, the slap would be explained; though, given Augustan legislation on marriage and the social and political sanctions which existed against celibacy, it is hard to see how Galba could have remained unmarried as late as 42, when Domitia Lepida's third husband was executed (S. *Claud*. 37.2; Dio 60.14.2-4). Furthermore, the silences of both S. and Tacitus make such a marriage improbable, and the most obvious explanation for Galba's holding of offices *ante legitimum tempus* (below, 6.1) is the existence of his children. On the other hand, given Livia's favour (5.2 below), the *Lex Iulia de maritandis ordinibus* could have been evaded, so that the possibility of this marriage is not completely ruled out.

**5.2** *observavit...Liviam Augustam*: Syme describes the private activities of Livia as 'deep and devious' (*RR* 385-6). Besides helping Galba in his early career, she secured entry into the Senate for M. Salvius Otho, grandfather of the later Princeps (see below, *O* 1.1) and also obtained a consulship for M. Plautius Silvanus (2 B.C.), the son of her close friend Urgulania (cf. *Ann*. 2.34; 4.21-22) and perhaps also for C. Fufius Geminus (A.D. 29; see *Ann*. 5.2.2: *is gratia Augustae floruerat*, which seems to parallel Galba's situation). After the death of Augustus, Livia, now Julia Augusta, was, of course, the *grande dame* of Rome. Her son was Princeps but he was not married between 14 and 29. Accordingly, Livia gave formal receptions, receiving members of the Senate and other notables in her own house, and the details of such occasions were published in the 'Court Circular' (Dio 57.12.2). Given her undoubted cool and penetrating intelligence, her influence is not surprising.

*sestertium namque quingenties,...sed quia notata*: numbers are a constant source of trouble in ancient texts, especially when numerical notation is used. S. is, of course, careful not to use it here and, given the point of the story, the copyists have managed likewise to resist the temptation. The principal difficulty lay in the fact that Roman numerical notation was based on seven signs only – 1, V, X, L, C. D, ∞. To simplify the writing of very large numbers, a bar at the top of the sign was used to indicate that the number was to be multiplied by 1,000; so $\overline{D}$ = 500,000. For even larger numbers, two vertical bars were added to the horizontal one, to indicate a multiplication by 100,000; so $|\overline{D}|$ = 50,000,000. However, fraudulent alteration of one number to another a hundred times larger was extremely simple, and common prudence therefore dictated that in important documents, as with modern cheques, figures should be written out in words as well as in numerical signs.

*herede Tiberio legatum ad quingenta revocante*: Tiberius, no doubt recognizing that his mother would not leave a mere HS 500 to her favourite, arbitrarily read the figure in her will as $\overline{D}$ rather than $|\overline{D}|$.

**6.1** *honoribus ante legitimum tempus initis*: in the light of our other information about Galba's career, this statement looks decidedly odd. Under the system evolved by Augustus for the holding of magistracies, a man became eligible for the quaestorship in his twenty-fifth year, the praetorship in his thirtieth (with the tribunate or aedileship coming somewhere about the middle of the five-year interval between the two), and, if he were a patrician, the consulate in his thirty-third year, or, if he were a plebeian, his forty-second (Syme, *RR* 369; *Tacitus* App. 18, modified by J. Morris, 'Leges Annales under the Principate', *LF* 86 [1963] 317-18, 323-36). As a result of the Lex Papia-Poppaea of A.D. 9, fathers were permitted to compete in elections as many years before the usual minimum age as the total number of their children (*Dig.* 4.4.2; cf. *Ann.* 2.51; Dio 56.10.1-3; H. Last, *CAH X* 452). If Galba held his junior magistracies *ante legitimum tempus*, this we should expect to have been because of his children, mentioned above (5.1).

*ludorum Floralium*: the *Ludi Florales* were celebrated in the Augustan period from 28th April till 3rd May. The cult of Flora was obviously very old since she had a *flamen*, but nothing is known of it prior to c. 241 B.C., when a temple was built for her as a result of consultation of the Sibylline Books. The games themselves became annual in 173 B.C.

The most distinctive feature of these games was their sexuality. Indecent mimes and public disrobing by prostitutes give clear evidence of this (Ovid *Fasti* 5.331, 347, 379-350; Val. Max. 2.10.8; Sen. *Ep.* 97.8; Schol. Iuv. 6.250); other activities, such as the hurling of chick peas, beans and lupins into the crowd and the hunting of hares and goats in the Circus Maximus, could have sexual significance (so R.M. Ogilvie, *The Romans and their Gods* [London, 1969] 83), but need not.

*novum spectaculi genus elephantos funambulos edidit*: on elephants for show, see J.M.C. Toynbee, *Animals in Roman Life and Art* (London, 1973) 48-9 and 352 nn. 103-10 (rejecting Galba's priority in displaying rope-walking elephants). See also H.H. Scullard, *The Elephant in the Greek and Roman World* (London, 1974) 250-9.

*exim provinciae Aquitaniae anno fere praefuit*: this governorship seems slightly odd, since *nobiles* in the period after Augustus usually governed *senatorial* provinces as praetorian proconsuls. Aquitania, however, was an important *imperial* province. According to the patterns described by E. Birley ('Senators in the Emperor's Service,' *PBA* 39 [1953] 197-214), Galba will have served as a legate of a legion after his praetorship and then as governor of a praetorian province. It looks as if, despite his patrician birth, and because of unusual favour or because of exceptional talents and loyalty, Galba was advancing in the Emperor's service as a budding *vir militaris*.

*consulatum per sex menses ordinarium gessit*: Galba was not consul until A.D. 33 and if 24th December, 3 B.C., was his date of birth, by 1st January, 33, he will have just celebrated his thirty-fourth birthday and was therefore in his thirty-fifth year. Morris has analysed the data concerning the known ages of approximately 180 consuls between 42 B.C. and A.D. 254 (*LF* 86 [1963] 323-36): this represents a sample of roughly ten per cent of those whose names are known to us and the conclusions are striking. *Patricians* usually reached the consulship at about the age of 32, and any patrician reaching it later than 33 probably did so because of a failure to obtain the praetorship at the first attempt (*op. cit.* 332, 334-6). However, these 'rules' were by no means rigid and the fact that Galba held an ordinary consulship certainly does not imply imperial disfavour; Galba's praetorship *may* have been delayed or he may have served a longer than average term as a *legatus legionis* after his praetorship.

*evenitque ut in eo ipse †L. Domitio patri Neronis, ipsi Salvius Otho pater Othonis succederet*: the father of Nero was Cn. Domitius Ahenobarbus; 'L.' is probably a scribal error with the mention of Nero leading to his name being substituted for that of his father. The coincidence is slightly more striking than S. allows: Cn. Domitius was *cos. ord.* in 32, Galba was *cos. ord.* in 33, his suffect in 33 was L. Salvius M.f. Otho, and one of the ordinary consuls of 34 was L. Vitellius, father of Otho's successor.

**6.2** *a Gaio Caesare... substitutus*: it is clear from the soldier's jingle a few lines below that Galba replaced Gaetulicus as *legatus* of the army of Upper Germany; accordingly, the text as printed represents a minimum supplement for the lacuna between *Caesare* and *...lici*. However, since a reference to the post involved is perhaps necessary, and since Upper Germany did not become a province until c. A.D. 90, we should probably read here *a Gaio Caesare legatus superioris Germaniae exercitus in locum Gaetulici substitutus...*

*Gaetulici:* Cn. Cornelius Lentulus Gaetulicus was *cos. ord.* in 26 (with C. Calvisius Sabinus) and in 29/30 was appointed legate of the army of Upper Germany, a post which he held until 39. In 28 his father-in-law L. Apronius was legate of the army of Lower Germany (*Ann.* 4.73.1, though it is not clear how long he held this post: *Ann.* 6.30.2, referring to 34, may imply that he was still there then, but need not). Gaetulicus and his father-in-law had been inefficient administrators and lax disciplinarians and Gaetulicus in particular had been popular with both armies (*Ann.* 4.72-74.1; 6.30.2; cf. 11.19.1; Dio 59.22.5) – so much so that he is alleged by Tacitus to have written to Tiberius in 34 demanding that he be allowed to keep his command indefinitely, adding that *successorem non aliter quam indicium mortis accepturum* (*Ann.* 6.30.3). In the late summer of 39 Gaius suddenly accelerated his plans for a northern campaign and made a hurried journey to Germany. Gaetulicus was apparently executed immediately after Gaius' arrival at his camp (cf. S. *Calig.* 44.1). A conspiracy was, naturally, alleged and news of its suppression reached Rome by 27th October, 39, when the Arval Brethren sacrificed *ob detecta nefaria con[silia in C. Germani]cum Cn. Lentuli Gaet[ulici...]*; see further C.J. Simpson in C. Deroux (Ed.) *Stud. in Lat. Lit. and Rom. Hist.* II (Bruxelles, 1980) 347-66.

*disce miles militare: Galba est, non Gaetulicus*: the metre is trochaic septenarius, which occurs several times in soldiers' jingles quoted by S., no doubt because of the opportunities for rhythmic chanting and stamping on the march; e.g. *DJ* 49.4:

> Gallias Caesar subegit, Nicomedes Caesarem:
> ecce Caesar nunc triumphat qui subegit Gallias,
> Nicomedes non triumphat qui subegit Caesarem.

and *DJ* 51:

> urbani, servate uxores: moechum calvom adducimus.
> aurum in Gallia effutuisti, hic sumpsisti mutuum.

**6.3** *veteranum ac tironem militem opere assiduo corroboravit*: on his arrival on the Rhine for his projected invasion of Germany, Gaius was faced with a major problem – the fact that, as a result of Gaetulicus' disciplinary laxness, the soldiers of the army of Upper Germany were simply not fit enough to engage in a major campaign. However, since Gaius was in Germany much sooner than he had originally intended, he had time to oversee some hard training during the last months of 39, so that the army would be ready for active service in the spring of 40. Furthermore, the commanders of the various detachments summoned from distant provinces were lackadaisical about arriving at the rendezvous point (Moguntiacum?) in time. The result therefore was a considerable tightening-up of discipline among both officers and men (S. *Calig.* 44.1; cf. 38, which may really refer to early discharge). The precise circumstances of Galba's appointment, e.g., whether he went to Germany in Gaius' suite or whether he was summoned from Rome after the execution of Gaetulicus, cannot be determined.

*matureque barbaris... coercitis*: the fact that marauding Germans were making raids beyond even the military district of Upper Germany into Belgica and possibly also Lugdunensis indicates how serious the weakness of the army of Upper Germany had become. The mere presence of a vigorous commander such as Galba combined with a few 'police actions' was no doubt sufficient to suppress the nuisance.

*praesenti quoque Gaio*: we must assume that Gaius toured the various army camps in both German provinces and that displays and field-days were put on to impress the Emperor with the fitness and battle-readiness of the units concerned. (On these manoeuvres, see R.W. Davies, *Historia* 15 [1966] 124-8; P. Bicknell, *Historia* 17 [1968] 496-505.) Gaius himself was present in Germany until about the beginning of December, 39.

*inter innumeras contractasque ex omnibus provinciis copias*: these words are exaggerated in order to enhance the picture of Galba's vigour and efficiency in 39-40. However, there is no doubt that the forces assembled in Germany in late 39 were considerable: Dio suggests 200,000 or 250,000 men (59.22.1), while S. in another passage emphasizes again the size of the force and adds that troops were widely levied on a large scale (*Calig.* 43: *dilectibus ubique acerbissime actis*). The brief notices in Tacitus confirm this (*Agr.* 13.2: *ingentes adversus Germaniam conatus*; *Ger.* 37.4: *ingentes C. Caesaris minae*; cf. Aur. Victor *Caes.* 3.11, Oros. 7.5.5). Although nothing came of either the German or the British expeditions of Gaius in 39-40, the legionary forces in Germany at the end of his principate were massive: *Lower Germany* (commanded by P. Gabinius Secundus): I, V, XX, XXI, XXII; *Upper Germany* (commanded by Galba): II, XIII, XIV, XV, XVI.

*campestrem decursionem scuto moderatus*: it is clear from this passage and from S. *Ner.* 7.2 that on field manoeuvres and at ceremonial drills the commander of a group of soldiers, moving with the men, would use his shield to signal commands in much the same way as the drum-major in a military band today uses his staff.

*ad essedum imperatoris... cucurrit*: there is no suggestion here that Galba *had* to do this. S. is merely stressing that in his forty-second year Galba was as tough as any legionary. However, elsewhere he tells us that Gaius made senators run behind his chariot as a form of humiliation (*Calig.* 26.2).

**7.1** *caede Gai nuntiata... quietem praetulit*: Gaius was assassinated on 24th January, 41. As in 44 B.C., the conspirators somewhat naively assumed that with the removal of the tyrant all would automatically be well and that 'liberty' would naturally return. Accordingly, no candidate for the Principate had been agreed upon. Inevitably, the

44

Senate, when summoned by the consuls, could not agree on the form
the new government should take, and on the following day Claudius
finally assented to the praetorians' oath of allegiance (S. *Calig*. 58, 60;
*Claud*. 10.1-4; Dio 59.30.3; 60.1.1-4).

We may presume that one of the first acts of the consuls after Gaius'
death was the dispatch of this news to provincial governors. The
message will have reached Moguntiacum by about the end of January,
though Galba may not have been there and his troops may not have
gone into winter quarters at all in 40-1: see J.P.V.D. Balsdon, *JRS* 24
(1934) 14-15 and *The Emperor Gaius* (Oxford, 1934) 194-5. Whoever
it was who urged him to make a bid for power, Galba had no desire
to move on the basis of what was, no doubt, a very preliminary and
sketchy report. Perhaps he was saved from the fate of Scribonianus
the following year (see below, *O* 1.2, n. on *motu Camilli*) by his desire
to see through to a satisfactory conclusion the business which he had
on hand in Germany (see Dio 60.8.7). However, this 'offer' to Galba
and the similar offers made to Verginius Rufus in 68 (see p. 52) may
perhaps explain why Galba put two particularly weak characters – A.
Vitellius and Hordeonius Flaccus – in charge of the German armies
in the latter part of 68.

*per hoc gratissimus Claudio receptusque in cohortem amicorum*:
perhaps the most striking psychological characteristic of Claudius
was his excessive timidity, which affected him from childhood on (Dio
60.2.4, 3.2-4; S. *Claud*. 35; 40.3). If the names of potential non
Julio-Claudian successors to Gaius were actually discussed in the
Senate on 24-25th January, 41 (Dio 60.3.2, but cf. the 'amnesty decree'
mentioned at S. *Claud*. 11.1), and if Galba's name was one of these,
we should expect Claudius to be exceedingly cautious towards him.
But Galba's obvious loyalty and his success in the summer of 41 will
have helped to reassure the Princeps. He was, however, recalled, as
*receptusque in cohortem amicorum* implies; the date is not certain –
perhaps late 41 or early 42.

*dilatus sit expeditionis Britannicae dies*: this probably refers to
Claudius' departure from Gesoriacum (Boulogne) for England,
perhaps in late August/early September, 43. Galba will have fallen ill
at or near Gesoriacum and, given the lateness of the season, any delay
to allow Galba to recover from even a trivial illness will argue great

solicitude and goodwill on Claudius' part. See further C.L. Murison, *Historia* 34 (1985) 254-6; on the Claudian invasion of Britain, see D.R. Dudley and G. Webster, *The Roman Conquest of Britain A.D. 43-57* (London, 1965) 15-19, 55-85; S.S. Frere, *Britannia* (London, 1967) 61-7; see also J.G.F. Hind, *G & R* 21 (1974) 68-70.

*Africam pro consule biennio optinuit*: the dates of Galba's proconsulship cannot be calculated precisely, but it probably began some time in 45 (cf. B. E. Thomasson, *Die Statthalter... Nordafrikas* [Lund, 1960] II 33).

*extra sortem electus*: this implies interference by Claudius in the normal process of drawing lots for the governorship of the 'senatorial' provinces (cf. Dio 60.25.6) and was not without precedent: for example, in A.D. 21 Tiberius had urged the Senate, because of disturbances in Africa, to choose a *vir militaris* as proconsul (*Ann* 3.32 and 35; cf. Syme, *JRS* 45 [1955] 25-6, 29-30; for sortition see Thomassen, *Die Statthalter... Nordafrikas* I 16-20)

*ad ordinandam provinciam... inquietam*: of the two reasons given for Claudius' interference, the second, *barbarorum tumultus*, is perhaps the more straightforward. An outbreak of the Musulamii (Aur. Vict. *Caes.* 4.2), perhaps the most troublesome to Rome of the nomadic tribes of North Africa, occurred in Mauretania and apparently spread to Numidia where Galba had to deal with it. The fact that he was subsequently awarded the *ornamenta triumphalia* (below, *G.* 8.1) confirms that he engaged in a military campaign, which brings us to S.'s first reason for his appointment to Africa – *intestina dissensio*. This could have arisen from difficulties of administration following the division of powers in the province of Africa imposed by Gaius in 39 between the *proconsul Africae* and the *legatus* of *legio III Augusta* (*H* 4.48; Dio 59.20.7). Galba clearly had full administrative *and* military powers (though Gaius' system was reintroduced afterwards). But at about this time Claudius re-organized the grain supply of the city of Rome. Tribute grain from the 'bread-basket' provinces (except Egypt and, therefore, involving principally Africa), previously the main source of revenue for the Senate's treasury, came increasingly under the oversight of imperial agents; this included attempts to improve the efficiency of the collection at source (cf. Dio 60.24.5) and the incorporation of the means of collection into the imperial administration. Possibly therefore Galba's posting to Africa was to oversee the transfer of the grain collection and to deal with any difficulties which might arise; cf. T.F. Carney in *Pro Munere Grates* (Festschrift H.L. Gonin, Pretoria, 1971) 39-57. Galba also, of course, had a family connection with the grain trade, since the largest granaries in Rome, the *Horrea Sulpicia*, were apparently founded by an earlier Servius Sulpicius Galba; cf. G. Rickman, *Roman Granaries and Store Buildings* (Cambridge, 1971) 165-8.

*ordinavitque magna severitatis ac iustitiae cura etiam in parvulis rebus*: the first anecdote illustrates Galba's *magna severitatis cura* and the latter his *magna iustitiae cura*. However, the story of the soldier and his rations (see next n.) is absurd and reveals complete ignorance of how the military commissariat operated.

**7.2** *militi qui...residuum cibariorum tritici modium centum denariis vendidisse arguebatur*: the provision of free rations was not a perquisite of service in the Roman army. This can most clearly be seen in the accounts of Nero's rewards to the praetorians in 65 after the detection of Piso's conspiracy: *addiditque sine pretio frumentum, quo ante ex modo annonae utebantur* (*Ann.* 15.72.1); cf. S. *Ner.* 10.1: *frumentum menstruum gratuitum*. The soldier had to pay for his rations and money was stopped out of his salary for this purpose; cf. *Pap. Gen. Lat.* 1, Recto 1 ( = MW 405). Since the soldier paid for his rations, presumably he became their legal owner and what he did with them thereafter was no one's business but his own.

*vetuit... a quoquam opem ferri; et is fame extabuit*: however, the point of the story is that in matters of military discipline, Galba had the reputation of being fully as strict as, for example, Corbulo was later; on whom cf. *Ann.* 13.35.9.

*cum de proprietate iumenti... ad quem sponte se a potu recepisset*: at first sight this looks like a familiar kind of folk tale. However, it turns out to have no parallel anywhere and may even be true.

**8.1** *ornamenta triumphalia*: these were invented by Augustus as a substitute for a triumph for those who had achieved signal victories but who were his *legati* and therefore not *suis auspiciis*. The *ornamenta* consisted of the right to wear triumphal garb – the *tunica palmata* and the *toga picta* – along with a laurel crown on public occasions and at the games. (Triumphal garb is depicted on several Augustan *denarii* from a Spanish mint: see *BMC Imp. I* cxi, pp. 69-70 and plates 8.20 and 9.1-2.) Furthermore, from 2 B.C. at least, a bronze statue of the recipient of these *ornamenta* was set up before the temple of Mars Ultor in the Forum Augusti (Dio 55.10.4; cf. Pliny, *NH* 35.27.1). See further Borszák, *RE XVIII* 1121-2, *s.v.* 'Ornamenta triumphalia'; L.R. Taylor, *JRS* 26 (1936) 168-70.

*sacerdotium triplex, inter quindecimviros sodalesque Titios item Augustales cooptatus*: the *quindecimviri sacris faciundis* looked after the Sibylline Books in the Capitoline temple of Jupiter and possessed general oversight of all foreign cults in Rome. *Duumviri* originally, they became *decemviri* c. 367 B.C. (half patrician and half plebeian), and their number reached fifteen during the last century B.C. A *sodalitas* was a lesser college of priests, whose members functioned only as a body (e.g. Luperci; Arval Brethren). For the *sodales Titii* and *Augustales*, see *Ann.* 1.54.1 and *H* 2.95.1; according to Tacitus, the *Augustales* were modelled on the *sodales Titii*, but on the origins in the regal period of the latter he is quite uncertain: they may have had a connection with augury (cf. Varro, *Ling.* 5.85) but the College had probably fallen into complete desuetude by the late Republic. The date of its restoration by Augustus, its size, organization and functions are all unknown. About the *sodales Augustales* we are somewhat better informed: the college was founded in A.D. 14 and consisted of twenty-one members, drawn from the most distinguished families in Rome, plus four members *extra ordinem* from the Imperial house. With the deification of Claudius in 54, the college became known as the *Sodales Augustales Claudiales* (and after the Year of the Four Emperors, new *sodalitates* were created for the various rulers or houses; e.g. *Flaviales, Hadrianales, Antoniniani*). Its activities were directed by three *magistri* and it ranked almost with the four major colleges of priests.

*atque ex eo tempore prope ad medium Neronis principatum in secessu plurimum vixit... decies sestertium in auro efferret*: if we accept that Galba returned to Rome from Africa in 47 *at the earliest*, the honours and decorations bestowed on him thereafter will probably fall in 47-8; but their lavishness makes it all the more surprising that suddenly thereupon Galba should simply drop out of affairs until c. 59-60, when he was offered and accepted the government of Hispania Tarraconensis.

The obvious fact that he feared for his life during this period gives us the clue to the cause of his eclipse – Agrippina, who wormed her way into Claudius' affections during the latter part of 48, after Messalina's execution (*Ann.* 12.3-5). After her marriage to Claudius early in 49 she exercised total control (*Ann.* 12.7.3: *versa ex eo civitas, et cuncta feminae oboediebant*). From this time on Galba clearly made himself as unobtrusive as possible, which was simply common prudence, for Agrippina was a good hater with a long memory. We can assume that Galba's resistance to her earlier overtures and the public humiliation which she had received from his mother-in-law (above, 5.1) will have rankled for years.

However, it is notable that soon after Agrippina's death in March, 59 (see below, *O* 3.1), Nero restored many of her victims from exile (cf. *Ann.* 14.12.3; 12.22.3). Accordingly, Galba's return to favour in 59-60 is fully consistent with Nero's behaviour at that time.

*Hispania Tarraconensis*: in 60 the largest of the three Spanish provinces, comprising the whole of northern and eastern Spain and a sizeable part of central Spain also – in total well over half of the Iberian peninsula. Pliny (*NH* 3.18-28) describes Tarraconensis as being divided into seven *conventus*, or assize districts, based on the towns of Carthago Nova, Tarraco, Caesaraugusta, Clunia, Asturica, Lucus Augusti, and Bracara. This indicates that pacification and Romanization had proceeded rapidly, even in the troublesome northwest.

*Hispania Tarraconensis oblata est*: why Nero decided to offer this province specifically to the now 'rehabilitated' Galba is unclear: he may have calculated that, although well past his prime, Galba would still be enough of a disciplinarian to lick the somewhat idle Spanish legions (in 60, *VI Victrix* and *X Gemina*) back into reasonable shape. In general, the standards of provincial government do not seem to have been particularly high at any point during the principate of Nero; for an examination of this question, see P.A. Brunt *Latomus* 18 (1959) 531-59, esp. 554-9.

**8.2** *duodecim secures, haud ambiguum summae imperii signum*: what was the *summa imperii*? Obviously the Principate, which is what the previous part of this paragraph suggests. And this, in turn, implies that twelve lictors bearing *fasces* with axes normally accompanied a princeps (*outside* Rome, presumably, from the reference to axes). Dio's statement (54.10.5) that in 19 B.C. Augustus received *consularis potestas*, ὥστε καὶ ταῖς δώδεκα ραβδοις ἀεὶ καὶ πανταχοῦ χρῆσθαι ['so that he could also use the twelve rods at all times and in all places'], would seem to confirm this idea. As *legatus Caesaris pro praetore* in Spain, Galba was entitled to five lictors (cf. Dio 53.13.8; Mommsen, *Staatsr. I*³ 385-6; 388).

**9.1** *per octo annos*: the length of time an imperial legate served as a provincial governor depended entirely on the princeps. The most extreme example of this occurs under Tiberius, whose practice is described by Tacitus (*Ann.* 1.80.1): *morum Tiberii fuit, continuare imperia ac plerosque ad finem vitae in isdem exercitibus aut iurisdictionibus habere*. In A.D. 11 C. Poppaeus Sabinus, grandfather of Otho's (and Nero's) wife Poppaea, became governor of Moesia. In 15 Achaea and Macedonia were added to his command (*Ann.* 1.80.1) and he seems to have died in his province at the end of 35 (cf. *Ann.* 6.39.3).

*varie et inaequabiliter provinciam rexit*: the anecdotes about Galba's conduct in Spain all emphasize his cruelty (cf. *G.* 10.5 below also); this would appear to reflect a source basically hostile to Galba (Cluvius Rufus, according to G.B. Townend, *AJP* 85 [1964] 367-8).

*nummulario non ex fide versanti pecunias*: this phrase makes the function of a *nummularius* perfectly clear: he is a money-*changer* (not a money-*lender*). Since coins of small denomination were minted in different areas of the Empire and would be accepted in a specific place only if they were familiar, the services of the *nummularius* would be required by travellers and traders. Also coins of silver and gold from earlier times would have varying values: the metal would have to be examined and records consulted before they would be exchanged for smaller denominations. The opportunities for cheating and unjust self-enrichment were considerable and Galba obviously decided to make an example of this man.

*tutorem, quod pupillum... veneno necasset*: *tutela* was the commonest type of guardianship in Roman law. The general principle was that every male who was *sui iuris*, (i.e., in no one's *potestas*) and under the age of puberty had to have a guardian (*tutor*). Where an infant child was named as heir in a will it was customary to name a substitute heir as well, in case, after inheriting, the child did not survive to an age when he himself could make a will, i.e., till puberty. In the case cited here, it would seem that the father was both careless and foolish – he let the name of his substitute heir be known and made that man his son's guardian.

*implorantique leges et civem Romanum se testificanti*: S. does not seem to doubt the man's guilt. Furthermore, there is no suggestion that Galba was acting *ultra vires*; rather, this is a particularly clear example of how Galba was *in coercendis quidem delictis vel immodicus*, because crucifixion was always regarded as a *servile supplicium*. However, there does not seem to have been a law forbidding its use on citizens, though perhaps the murderer here thought otherwise. See further P. Garnsey, *Social Status and Legal Privilege in the Roman Empire* (Oxford, 1970) 70-1, 82-5, 267-71.

*paulatim in desidiam segnitiamque conversus est*: was it merely advancing age which caused Galba to become slacker as the years went by? The only event in Spain (apart from the material above) about which we have definite information is the transfer of Legio *X Gemina* to Pannonia (Carnuntum) in about 63. We must ask ourselves, however, why it was from Spain that a legion was drawn to make up the complement in Pannonia. Probably the tranquillity of the province and its rapid Romanization contributed most to this decision, but Galba may have interpreted it as a warning that his excessive vigour was regarded with some suspicion in Rome.

## THE REVOLT OF VINDEX AND THE FALL OF NERO (9.2-11)

In these chapters S. describes the revolt of Vindex from the point of view of Galba in Spain. Similarly, in *Ner.* 40.1-49.4 he describes events from the point of view of Nero in Italy. Given this strictly biographical approach, important details about events in Gaul and elsewhere are inevitably lacking. To supplement S., we must turn to Plutarch (*Galba* 2-7), Dio (63.22-46.1) and to numerous references in the *Histories* of Tacitus, whose main narrative begins on 1st January, 69.

In recent years almost every aspect of what Tacitus calls the *bellum Neronis* (*H.* 2.27.2) has become controversial (although an old controversy, on the aims of Vindex, seems largely to have died away: Vindex, as a Roman senator, wished to overthrow Nero and replace him by another, more worthy, emperor). This is especially true of the chronology of the revolt and of the conduct of L. Verginius Rufus, army commander in Upper Germany.

Briefly, C. Iulius Vindex, governor of Gallia (?) Lugdunensis, started a revolt against Nero about the middle of March, 68. He had sounded out other provincial governors beforehand, but with the exception of Galba they all informed Nero of his overtures. Galba's adhesion to the revolt in early April threw Nero into a panic and by mid-April he had summoned to Italy large numbers of troops from the Danubian area, along with detachments from Egypt and Africa; he also set about raising a new legion in Italy. Verginius Rufus in Upper Germany had apparently conferred with Fonteius Capito, commander in Lower Germany, and an expeditionary force consisting of units from both German districts was assembled and marched south under Verginius' command. Eventually – perhaps as late as mid-May – a battle occurred at Vesontio (in Gallia Lugdunensis in 68) and Vindex and most of his Gallic levies perished. This should have been the end of the matter, but Verginius seems to have been wavering in his loyalty to Nero and his troops tried to proclaim him Emperor, perhaps even *before* the battle of Vesontio. He argued that the choice of an emperor was up to the Senate and the people – and stuck to this position. The forces from the Danube area arrived in Italy late in May and they too abandoned Nero and tried to persuade Verginius to accept a 'call'. Finally, Galba's agents in Rome won over Nymphidius Sabinus, the praetorian prefect; he persuaded the Guard to abandon Nero and declare for Galba. That finished Nero: the Senate proclaimed him a public enemy, he committed suicide on 9/11th June, and the various army groups then, more or less reluctantly, accepted Galba.

Of the many studies of this episode, for differing views see P.A. Brunt, *Latomus* 18 (1959) 531-59 and B. Levick, *RhM* 128 (1985) 318-46 (with copious bibliography).

**9.2** *Carthagine nova*: Carthago Nova (modern Cartagena) was originally Mastia, capital of the Mastieni, an Iberian people. About

228 B.C., it became the main Punic base in Spain. After the second Punic War Carthago Nova remained for some time the key position in the new Roman province of Hispania Citerior. During the last century of the Republic it grew and prospered as a commercial and manufacturing centre and as a base for fishing and shipping operations. Though it became a Roman colony in the time of either Julius Caesar or Augustus, it was gradually overshadowed by Tarraco, the other large base in Hispania Citerior, which in the time of Augustus was renamed Hispania Tarraconensis.

*legato Aquitaniae auxilia implorante*: this phrase is somewhat ambiguous. Was the governor of Aquitania seeking Galba's help in order to protect his province from possible uprisings or invasion by supporters of Vindex (who was himself descended from Aquitanian royalty), or as a participant in the revolt was he trying to win Galba over to the rebel cause? Probably the former.

*Vindicis litterae*: cf. Plut. *G.* 4.5; Dio 63.23. This may have been some kind of political pamphlet, represented perhaps as an open letter to Galba, and it was probably as close as Vindex came to proclaiming Galba Princeps. He seems to have urged Galba to claim the Principate and to have offered his own services to that end.

*humano generi assertorem*: this phrase calls to mind one of the best-known features of a *causa liberalis* in the Roman courts. When an action was brought to prove the liberty of a person held as a slave, an *adsertor libertatis* – a citizen who approached the court on behalf of the slave – was necessary. The analogy here is obvious: Nero as a *dominus* had enslaved the whole human race and action was necessary to restore its *libertas*. Galba therefore was to be its *adsertor libertatis*. However, he was not the only person to be hailed as, or to claim to be, an *adsertor libertatis* in connection with the events of A.D. 68: Pliny (*NH* 20.160) described Vindex as *adsertor ille a Nerone libertatis*; and Verginius Rufus in his own epitaph asserted *imperium adseruit non sibi sed patriae* (Pliny, *Ep.* 6.10.4).

*nec diu cunctatus*: Galba alone had failed to report the original soundings made to provincial governors by Vindex (Plut. *G.* 4.4) and so found himself in a completely exposed position once the revolt in Gaul began. However, it is clear from the numbers and the distribution of his allies once he revolted (e.g., T. Vinius in Tarraconensis, M. Salvius Otho in Lusitania, A. Caecina Alienus in Baetica, (?) Ti. Iulius Alexander in Egypt and others in Rome, perhaps part of the general opposition to Nero that had been building for some time) that he had come to feel threatened and had begun to build *partes* in the traditional Roman manner, perhaps since the deaths of *viri militares* such as Corbulo and the brothers Scribonii in 66-67 (Dio 62.17.2-6; cf. *H.* 4.41.3). This 'movement' was probably separate from that of Vindex, since S. *seems* to imply (previous sentence) that news of the outbreak of the revolt came as a surprise to him. His failure to report the overtures of Vindex, the news that Nero had ordered his death, and then finally the open appeal from Vindex, all combined to force his hand prematurely. See further G.E.F. Chilver, *JRS* 47 (1957) 31-2; R. Syme, *Historia* 31 (1982) 460-83.

*condicionem... recepit*: Galba's appraisal of the situation and his conclusion that there would not be another opportunity for him cannot have taken long. However, the 'declaration of candidacy' will have required careful stage-management. A good deal of staff work was obviously done very rapidly: perhaps at a minimum ten days were necessary to get gossip and rumour going satisfactorily. Also, the actual 'declaration' itself had to be orchestrated with care (below, 10.1).

*mandata Neronis... clam missa*: this may have been Nero's response to Galba's failure to report the approaches made to him by Vindex. It is also possible that Nero's agents discovered something of Galba's political soundings and *partes*-building. There was at least one other attempt on Galba's life (below, 10.2).

*confirmabatur cum secundissimis auspiciis et ominibus*: this religious propaganda must have started almost as soon as Galba decided to make his bid for power. S. has distributed the material over several chapters, so that it does not seem as obtrusive as it would were it all in one place: 4.1-3; 6.1; 8.2; 9.2; 10.4; cf. Dio 64.1.1-3. All these stories, with their varying levels of sophistication, aimed no doubt at different strata of society, had but one aim: *ut nemini dubium esset iustum piumque et faventibus diis bellum suscipi* (below, 10.4); cf. the very similar procedures followed later in the East on Vespasian's behalf (e.g. *H.* 4.81-82).

*Cluniae*: near the modern Coruña del Conde in north-central Spain, by the later Julio-Claudian period Clunia was the centre of one of the seven *conventus* of Hispania Tarraconensis (Pliny, *NH* 3.18 and 26) but was, apparently, not a colony. Galba retired here in 68 after the battle of Vesontio (Plut. *G.* 6.6) and there is epigraphic evidence to suggest his presence (*CIL II* 2779).

**10.1** *cum... conscendisset tribunal*:  our sole evidence for the date of the proclamation at Carthago Nova is Dio's statement (64.6.5²) that Galba lived seventy-two years and twenty-three days of which he was Princeps for nine months and thirteen days. Even if we accept the 24th December (3 B.C.) as his birth date (cf. above, *G.* 4.1) and calculate to 15th January (A.D. 69), such is the peculiarity of Roman calendric calculation that *either* 2nd *or* 3rd April could be the date of Galba's proclamation, depending on whether nine months and thirteen days are calculated *backwards* from 15th January or *forwards* from 3rd April. Romans tended to be superstitious about days following the Kalends, Nones and Ides, so 3rd April is more likely. See L. Holzapfel, *Klio* 12 (1912) 489-91; W.F. Snyder, *Klio* 33 (1940) 39-44; 47.

*consalutatusque imperator legatum se senatus ac populi R. professus est*: S.'s picture of events on this day is extremely brief: Galba stands up in public, deplores the state of the times and is immediately hailed as Imperator by the crowd which was presumably present; cf. Plutarch (*G.* 5.1-2) for a fuller and more convincing picture. In strict theory, the emperors received their powers from the Senate and people (by a decree of the Senate subsequently confirmed by a series of popular votes); the novelty in April 68 was that Galba was offering himself for a position still held by the previously (and properly) 'elected' incumbent. The irony of this situation lies in the fact that Galba was nearly brought to ruin (cf. below, 11) by a similarly rigid and doctrinaire approach on the part of Verginius Rufus, an approach for which he could find no reasonable fault with Verginius.

**10.2** *e plebe quidem provinciae legiones et auxilia conscripsit super exercitum veterem*: the new legion enrolled by Galba (one only, *pace* S.) was given the number *VII* and was originally called *Galbiana* or *Hispana*, perhaps unofficially. It was subsequently known as *VII Gemina. e plebe quidem provinciae* suggests that the recruits were taken fairly indiscriminately, since it was obviously done in a hurry, and we may presume that those who were enrolled were granted citizenship when the new unit became a *iusta legio* (the *dies natalis* of the *aquila* was 10th June, 68). Galba took it with him to Rome (*H*. 1.6), but almost immediately thereafter he sent it to Pannonia and there it took the place of *X Gemina* at Carnuntum (*H*. 2.11, 2.67). Little is known of the new *auxilia* enrolled by Galba except for a mention of *Vasconum lectae a Galba cohortes* who performed well during the revolt of Civilis (*H*. 4.33).

*e primoribus prudentia atque aetate praestantibus vel instar senatus... instituit*: this move should be viewed in the light of Galba's constitutionalist pretensions. Presumably this 'kind of Senate' represented a widening of Galba's *consilium* and the implication was that had he been in Rome, the Senate itself would have been fulfilling this rôle. Clearly it was not intended to be an 'anti-Senate' of the type established by Sulla in Greece or Sertorius in Spain.

**10.3** *manente anulorum aureorum usu*: *equites* who served in the legions or as centurions lost their equestrian status. For the *ius anulorum* see below, 14.2, n. on *paulo ante anulis aureis et Marciani cognomine ornatus*.

*etiam per provincias edicta dimisit... ut qua posset quisque opera communem causam iuvarent*: cf. Plut. *G*. 6.1. These appeals were very broadly based and sought more than just political support from those to whom they were addressed. Money was obviously important: Galba confiscated and sold all of Nero's property in Spain (Plut. *G*. 5.6). He obtained a large amount of gold and silver from Otho (Plut. *G*. 20.3), which he used for coinage; furthermore, he seems to have demanded contributions of predetermined size from cities and communities in both Gaul and Spain (cf. below, 12.1; *H*. 1.8.1 and 1.53.3). In addition to those mentioned above (9.2, n. on *nec diu cunctatus*) Galba seems to have gained the support of Lucceius Albinus in Mauretania Caesariensis, the *proconsul Africae* (identity unknown) and perhaps the governor of Achaea (?Q. Vaternius Pollio). In addition there is some evidence about assistance to Galba's cause rendered by individuals. Pedanius Costa, a senator, was possibly a *legatus legionis* in Upper Germany in 68: Tacitus tells us that, *adversus Neronem ausus*, he had tried to persuade Verginius Rufus to declare for Galba (*H*. 2.71.2); Cornelius Fuscus persuaded his home town to come over to Galba, and for this he was rewarded by being appointed imperial procurator in Illyricum (*H.* 2.86.3-4).

**10.4** *Alexandrina navis Dertosam appulit*: cf. S. *Ner.* 45.1 for *Alexandrina navis* meaning 'a ship outward bound from Alexandria'. The significance of this ancient 'Mary Celeste' is hard to grasp today. The story as circulated was perhaps deliberately left rather vague, so that different people might interpret it to their satisfaction in different ways.

**11.1** *accessit...mors Vindicis*: estimates of the date of the battle of Vesontio range from mid-April to mid-June; while certainty is not possible, consideration of the various factors involved makes a date towards the middle of May appear most likely.

*non multum afuit quin vitae renuntiaret*: this must have been an immediate panic-reaction to news of the battle of Vesontio and the death of Vindex. Galba presumably interpreted these events as a sign that Verginius had decided to seize supreme power for himself. In such an event Galba would, of course, have stood no chance of prevailing: hence his alarm and despondency, and the letter which Plutarch tells us (*G.* 6.5-6) Galba sent to Verginius inviting him to make common cause with him. However, receipt of detailed information about the battle, and possibly even a reply from Verginius, who followed a strictly 'constitutionalist' line (cf. above, 10.1, n. on *consalutatusque...professus est*), will have shown him that his chances were not appreciably weakened.

### THE PRINCIPATE OF GALBA (11-17)

The evidence for the principate of Galba is unsatisfactory: as biographers, both Suetonius and Plutarch concentrate mainly on the personality of the Princeps and do not give either a balanced account of his policies or a narration of his actions with a firm chronological base. Tacitus concentrates on the last two weeks of Galba's life starting with 1st January, 69, and details of events and policies from the earlier part of the principate are given either in summaries or in asides. In spite of this, however, Tacitus remains the most useful of the literary sources; the epitomes of Dio are rather scrappy, and whilst inscriptions, coins and papyri are useful and informative, they cannot serve as a remedy for what is lacking in our other evidence. It follows, therefore, that a detailed *history* of the principate of Galba cannot be written.

As administrators generally, and especially in armed provinces near Italy, Galba preferred to have rather sluggish nonentities in the top jobs, partisans if possible, but men at all costs who were unlikely to want to make a bid for power. In the middle- and lower-ranking positions Galba sought to place energetic supporters, who would keep control of their men and report on the senior officers; he doubtless expected that these men would not themselves pose any sort of threat. However, some of these supporters were thoroughly disreputable, and this problem actually became more acute during his principate: the behaviour of his henchmen in Rome was a public scandal. This will have given his administration a rather raffish aspect. It may also have caused difficulties when Galba sought to make appointments from the pool of available administrative talent in Rome: some people will, no doubt, have felt slighted at being passed over for a particular job, to which they may have felt entitled, in favour of one of Galba's partisans, while others will have been reluctant to become involved with Galba's administration at all. Thus Galba may have been in the awkward position of having a large number of political debts to pay, and yet at the same time of suffering from a shortage of suitable people to appoint to administrative positions (see further below, 15.1, n. on *existimabatur etiam senatoria et equestria officia... invitis ac recusantibus*).

However, given that there was a large number of supporters whom he had to reward, the system which he established for his provincial government was generally sound, and, with regard to the German armies, he could reasonably have expected little further trouble. As it turned out, he had bad luck in Germany, but if he had not made the fatal mistake in Rome of alienating the praetorians, he might well have met and overcome the challenge from Vitellius. In fact, by January 69, Galba was out of touch with most aspects of both military and civil affairs and he seems no longer to have had sufficient drive and energy for the task which he had undertaken.

**11.1** *supervenientibus ab urbe nuntiis*: S. here has simplified a somewhat complex process. We learn from S. and Plutarch (*G*. 7.1-3) that the first word was brought by Galba's freedman Icelus, who had made the journey from Rome to Clunia (to which Galba had gone after Vesontio; cf. Plut. *G.* 6.6) in seven days (*sc.* from Nero's death), a remarkable time for a journey of something over 1100 *mp* by road. (This is probably impossible; he will have made a fast voyage from Ostia to Tarraco in about five days and then ridden to Clunia.) Two days later official messengers arrived with the exact text of the Senate's decrees (Plut. *G.* 7.5): they would have taken the regular route from Rome to Spain, leaving a little later than Icelus. Their average speed of c. 122 *mp* per day is quite feasible for official dispatches.

*occisum Neronem*: cf. S. *Ner.* 47-49; Dio 63.27.2-29.2. Nero probably died on 9th June, A.D. 68: see the calculations of L. Holzapfel, *Klio* 12 (1912) 484-9. However, a case can also be made for 11th June: see B. R. Reece, *AJP* 90 (1969) 72-4; O. Neugebauer and H. B. van Hoesen, *Greek Horoscopes* (Philadelphia, 1959) 78-9.

*deposita legati suscepit Caesaris appellationem*: by A.D. 68 'Caesar' was probably as much a title as a name, and by assuming it along with 'Imperator' and 'Augustus', which had never been anything but titles, Galba was apparently laying claim to the entire inheritance of the Julio-Claudian house – their *auctoritas*, their *patrimonium* and, especially, their *clientela*. However, it seems likely that he proceeded cautiously; Dio 63.29.6 (cf. Zonaras 11, 13 p. 42, 10-20 D) speaks of the Senate voting him τὴν ἀρχήν (i.e., the *imperium* of Emperor), and adds, perhaps correctly, that he did not adopt the name of Caesar until the Senate's envoys met him (at Narbo, according to Plut. *G.* 11.1); Plut. (*G.* 7.5) speaks of 'resolutions' (τὰ δόξαντα) of the Senate (cf. 7.2 where it is reported that the army, Senate and people proclaimed Galba Emperor). On coins Galba is usually SER. GALBA IMP. CAESAR AVG. TR.P (e.g. MW 28). The title P.M. was conferred by 22nd December, 68 (MW 396) and P.P. occurs only on the 'posthumous' coinage (*BMC Imp. I* ccxv).

*iterque ingressus est paludatus... pectus*: Galba will not have left Spain until he had settled affairs there (cf. below, 12.1) and made arrangements for its government. On his journey he sent Hordeonius Flaccus to replace Verginius Rufus in Upper Germany; Verginius then met Galba on his march and joined his suite (apparently before Galba reached Narbo: Plut. *G.* 10.6-7; cf. 11.1). The picture of the aged Galba doggedly acting as a soldier on the march (*paludatus*) may seem to us at best only slightly comical; but by Dio's time it was regarded as incurring πάνυ πολὺν γέλωτα ['a great deal of mirth'] (64.3.4). For the significance of the dagger worn by Galba, see below *Vit*. 15.4, n. on *tunc solutum a latere pugionem*.

*nec prius usum togae reciperavit... legatis*: until he was sure that all threats to his authority had been crushed, Galba preferred to present himself as a *vir militaris*, an *imperator* rather than a *princeps*. Perhaps this was intended to palliate somewhat the questionable legality of the executions carried out during this period (cf. below 12.1).

*praefecto praetori Nymphidio Sabino Romae*: only Plutarch gives a detailed account of events in Rome prior to Galba's arrival (*G*. 2; 8-9; 13-15). Nymphidius had hoped to be able to act as the real power behind Galba; he ordered his colleague Tigellinus to resign and fabricated a 'spontaneous' demand from the praetorians to Galba that he should be appointed sole praetorian prefect for life. The Senate deferred to his pretensions, and he started to aspire to the principate. When Galba ignored him, he decided to launch a *coup* by presenting himself to the praetorians, an attempt which misfired badly: Antonius Honoratus, one of the praetorian tribunes, rallied the men and they killed Nymphidius when he came to the camp. Galba subsequently ordered the executions of such of Nymphidius' followers as had not committed suicide.

*in Germania Fonteio Capitone*: Fonteius was *consul ordinarius* in 67 and apparently became *legatus* of the army of Lower Germany later that year. After taking up his post he executed Julius Paulus of the Batavian royal family on a trumped-up charge of rebellion (*H*. 4.13.1 – perhaps in connection with the revolt of Vindex, though the Tacitus context makes this doubtful), and Tacitus describes him as *avaritia et libidine foedum ac maculosum* (*H*. 1.7.2). His relations with his senior officers seem to have been bad: Julius Burdo, prefect of the German fleet, invented some sort of accusation and subsequently plotted against his life (*H*. 1.58.1-2); and two of his legionary legates, Cornelius Aquinus and Fabius Valens, actually killed him, without receiving instructions so to do. Tacitus is scathing about Galba's failure to make any inquiry into this affair (*H*. 1.7.1), and twice suggests that Fonteius was killed because he would not conspire against Galba (*H*. 1.7.2; 3.62.2; cf. Dio 64.2.3).

*in Africa Clodio Macro*: in the senatorial province of Africa, authority had been divided (since 39; cf. *H*. 4.48) between a proconsul (identity unknown in 68) on the civil side and a *legatus Caesaris* in charge of legion III *Augusta* (in 68, L. Clodius Macer). Troops were apparently sent from Africa to Italy in response to Nero's summons (*H*. 1.70.1), which appears to have been issued towards mid-April, when news of Galba's revolt reached Rome. These troops had arrived in N. Italy by the time of Nero's death; so the authorities in Africa were still loyal to Nero in about late April. According to Tacitus (*H*. 1.73) Calvia Crispinilla, a former mistress of Nero (cf. Dio 63.12.3-4) crossed to Africa *ad instigandum in arma Clodium Macrum*: this might imply that she was sent to keep Macer loyal to Nero and to persuade him to take action against the proconsul, who had gone over to Galba (cf. *BMC Imp. I* pp. cxciii and 293 no. 15 = Smallwood no. 74); for another interpretation, see K.R. Bradley, *AJP* 93 (1972) 451-8. Eventually, however, Macer launched a movement of his own (Plut. *G*. 6.1), seized Carthage, issued coins from the mint there (perhaps after killing the proconsul) and planned to seize Sicily in order to cut off its grain supplies to Rome (cf. *BMC Imp. I* pp. 285-7; Smallwood no. 73; K.V. Hewitt, *NC* 143 [1983] 64-80); he also recruited a new legion (*H*. 2.97.2). Macer's line in Africa was basically similar to Galba's in Spain; however, his movement failed because of his meagre resources and his failure to attract any support outside Africa. He was subsequently murdered on Galba's order (*H*. 1.7.1, 11.2; 4.49), probably before Galba arrived in Rome, as implied by S.'s placing of this event (cf. below, 12.2; see also Plut. *G*. 15.3, 15.5 and *H*. 1.37.3). It would appear that in this sentence S. places the deaths of Nymphidius, Fonteius and Clodius in their correct chronological order.

**12.1** *praecesserat de eo fama saevitiae simul atque avaritiae*: this chapter and its successors (to the end of 15), which credit Galba with no forward-looking policies whatsoever, seem to represent the common opinion of him which (presumably) developed and found literary expression during the Flavian period. Likewise, although S. also says (below, 14.1), ... *quamquam multa documenta egregii principis daret*, he does not give a single specific example. For a careful reading and interpretation of this section, see P. Le Roux, *Pallas* 31 (1984) 113-24, esp. 119.

*civitates Hispaniarum Galliarumque...punisset*: there is here no suggestion that Galba *rewarded* anyone for supporting him, and yet, on balance, there is more evidence about this than there is about punishments. In Spain, apart from the remarks below about Tarraco and its golden crown, there is no evidence of punishment meted out to Spanish *civitates*. (On Clunia, see above, 9.2, n. on *Cluniae*). For a general statement of Galba's policy in Gaul, as elsewhere, of distributing rewards and punishments on a strictly party basis, see *H.* 1.8.1, which mentions a grant of Roman citizenship and a reduction of taxation, as well as confiscation of lands from some tribes close to the German armies (cf. *H.* 1.51.4). In general, Gaul appears to have been treated more generously than Spain; but Gaul had suffered much more during the revolt of Vindex and Romanization had advanced further.

*praepositos procuratoresque...cum coniugibus ac liberis*: Galba announced reduction of taxes in Spain by means of a coin which depicted three men with their hands tied behind their backs (*BMC Imp. I* p. 345 no. 205; cf. MW 29). That this beneficence should be proclaimed in a context signifying the punishment of those who had mishandled the collection of revenues during the previous admin-istration seems entirely appropriate, especially in view of what S. tells us here. The word *praepositos* is vague: it may apply not only to governors, but also to army officers and almost any type of official. Equally vague is *supplicio capitis*: in strict law, the word *caput* means not only one's life but all one's rights, privileges and duties as a citizen, and any loss of these privileges was *capitis deminutio*. For example, there were two types of exile which involved what might be termed *capitis supplicium: aquae et ignis interdictio*, where no specific place of exile was designated but the victim lost his citizenship and had his property confiscated, and *deportatio* (which tended to replace *interdictio*) which involved all this plus forcible removal to an island or some other appointed place. Wives and children certainly did accompany husbands and fathers into exile (cf. *H.* 1.3.1; Pliny, *Ep.* 7.19.4) and S.'s comments here, taken literally, may mean no more than this, though undoubtedly the aim is to create a different impression.

**12.2** *ut primum urbem introiit*: the date of Galba's arrival in Rome can only be estimated. If we allow him one month in Spain after receiving word of his acceptance at Rome (16/18th June; cf. Plut. *G.* 7.1) to settle his affairs there and make new arrangements for the administration of the province, and if we assume that he travelled from Tarraco to Rome by the coastal, the most direct route, the *via Augusta*, which passes through Narbo Martius (Plut. *G.* 11.1), his journey was one of 987 *mp*. Since there were doubtless official receptions at numerous points on the route (cf. below 18.1) and since Galba had his new legion with him (cf. *H.* 1.6.1), we are probably justified in assuming a maximum speed of c. 15 *mp* per day, which means a journey of about sixty-six days, and an arrival in Rome about 20th September, 68. It should be stressed that this merely provides a *terminus post quem* and that there are other considerations: from *H.* 1.23 it is clear that Galba's route involved an Alpine crossing; moreover, coming along the Riviera coast of France one does not 'struggle over' the Alps. We may therefore assume that Galba did not come by the coast road, and if he did not, we may also assume that he visited some areas in the interior of Gaul – probably Vienna and possibly even Vesontio (cf. Plut. *G.* 22.2). The probable route by Vienna gives a total distance of some 1,170 *mp* and a *terminus post* for his arrival in Rome of 2nd October; a detour to Vesontio would imply a journey of more than 1300 *mp* and a *terminus post* of 12th October. It should be stressed that these are earliest possible dates only.

*nam cum classiarios... decimavit etiam*: cf. *H.* 1.6.2; Plut. *G.* 15.5-9; Dio 64.3.1-2. There is some problem with the identity of the men involved in this incident: Dio speaks of Nero's praetorians, which is almost certainly wrong; Plutarch speaks of rowers whom Nero had collected into a single legion and called soldiers. The latter would appear to be a reference to the newly formed Legio *I Adiutrix,* but the identification is unlikely, given Tacitus' narrative: he refers to *trucidatis tot milibus inermium militum* and in the very next sentence, speaking of legions in Rome, mentions *remanente ea quam e classe Nero conscripserat*, which is of course Legio *I Adiutrix*. It is clear from S.'s information here about *classiarii* refusing to return *ad pristinum statum* and demanding *aquilam et signa*, that, although they had been undergoing training (*quos Nero... iustos milites fecerat*), they were not yet a regularly constituted legion. Nero had presumably intended to create a Legio *II Adiutrix* but the necessary arrangements had not been completed by June of 68.

In this episode casualties were no doubt high, but Dio's 7,000 and Tacitus' *tot milibus* must be exaggerations. Both Dio and Tacitus (*H.* 1.37.3) share with S. references to decimation – perhaps the casualties were such that they were equivalent to decimation. Finally, we should note that only Dio speaks approvingly of Galba's action: no doubt this would have become the official line on the incident if Galba had survived.

*Germanorum cohortem... dissolvit*: there may also have been an element of constitutional propriety in this act, on the grounds that it was unrepublican for a commander-in-chief to have anything more than a *cohors praetoria*. However, the tradition of 'barbarian' *corporis custodes* goes back to Marius (App. *BCiv.* 1.70-71), and Caesar, Decimus Brutus and Octavian before Actium all had something similar (S. *DJ* 86; App. *BCiv.* 3.97; S. *Aug.* 49.1). It was Augustus who chose Germans, principally Batavians, to serve as these *custodes*. Although they were dismissed after the Varus disaster (S. *Aug.* 49.1), we hear of them at the beginning of Tiberius' principate (*Ann.* 1.24.2), under Gaius, whose life they failed to save in A.D. 41 (S. *Calig.* 43 and 58.3), and Nero (*Ann.* 13.18.3; 15.58.2; cf. S. *Ner.* 34). Galba's dismissal of these *custodes* seems to have been permanent; cf. *Ann.* 1.24.2...*Germanorum qui tum custodes imperatori aderant*. See further, P.R.C. Weaver, *Familia Caesaris* (Cambridge, 1972) 83.

*Cn. Dolabellae*: cf. Groag, *RE IV s.v.* 'Cornelius' no. 136; S. appears to have made a mistake about his *praenomen*, which should be Publius (cf. Groag, *PIR$^2$* C 1347, with stemma facing p. 318). He was related to Galba (*H.* 1.88.1) and his wife Petronia (probably the granddaughter of P. Petronius, *cos. suff.* A.D. 19) had previously been married to A. Vitellius, Otho's successor as Princeps (*H.* 2.64.1). When Galba was considering whom to adopt as his successor, Dolabella's name was put forward (Plut. *G.* 23.2). Galba rejected it and the German guard was dismissed (n. immediately preceding) because its loyalty had apparently been tampered with. He was eventually murdered after Otho's death, to the great disrepute of Vitellius' new regime (*H.* 2.63-64).

**12.3** *illa quoque verene an falso per ludibrium iactabantur*: S. concludes this chapter on Galba's *saevitia* and *avaritia* with a few anecdotes highlighting Galba's stinginess. They are not really hostile, but we may note that in Plutarch's version of the story of Canus the *choraula* (*G.* 16.2) the reward was gold pieces and Galba stressed that the money was his own and not the state's. This does not serve the purposes of *ludibrium* as satisfactorily as do the five *denarii*, but it illustrates well Galba's concern in the matter of state finance. The level of public resources was clearly low after the extravagance of Nero's last years (cf. S. *Ner.* 31-32) and Galba had to retrench on public expenditure. While much of what he did was sound and sensible, he did tend to carry his *severitas* to extremes: it was reasonable to attempt to recover some of Nero's more excessive gifts (see below, 15.1, on *liberalitates Neronis... solvere nequirent*), but it was patently unfair to seize property from those who had in good faith purchased it when the recipients of Nero's largesse had chosen to convert the gifts into cash. Similarly, it was unfair (and, in the event, fatal) to refuse to pay the military donative (below, 16.1), since this had become traditional (cf. S. *Claud.* 10.4; *Ann.* 12.69.2).

**13.1** *proximo spectaculo apparuit*: as we saw above (12.2, n. on *ut primum urbem introiit*) the earliest possible date for Galba's arrival in Rome would be c. 20th September, 68, and it is likely that he did not arrive until mid- or even late October. The reference will, therefore, be to the *ludi scaenici* held on 4-12th November as part of the Plebeian Games.

**14.1** *maiore adeo et favore et auctoritate adeptus est quam gessit imperium*: cf. *H.* 1.49.4: *maior privato visus dum privatus fuit, et omnium consensu capax imperii nisi imperasset.* Whether S. or Tacitus more closely reflects the 'common source' is impossible to determine. Opinions about Galba obviously changed: by the end of 69 after Otho and, especially, Vitellius, he will have seemed better than he did in January, 69, particularly to members of the Senate (cf. below, 23). What we have here appears to be a *communis opinio* which probably developed in the Flavian period.

*sed nequaquam tam grata erant, quam invisa quae secus fierent*: however, no 'good' deeds of Galba are specified by S.; cf. *H.* 1.7.2: *et inviso semel principi seu bene seu mala facta parem invidiam adferebant.* On the other hand, in his obituary notice (*H.* 1.49) Tacitus does try to balance Galba's good points with his faults; cf. Dio 64.2.1-3.4.

**14.2** *regebatur trium arbitrio, quos… paedagogos vulgo vocabant*: S. has in a sense summarised the information about Galba's principal aides which appears in a rather more scattered form in our other sources. He has also perhaps oversimplified matters somewhat; from Tacitus (*H.* 1.6.1, 13) it appears that Titus Vinius and Cornelius Laco were the leading powers behind the throne with Icelus as the leading freedman and a somewhat junior member of the trio. This may represent the impression gained by people at the time.

*T. Vinius legatus… cupiditatis immensae*: there is no disagreement among our sources as to the character of T. Vinius Rufinus. He was born in A.D. 21/22 and from the very beginning his career moved erratically from one scandal to another (see *H.* 1.48 and Plut. *G.* 12 for details; cf. Dio 59.18.4). He was undoubtedly able and in 68 he was *legatus* of VI *Victrix* in Spain and urged Galba to involve himself in the revolt of Vindex (Plut. *G.* 4.6-7). After Galba's arrival in Rome Vinius became, in effect, minister of finance and proceeded to line his own pocket at astonishing speed even for a man of his rapacity. He championed Otho as Galba's possible heir when the question of the succession first arose (late in 68): it was rumoured that Otho had agreed to marry Vinius' daughter in return for his support. His power and influence reached its peak in the first few days of 69 when he was *consul ordinarius* along with the Princeps. However, on 10th January Galba decided to adopt Piso Licinianus, who was hostile to Vinius. Thereafter Otho plotted and executed his coup, and it is possible that Vinius was privy to this: however, he was killed and his property was confiscated. Tacitus' summing up is masterly:…*audax, callidus, promptus et, prout animum intendisset, pravus aut industrius, eadem vi* (*H.* 1.48.4); see further G.V. Sumner, *Athenaeum* 54 (1976) 430-6.

*Cornelius Laco ex assessore praefectus praetorii, arrogantia socordiaque intolerabilis*: of his background nothing is known except for what S. tells us here. His appointment as praetorian prefect implies that he was of equestrian status, which he may of course have recently acquired. Again our sources are agreed on his undesirable qualities: *mortalium… ignavissimus* (*H.* 1.6.1); *socordiam* (*H.* 1.24.2); *ignarus militarium animorum* (*H.* 1.26.2). He opposed and even hated T. Vinius (*H.* 1.13.2; Plut. *G.* 26.1; *H.* 1.33.2) and is said to have contemplated killing him on 15th January, 69 (*H.* 1.39.2). As praetorian prefect Laco appears to have been useless: he knew nothing of the bitter mood of his troops and though rumours of Otho's coming *coup* were widespread and even reached Galba's ears, he either failed to notice them or else played them down (*H*. 1.24.2; 1.26.2). There is, however, little evidence of much personal corruption or venality on Laco's part. He appears to have been a somewhat stubborn man of limited talents, who found himself hopelessly out of his depth as praetorian prefect.

*libertus Icelus*: after Galba's accession (see above, 11, n. on *supervenientibus... nuntiis*) Icelus was the most powerful of his freedmen and had considerable opportunities for personal enrichment, which he certainly seems to have seized; for in his speech to the praetorians, Otho says that in seven months Icelus had stolen more than all Nero's favourites had squandered (*H*. 1.37.5; cf. 2.95.3). He opposed Vinius' proposal that Otho be adopted by Galba (*H*. 1.13.2), even though Otho paid court to him and asked him for favours (Plut. *G*. 20.6). Once Otho became Princeps, as heir to Galba's *patrimomium* and *clientela* he became Icelus' *patronus* and had him executed (*H*. 1.46.5).

*paulo ante anulis aureis et Marciani cognomine ornatus*: it would appear that Icelus was given equestrian status shortly after he brought the good news from Rome to Clunia (*G*. 7.6; cf. *H*. 1.13.1). After A.D. 23 the mere possession of equestrian status with the *ius anulorum* implied possession of the equestrian census and three generations of free birth in the male line, along with eligibility under the *Lex Iulia theatralis* for a seat in the first *XIV* rows in the theatre (Pliny, *NH* 33.32). In Icelus' case *ingenuitas* was a patent fiction but the right to bestow it like a decoration seems to have been formally recognized as part of the princeps' prerogative with the passage of the *Lex Visellia* of A.D. 24 (*Cod. Iust.* 9.21; cf. Charlesworth, *CAH X* 616). As for 'Marcianus', presumably Galba gave him the name (or Icelus took it for himself; cf. *H*. 1.13.1; Plut. *G*. 7.6; P.R.C. Weaver, *Familia Caesaris* [Cambridge, 1972] 87-90), so that instead of becoming 'Servius Sulpicius Icelus' he became 'Servius Sulpicius Marcianus', which served to some extent to mask his servile origin.

*iam summae equestris gradus candidatus: summae equestris gradus* undoubtedly means the office of *praefectus praetorio* (cf. Vell.Pat. 2.127.3: Seius Strabo is *princeps equestris ordinis*; *Ann.* 4.40: the prefecture is *fastigium equestre*).

*candidatus* is perhaps slightly ambiguous. It probably means that Icelus was hoping that Galba would make him colleague to Cornelius Laco.

*principi electo*: Galba appears to have stressed this aspect of his acquisition of the Principate, in contrast to the 'dynastic' practices of the Julio-Claudians; cf. *H*. 1.16.1:...*unius familiae quasi hereditas fuimus: loco libertatis erit quod eligi coepimus*; see also Dio 64.2.1.

**14.3** *quosdam claros ex utroque ordine viros suspicione minima inauditos condemnavit*: S. here carefully defines the people about whom he is talking by means of a complex series of epithets. If the basic sentence is *viros... condemnavit*, then there are five separate qualifications – *quosdam, claros, ex utroque ordine, suspicione minima, inauditos*. However, the intention in this case is not to restrict the reference through careful definition, but to create the impression of a bloodthirsty tyrant on the rampage, since the five epithets are in an emotively ascending sequence. A comparison with Plut. *G*. 15.1-4 and *H*. 1.6.1 and 1.37.3-4 shows that the total list of people involved is: Nymphidius Sabinus, Fonteius Capito, Clodius Macer, Mithridates of Pontus, Obultronius Sabinus, Cornelius Marcellus, Betuus Cilo, Cingonius Varro and Petronius Turpilianus; all of these (except Nymphidius and Mithridates) were apparently of senatorial rank, and while it is not unlikely that others, possibly of equestrian rank, were purged after the deaths of Fonteius, Nymphidius and Macer, their names were not preserved.

*civitates R. raro dedit*: a somewhat vague phrase; we may ask 'compared with whom?' (Nero? or possibly Otho? cf. *H*. 1.78.1). It is certainly not true as regards Gaul, or perhaps Spain either; furthermore, Pliny (*NH* 3.37) mentions that Galba (presumably while he was in Gaul) gave Roman citizenship to two Alpine tribes, the Avantici and Bodiontici (or Brodiontii; cf. *NH* 3.137).

*iura trium liberorum vix uni atque alteri ac ne is quidem nisi ad certum praefinitumque tempus*: under Augustan legislation designed to promote marriage and stimulate the birth rate (esp. the *Lex Iulia de maritandis ordinibus* of 18 B.C. and the *Lex Papia Poppaea* of A.D. 9) neither a man nor a woman was completely free of legal disabilities of various kinds unless and until they had begotten or borne three children (for details, see Last, *CAH X* 448-56). However, the emperors could grant exemptions from these regulations by a grant of the so-called *ius trium liberorum*. At the insistence of Pliny the Younger, S. himself received such a grant from Trajan *ea condicione qua adsuevi* (revocation on re-marriage? Pliny, *Ep.* 10.94, 95; cf. A.N. Sherwin-White, *Commentary on the Letters of Pliny* [Oxford, 1966] *ad locc.*). Galba's imposition of terms does not really seem unreasonable.

*iudicibus sextam decuriam adici precantibus*: the *locus classicus* on the *decuriae*, or jury panels, in the *iudicia publica* is Pliny *NH* 33.29-33 (brilliantly analysed by M.I. Henderson, *JRS* 53 [1963] 65-70). To the four *decuriae* existing by A.D. 5 (whose members were all formally recognized as *equites* in 23) Gaius added a fifth, and with the social prestige attached to the *ius anulorum*, even freedmen made attempts to slip into the *decuriae* (Pliny, *NH* 33.33). By 68 the members of the five panels presumably felt overworked and requested the establishment of the additional *decuria*.

*non modo negavit, sed et... beneficium... eripuit*: clearly S. sees Galba's refusal to agree to the creation of a sixth *decuria* as symptomatic of his general niggardliness with regard to privileges of any sort. The beneficium conferred by Claudius is not altogether clear: Augustus had excused the *iudices* from duty in November and December (S. *Aug.* 32.3). S. here says that under Claudius they were not summoned in winter or at the beginning of the year; however, at *Claud.* 23.1 he says: *rerum actum divisum antea in hibernos aestivosque menses coniunxit*. If any consistency is to be assumed, we must conclude that at some time after Augustus the courts had had a further vacation inserted in their calendar, perhaps in the early summer. Claudius eliminated this, but extended the winter vacation to include not only November and December but also the *initium anni* (perhaps January-February?).

**15.1** *existimabatur etiam senatoria et equestria officia... vitis ac recusantibus*: this sentence in S. may represent a distortion of the policy which Galba perhaps considered adopting because of the shortage of officials who were both willing and, in Galba's own estimation, able and reliable (cf. p. 58). The two-year term of office may have been a promise from Galba to those whom he more or less conscripted into his administration. This would have suited both sides, since Galba himself knew from his own long tenure in Spain that such things were potentially dangerous. As for appointing people unwilling to serve, Galba must have known that a conscientious official, even if performing his duties somewhat reluctantly, would probably help to provide efficient government in the provinces, while over-eagerness to serve might well indicate an enthusiasm for perquisites and self-enrichment.

*liberalitates Neronis non plus decimis concessis... revocandas curavit*: for this curious episode, cf. *H.* 1.20.1-2 and Plut. *G.* 16.3-4. Nero had squandered HS 2,200 million on largesse of one sort or another for his favourites. Most of this seems to have been goods or property confiscated from his victims. There is some doubt as to what exactly happened to the recipients of this bounty: S. here states that gifts given to *scaenici* and *xystici* were to be recovered even from third parties and Plutarch says essentially the same thing. Tacitus is less specific: in general, the recipients had remaining scarcely the one-tenth they were to be allowed to keep, while others (*rapacissimus quisque ac perditissimus*) had not even that. One notable exception to the general rule of squander and dissipation among Nero's beneficiaries was the Pythia at Delphi: Nero had given her HS 400,000, all of which, apparently, Galba recovered (Dio 63.14.2).

*per quinquaginta equites R.*:  it is not clear how this group was supposed to function (as an adjudication committee? as directors of investigation? or as actual snoopers themselves?). Tacitus (*H.* 1.20) says: *exactioni triginta equites Romani praepositi*, and though all the commentators on Tacitus mention the variant to be found in S., the assumption appears to be that Tacitus is, of course, correct: cf. Stevenson, *CAH X* 814. There is no decisive way of judging between the figures given us. We should, however, remember the magnitude of the task, which may perhaps dispose us to regard S.'s figure as more likely to be correct; furthermore, as an administrative secretary himself, he might be more inclined to accuracy in details of this sort.

*ut... auferretur emptoribus, quando illi pretio absumpto solvere nequirent*: S. sees this particularly unfair action as part and parcel of Galba's establishment of the commission. Plutarch (*G.* 16.3-4) indicates that it was supplementary to Galba's original scheme and that it came about because the commission was recovering very little.

**15.2** *nihil non per comites atque libertos pretio addici aut donari gratia passus est*: insofar as Galba did not stop them, this statement is true and there is ample evidence that his principal advisers, especially Vinius and Icelus, were corrupt (cf. 14.2; Plut. *G*. 18.1-2), but Galba did not himself connive at any financial irregularities that came to his attention. In fact, his readiness to prosecute Caecina in Germany for embezzlement (*H*. 1.53.1-2) may well have contributed substantially to his downfall.

*quin etiam populo R. deposcente supplicium... increpuit*: because of the excessive influence wielded over him by corrupt figures such as Vinius and Laco, Galba's policies were applied in a glaringly inconsistent manner (cf. 14.2: *ut vix sibi ipse constaret*). Thus because for a price they had obtained the protection of Galba's favourites, Halotus and Tigellinus (on whom see immediately below) were safe for a while. However, S. does not mention that Galba *did* make away with some of Nero's most notorious agents – Helius, Polycleitus, Petinus, Petrobius, Narcissus and the poisoner Locusta (Plut. *G*. 17.2-3; Dio 63.3.4[1]; cf. B. Baldwin, *PP* 22 [1967] 428, and *CQ* 20 [1970] 364). We may conclude therefore that while Galba's inclinations were in favour of eliminating Nero's creatures, he allowed himself in this instance as in others to be overruled by his *paedagogi*.

*Haloti*: a eunuch who served as food-taster to Claudius, he was employed by Agrippina to administer the famous poisoned mushrooms which led to that Princeps' death in A.D. 54 (*Ann*. 12.66.2; cf. S. *Claud*. 44.2). Very little is known of his activities during Nero's principate, but it is clear from S.'s words here that his influence was remembered as wholly malign: possibly he was protected by Icelus.

*Tigellini*: Ofonius Tigellinus was perhaps the most generally hated of Nero's ministers. Plutarch describes him as τὸν διδάσκαλον καὶ παιδαγωγὸν τῆς τυραννίδος ['the teacher and watchdog of the tyranny'] (*G*. 17.2), a judgement widely echoed in our sources (cf. *Ann*. 14.51.2-3; 15.50.3; Dio 62.13.3; 63.12.3). After a scandal-filled youth and a period of exile in Greece, Tigellinus became a horse-breeder in S. Italy and gained Nero's friendship. After serving as *praefectus vigilum* in Rome he was appointed *praefectus praetorio* in A.D. 62; from then on his influence was paramount and he was, in effect, head of the security police in a totalitarian state. However, after the detection of the Pisonian conspiracy in 65 Nymphidius Sabinus became his colleague as praetorian prefect, and in 68 it was Nymphidius who took the lead in inducing the praetorians to desert Nero: he subsequently forced Tigellinus to resign (Plut. *G.* 2.1-2; 8.3). Since Tigellinus was probably already suffering from an incurable disease (cf. Plut. *G.* 17.5; *O.* 2.1-2 – perhaps tuberculosis or cancer), his powers may well have been failing and he may perhaps have hoped to be allowed to live out the remainder of his life in quiet depravity. He ensured his safety under Galba by bribing T. Vinius (see above, 14.2, n. on *T. Vinius... cupiditatis immensae*). However, after Otho came to power he was ordered to commit suicide and, to universal rejoicing, he cut his throat with a razor (Plut. *O.* 2; cf. *H.* 1.72: *infamem vitam foedavit etiam exitu sero et inhonesto*). For a somewhat different view of Tigellinus, see T.K. Roper, *Historia* 28 (1979) 346-57.

*solos... vel maleficentissimos*: *solos* here does not mean 'only' or 'alone' but represents simply a plural form of *unus* with a superlative; cf. H.C. Nutting, *CW* 28 (1935) 182.

*Halotum procuratione amplissima ornavit*: this may be referred to in *CIL VI* 8833 (= MW 198), where a *Halotus Aug(usti) l(ibertus) proc(urator)* is mentioned.

**16.1** *per haec prope universis ordinibus offensis vel praecipua flagrabat invidia apud milites*: in this sentence S. summarizes and reinforces the impression he has attempted to create in chapters 14 and 15, which have served as his account of Galba's policies and practices after his arrival in Rome. This account, as we have seen, is biased, since it concentrates solely on the negative aspects of Galba's actions and suppresses completely anything which might enable us to see Galba in a favourable light.

At the end of this sentence with the emphatically-placed words *apud milites* S. turns our attention to the soldiers – not only to the Praetorians, though these are the most important element in the last two weeks of Galba's life, but also to the army of Upper Germany, since it started the chain of events which brought Galba down. The soldiers remain for the time being the unifying idea in S.'s narrative: in this chapter their attitudes are explained in some detail, and in chapters 17 and 18, which ostensibly deal almost exclusively with other subjects, in each case towards the end of the chapter soldiers are mentioned, as if to remind the reader of the brooding presence always in the background.

*nam cum... donativum grandius solito praepositi pronuntiassent*: again the word *praepositi* is somewhat vague (cf. above 12.1, n. on *praepositos... adfecisset*). Plutarch speaks of Nymphidius Sabinus promising HS 30,000 to each of the praetorians and other urban troops and HS 5,000 for those serving in the legions (*G.* 2.1-2). Presumably the defection from Nero and the sum to be promised were agreed on beforehand between Nymphidius and at least some of the praetorian tribunes, but no precise information on the point survived – hence S.'s vagueness; cf. Tacitus' use of the passive: *donativum sub nomine Galbae promissum* (*H.* 1.5.1).

The sum promised was twice as large as anything hitherto known. *Donativa* seem to have been regarded during the Julio-Claudian period (and after) as the military equivalent of *congiaria*: they were given either to celebrate joyful events in the life of the state, or else they were sums of money left to the soldiers by a princeps in his will. This practice led them to be regarded as an 'accession bribe,' since in A.D. 14 and A.D. 37 Tiberius as Augustus' heir and Gaius as Tiberius' heir respectively paid the sums, and no doubt the money tended to be regarded as a gift from the new princeps rather than a legacy from the old. In 41 Claudius on his accession personally promised HS 15,000 to each of the praetorians, and Nero promised the same in 54 when he too succeeded to the Principate in rather dubious circumstances. Nymphidius may have felt that twice the amount of A.D. 41 and 54 was necessary to induce the *miles urbanus longo Caesarum sacramento imbutus* (*H.* 1.5.1) to overthrow a dynasty.

*in verba eius absentis iurantibus*: the key word is *absentis*. This had not happened before, as far as the praetorians were concerned, in the history of the Principate and the word underlines what Tacitus means by the *imperii arcanum* which was now revealed: *posse principem alibi quam Romae fieri* (*H.* 1.4.2). The implications of this change were not immediately apparent (in June, 68), but by January, 69 there was undoubtedly a feeling both in Rome and among the frontier armies that a fundamental power shift of some sort had taken place (see

further, however, below, 16.2, n. on *displicere imperatorem...
comprobarent*).

*neque ratam rem habuit*: Galba may have been technically within his
rights in refusing to pay the donative promised without his knowledge.
However, he was completely in the wrong morally, and any excuses
that may have been put forward would certainly have been regarded
as mere sophistry. Galba, however, would have felt that the Principate
was in a most unhealthy state if the succession was to be decided in
this way; he failed to realize that *he* was not in a position to put a stop
to it.

*subinde iactavit legere se militem, non emere consuesse*: S.'s *subinde*
may well be true, for this remark is preserved in all our sources: cf.
Plut. *G.* 18.4; *H.* 1.5.2; Dio 64.3.3. The tragic aspect of Galba's
stubbornness is that even a partial payment of the donative would
probably have satisfied the praetorians (cf. *H.* 1.18.3): Galba had a
formidable reputation as a disciplinarian and the soldiers might have
respected this up to a point.

*omnis, qui ubique erant, exacerbavit*: contact between army units at an
'unofficial' level seems to have been fairly regular (cf., for example,
*H.* 2.82.3, 85.1, 86.4, 98.1). In addition, gossip and rumour travelled
quite rapidly along the main routes of the Empire since the
messengers using the *vehiculatio* (later called the *cursus publicus*)
would have been asked for general news at every way-station. It is
clear, therefore, that the legionary troops were no more successful in
obtaining their donative than were the praetorians. This was,
however, hardly a major factor in causing the revolt in Germany;
rather, it helped to confirm pre-existing feelings of dissatisfaction.

*removens subinde plerosque ut suspectos et Nymphidi socios*: S. here
concentrates on *Galba's* attitudes, (in marked contrast to Tacitus'
*manebat plerisque militum conscientia*: *H.* 1.5.2), and through them
comes to the *metus* and *indignitas* which the praetorians felt. His use
of *praetorianos...plerosque* implies that men as well as officers were
dismissed, and we can see from our other sources that this
combination of justifiable fear and anger was not restricted to the
praetorians (cf. *H.* 1.20.3 for the dismissal of two praetorian tribunes
along with officers in the urban cohorts and *vigiles*, and for further

comments on the poisonous atmosphere among the city troops).

**16.2** *sed maxime fremebat superioris Germaniae exercitus fraudari se praemiis navatae adversus Gallos et Vindicem operae*: S. rightly emphasizes the attitudes of the army of Upper Germany. It had been mainly responsible for the suppression of the revolt of Vindex (cf. *H.* 1.57.2; above, pp. 52, 57), and it was particularly unfortunate that this victory destroyed the ally of the man who ultimately came out on top. This meant that the promotions to centurionships and tribuneships, the new postings to better climates, to easier jobs and, most desirable of all, to the Praetorian Guard, all of which could reasonably be looked for after the crushing of a provincial revolt, were not in this case available. This affected ordinary soldiers and junior officers just as much as legionary commanders and army legates. Furthermore, their friends, the Gallic tribes living nearest to them, had been punished for opposing Vindex (*H.* 1.53-54), and they had lost their admired commander, Verginius Rufus, and had seen him replaced by the useless Hordeonius Flaccus (*H.* 1.9; 1.54). This army was undoubtedly in a greater state of tension than the army of Lower Germany and its discontent was deliberately exacerbated with rumours of decimations and dismissals (*H.* 1.51.5; see also below, *Vit.* 8.2, n. on *consentiente deinde... defecerat*).

*ergo primi obsequium rumpere ausi Kal. Ian. adigi sacramento... recusarunt*: Tacitus tells the same story in more detail (*H.* 1.55-56). Initially, although there was some trouble in Lower Germany, the revolt was confined to the legions IV *Macedonica* and XXII *Primigenia* stationed at Moguntiacum in Upper Germany, and of the seven legions in Germany only they actually refused to take the oath of allegiance to Galba.

*nisi in nomen senatus*: cf. *H.* 1.55.4: *ac ne reverentiam imperii exuere viderentur, senatus populique Romani oblitterata iam nomina sacramento advocabant...*

*statimque legationem ad praetorianos cum mandatis destinaverunt*: this sentence proves the extent of Galba's real debt to the praetorians. In A.D. 41 and 54 the practice had been established that the praetorians chose the princeps and that the Senate and people should thereafter ratify their choice. The German armies (and others, by implication) had recognized and accepted this practice by their acquiesence in the praetorians' choice of Galba in the summer of A.D. 68.

*displicere imperatorem in Hispania factum; eligerent ipsi quem cuncti exercitus comprobarent*: this is simply a more realistic version of the senator's *superioris Germaniae legiones... imperatorem alium flagitare et senatui ac populo Romano arbitrium eligendi permittere* (*H.* 1.21.1). The fact that an emperor could be 'made in Spain' should immediately have suggested that one could also be made in Germany or anywhere else. However, the fact that Galba had made no move until he was recognized at Rome may have served to mask this possibility. Indeed, for a century Augustus' propaganda had prevailed, that Rome was the real centre of power and that Rome's word was what counted. The recognition that this was a myth did not come equally quickly in all parts of the Empire; cf. *H.* 1.76.2: *longinquae provinciae et quidquid armorum mari dirimitur penes Othonem manebat, non partium studio, sed erat grande momentum in nomine urbis ac praetexto senatus...* The secret was not fully revealed (cf. above, 16.1, n. on *in verba eius absentis iurantibus*) until Vitellius had fought his way to supreme power – opposed totally by the Guard and by the Senate and people at Rome.

**17.1** *quod ut nuntiatum est*: since the formal adoption of Piso took place on 10th January, 69 (*H.* 1.18.7) and according to S., in the morning (cf. below, *e media salutantium turba*), we may assume that word reached Galba of the trouble in Germany by the evening of the 9th. The message that reached him came from Pompeius Propinquus, imperial procurator in Gallia Belgica and was that two legions in Upper Germany were in revolt (*H.* 1.12.1, 16.3, 18.2). It contained no word of the spread of the revolt to Lower Germany or of any involvement of Vitellius, which happened on 2nd January; the message must therefore have been sent on 1st January. (This, incidentally, serves to demonstrate the speed with which messages could be sent over long distances: depending on variations in the route followed, the distance from Trier to Rome is between 950 and 980 *mp* and since the journey took eight days at most, the daily average is 120-125 *mp*.)

S. here suggests that Galba's formal adoption of Piso came about as a direct consequence of the news of the outbreak in Germany; Tacitus

states this as a fact: *sed Galba post nuntios Germanicae seditionis...
quod remedium unicum rebatur, comitia imperii transigit (H.* 1.14.1; cf.
Dio 64.5.1). Plutarch, however, gives us an account with considerably
more background material. He indicates that Galba began to think
about a successor some time late in 68 (*G.* 19.1-21.4) and that the
general unrest then among the German armies, rather than a specific
outbreak, was the reason for the discussions which took place.

*despectui esse non tam senectam suam quam orbitatem ratus*: though
these words appear to be a direct quotation from the 'common source'
(cf. Plut. *G.* 19.1), can Galba really have thought this? The revolt in
Germany was in response to his policy of rewarding friends and
punishing enemies and perhaps, more generally, to his *saevitia*. His
age and childlessness had little, if anything, to do with it and as he had
already received news of discontent in Germany (Plut. *G.* 18.7-19.1)
we may presume that some information about the reasons for it was
available to him. Accordingly, the fact that he responded to the news
of the revolt by proceeding immediately to adopt his heir suggests not
that he thought that this would serve as any sort of placatory response
to the German armies, but rather that it would tell them that he was
master of affairs in Rome, that he would arrange things as he saw fit,
and that such matters were none of their business!

*Pisonem Frugi Licinianum nobilem egregiumque iuvenem*: his full
name was L. Calpurnius Piso Frugi Licinianus (hereafter referred to
as 'Piso Licinianus'). He was the son of M. Licinus Crassus Frugi (*cos.
ord.* A.D. 27 and, it would appear, a descendant by adoption of
Crassus the 'triumvir') and of Scribonia, a direct descendant of
Pompey the Great. The family was prominent in the 'senatorial
opposition' to the later Julio-Claudians and suffered accordingly (see
D. McAlindon, *AJP* 77 [1956] 113-32, esp. 126-8): for example Piso
Licinianus, born in A.D. 38 (cf. *H.* 1.48.1), was only about eight years
old when his parents and eldest brother were executed. Tacitus tells
us that he was *diu exul* (*H.* 1.48.1; cf. *H.* 1.21.1; 1.38.1 and this would
certainly explain why he had held no offices. His character was
undoubtedly shaped by adversity: *vultu habituque moris antiqui, et
aestimatione recta severus, deterius interpretantibus tristior habebatur*
(*H.* 1.14.2; cf., more favourably, Plut. *G.* 23.2). At any rate, at the time
of his adoption and immediately after, he made little or no impression
on anyone, acting *quasi imperare posset magis quam vellet* (*H.* 1.17.1;

cf. Plut. *G*. 23.5). The majority of the Senate was indifferent (*H*. 1.19); and Piso's speech to a praetorian cohort on 15th January (*H*. 1.29.2-30.3) had no effect on the outcome of events (*H*. 1.31.1).

*sibi olim probatissimum*: that Galba should have thought highly of Piso, given Piso's upright, dignified, rather old-fashioned character, need occasion no surprise. Moreover, the fact that he recalled Piso from exile (*H*. 1.21.1; 1.38.1) and was prepared to adopt him as his successor, in spite of his lack of experience and in spite of a general clamour for the adoption of either Otho or Dolabella (cf. *H*. 1.13; Plut. *G*. 21; 23.2), argues strongly that Galba knew both him and his family well: indeed, Piso's father (*cos*. A.D. 27) and Galba (*cos*. A.D. 33) were probably near contemporaries. Finally, S.'s words *olim probatissimum* suggest an admiration of long standing (cf. next n.).

*testamentoque semper in bona et nomen adscitum*: in his will, a childless Roman might direct that, as a condition of inheritance, his principal heir take his name (cf. E.J. Weinrib, *HSCP* 72 [1967] 253-61, with full legal bibliography [nn. 27,35]: his conclusion is that 'testamentary adoption' was usually nothing more than the institution of an heir with a *condicio nominis ferendi*; see also R. Syme, *Tituli* 4 [1982] 397-410). That Galba, as a wealthy Roman of proud and ancient lineage, should have wished his name to continue (cf. above, 5.1), is hardly surprising; that for this he should have picked a young man of distinguished ancestry and sterling character could almost be predicted.

When would Galba have drawn up his will? Romans seem to have revised or re-drawn their wills before major changes in their lives or at the onset of possible danger. Accordingly, it may be that Galba drew up a will, in which he 'adopted' Piso, before leaving for Hispania Tarraconensis in A.D. 60, and that, whatever changes were made in his legacies and bequests during his years in Spain, Piso remained his principal heir throughout. Of course, when Galba himself became Princeps, the will which he had made as a *privatus* would have assumed great political significance in the event of his sudden (natural) death. He recalled Piso from exile and may have wished to give him experience in public life before formally adopting him as his successor. In the meantime, if he were to die suddenly, Piso would certainly be in no worse position than Octavian in 44 B.C. We can now, perhaps, appreciate why Galba, unlike almost everyone else in Rome (cf. *H.* 1.12.2 – *non sane crebrior tota civitate sermo per illos mensis fuerat*), was in no hurry to see a successor nominated.

*repente e media salutantium turba adprehendit*: the precise reference of *repente* is not wholly clear. It could refer to the apparent suddenness of Galba's decision to adopt Piso formally (seemingly made overnight, 9-10th January, A.D. 69; cf. above, 17, n. on *quod ut nuntiatum est*), or it could refer to the suddenness with which Piso found himself 'Servius Sulpicius Galba Caesar' (*AFA* for 10th January, 69 = MW 2).

The *salutantium turba* implies *amici principis* (and others) who were admitted to the Emperor's presence each morning. As for what actually happened, we may prefer to accept S.'s story over Tacitus' implausible account of *comitia imperii*, where Galba sought no advice nor asked for opinions about Piso as a potential successor (*H.* 1.14.1). At the morning *salutatio*, Galba appears simply to have announced that he had decided to adopt a successor, asked that Piso be brought to him, and called him his son; on the other hand, cf. B. Baldwin, *Suetonius* (Amsterdam, 1983) 538: 'Suetonius offers a silly scene...'.

*filiumque appellans perduxit in castra ac pro contione adoptavit*: where, exactly, did Galba adopt Piso? In the palace (*filiumque appellans*) or in the praetorian camp (*pro contione adoptavit*)? Since the main verb *adoptavit* refers to the camp, S. presumably intends us to understand that the decisive act took place there (cf. Plut. *G.* 23.3). But *adrogtio*, the adoption of a person *sui iuris*, was a solemn and formal act and, legally, it could not take place either *inter amicos* or *apud milites*. It required the summoning *arbitris pontificibus* of the *comitia curiata*, under the presidency of the *pontifex maximus*. Of course, the *comitia curiata* had long since ceased to operate at a genuine assembly of the people and the original thirty *curiae* were represented by thirty lictors (cf. Cic. *Leg. Agr.* 2.12.31), but the legal forms were still strictly observed: the procedure is described by Gellius (*NA* 5.19) and by the jurist Gaius (1.98-107), both of whom wrote in the second century A.D. and both of whom use the *present* tense in their accounts. As *pontifex maximus* Galba could not dispense with the traditional forms and in the opening sentence of his 'speech' to Piso as given by Tacitus (*H.* 1.15) – *si te privatus lege curiata apud pontifices, ut moris est, adoptarem...* – the emphasis is not on *lege curiata*, but on *privatus*. Galba is, of course, doing more than *merely* adopting Piso: he is making him his successor in the Principate as well. But this does not imply that he has dispensed with the necessary legal forms for *adrogatio*.

On the other hand, given that the actual legally-required ritual of adoption was now the merest of formalities, the important step was the public announcement of it. Furthermore, the fact that the soldiers were given precedence over the Senate and the people simply reflected political reality. The actual legal formalities appear to have been carried out on 10th January, probably after the speeches in the camp and the *curia*: cf. Tacitus' use of *adoptari* rather than *adoptatum esse* in *H*. 1.18.2, and the words *adoptio facta* and *ob ad]optione[m Ser. Sulpici Gal]bae C[aesaris* in the *AFA* for 10th January, 69 ( = MW 2, lines 24, 27).

*ne tunc quidem donativi ulla mentione facta*: this was crucial. Both Plutarch (*G*. 23.4) and Tacitus (*H*. 1.18.2) make the same point, and Tacitus' comment shows how easily Galba could have ensured his own and Piso's safety: *constat potuisse conciliari animos quantulacumque parci senis liberalitate*.

*M. Salvio Othoni*: S. introduces Otho at this point with great skill. (His previous mention of him, at *Galba* 6.1, is merely an aside.) The use of the *tria nomina* lends weight to the introduction, which is immediately clarified by the words *praebuit perficiendi conata intra sextum adoptionis diem*. This is all that the reader needs to know about Otho at this point: his background, early life and career to date can wait until his *Life* is reached, since to introduce such personal details at this point would ruin the flow of S.'s rapid narrative.

### THE FALL OF GALBA (18.1-20.2)

S.'s account of the fall of Galba and the events of 15th January, 69, is predictably divided between *G*. 18.1-20.2 and *O*. 5.1-7.1. With his view firmly focussed on first Galba and then Otho, his account is much simpler and less emotionally affecting than the accounts of either Tacitus (*H*. 1.21-49) or Plutarch (*G*. 23.5-29.5); it is also briefer than either. Dio's account of Galba's fall consists essentially of one epitome (64.4.1-6.5), which describes the rising of Vitellius in Germany,

Galba's adoption of Piso and Otho's reaction to it, and then the murder of Galba.

Inevitably the main question which arises when we consider these versions of events is: how many separate sources underlie our extant accounts, and who used which? These questions are simply unanswerable, because although it is possible to form some estimate of the number and type of the lost literary works on A.D. 68-9, it is not possible to form any impression of the *eye-witness* accounts of events in Rome on 15th January, 69, on which Pliny the Elder or Cluvius Rufus or Tacitus or Plutarch or Suetonius might have drawn. Pliny the Younger's letters to Tacitus on the eruption of Vesuvius (*Ep.* 6.16, 20) provide one example of this kind of account, while Plutarch's remarks about his patron Mestrius Florus (*O.* 14) provide another. Finally, Tacitus himself as a boy of about thirteen or fourteen may have been in Rome on that day and may have retained vivid personal impressions of the course of events.

**18.1** *magna et assidua monstra iam inde a principio exitum ei qualis evenit, portenderant*: this collection of omens and portents is unique to S.; none of the other sources contains any of those listed in this chapter.

*taurus securis ictu consternatus... essedum eius invasit*: it was considered extremely unlucky if a half-killed beast broke away. The sacrifice was ruined; cf. S. *DJ* 59, for Caesar's disregard of such an omen. Vitellius, however, in late 69 was not so bold: when he moved from Rome to Mevania to take command of the forces facing the advancing column of Antonius Primus, he was confronted by this same omen and immediately returned to Rome (*H.* 3.56.1-2).

*urbem quoque et deinde Palatium ingressum excepit terrae tremor et assimilis quidam mugitui sonus*: earthquakes were *always* regarded very seriously: they were *prodigia publica* and were therefore of national significance; cf. Pliny, *NH* 2.200: *numquam urbs Roma tremuit ut non futuri eventus alicuius id praenuntium esset*. For the *assimilis quidam mugitui sonus*, cf. Evans' description of the earthquake of 26th June, 1926, which caught him in the basement of the Villa Ariadne at Knossus (*Palace of Minos II* [London, 1928; repr. New York, 1964] 316, 325): 'A dull sound rose from the ground like the muffled roar of an angry bull...It is something to have heard with

81

one's own ears the bellowing of the bull beneath the earth who, according to a primitive belief, tosses it on his horns.'

**18.2** *ad ornandam Fortunam suam Tusculanam*: for Galba's statuette of Fortune and its shrine in his villa at Tusculum, see above 4.3 and nn. Galba seems to have been particularly superstitious about dreams, though not about other types of omen (see below, 18.3, n. on *adoptionis die*).

*Capitolinae Veneri*: apart from a reference in S. *Calig.* 7, 'Capitoline Venus' is otherwise unattested; there was an altar or shrine to Venus Victrix on the Capitol; there was also a temple of Venus Erycina dedicated by Q. Fabius Maximus in 215 B.C.

**18.3** *Kal. Ian. sacrificanti*: other sacrifices were performed on 1st January, 69, by the Arval Brethren (see MW 2).

*coronam de capite excidisse*: cf. below *Vit.* 9: *laurea, quam religiossime circumdederat, in profluentem excidit.* Alexander the Great encountered a similar omen not long before his death (Arr. 7.22; Diod. 17.116.6).

*auspicanti pullos avolasse*: they were supposed to *eat* and the more greedily, the better, so that food would fall from their mouths (cf. Cic. *Div.* 1.15.27-28; 2.34.72); cf. S. *Tib.* 2.2 for the famous story of P. Claudius Pulcher, *cos.* 249 B.C., off Drepanum.

*adoptionis die*: the omens here recorded by S. seem trivial in comparison with what we have from Tacitus (*H.* 1.18.1): *Quartum Idus Ianuarias, foedum imbribus diem, tonitrua et fulgura et caelestes minae ultra solitum turbaverant* (cf. Plut. *G.* 23.3 for essentially the same thing). Tacitus adds that Galba was *contemptorem talium ut fortuitorum, seu quae fato manent, quamvis significata, non vitantur.*

**19.1** *prius vero quam occideretur sacrificantem mane haruspex identidem monuit... abesse*: for this dramatic scene, see below *O.* 6.2 and n. on *etiam sacrificanti interfuit audivitque praedicta haruspicis.*

*haud multo post cognoscit teneri castra ab Othone*: S. is suitably vague about the time involved here. Otho left Galba at the Temple of Apollo on the Palatine and went through the palace (presumably the *domus Tiberiana*) and out the 'back door' (i.e. the side furthest away from the forum). He then made for the Velabrum and thence headed for the forum and the Golden Milestone, where he was met by some soldiers and hustled off to the praetorian camp in a litter (see below, *O*. 6.2-3 and nn.). The exact distance covered is hard to estimate but it would seem to be at least 2 *mp*, and since it was not all covered at a particularly brisk rate, Otho would not have arrived in the camp until at least half an hour after he left Galba and word could hardly have reached Galba until about one hour after Otho's departure. Accordingly, the picture of Galba standing on the Palatine beside the *haruspex* who was still holding the entrails when word came of the revolt (Plut. *G*. 25.7; *H*. 1.29.1) may be dramatic, but it is scarcely credible – unless the *haruspex* was exceptionally slow.

*nihil amplius quam continere se statuit et legionariorum firmare praesidiis, qui multifariam diverseque tendebant*: S. omits any mention of the decision to send Piso, Galba's heir, to test the feelings of the praetorian cohort on guard at the palace (Plut. *G*. 25.8; *H*. 1.29.1-31.1), no doubt because it came to nothing, and also because it would take the focus of attention away from Galba (see also G.B. Townend, *AJP* 85 [1964] 357).

There were, it seems, numerous legionary and auxiliary soldiers in Rome in January, 69: the legion which Nero had enrolled from the fleet (Legio *I Adiutrix*, which Galba had made a *iusta legio*: *H*. 1.6.2; cf. *CIL XVI* 7 = MW 396), and many detachments from Germany, Britain and Illyricum (which Nero had sent to the east for his projected war with Parthia and which he had subsequently recalled to Italy at the time of the revolt of Vindex, though they had not arrived in Italy until after Nero's death). In the event, none of these troops provided any assistance to Galba (cf. *H*. 1.26.1, 31.2-3; and see below 20.1); indeed, Piso was murdered by Sulpicius Florus, a soldier from the British auxiliaries (*H*. 1.43.2) and Galba himself seems to have been killed by one Camurius, a legionary from *XV Primigenia*, who was obviously part of the German detachment (*H*. 1.41.3; cf. Plut. *G*. 27.2).

*loricam tamen induit linteam*: linen corslets are attested among the Greeks from the Archaic Period on, although there is usually an element of the exotic about them and they appear, in general, to be regarded as oriental – either Egyptian or Persian; cf. S. Törnkvist, *ORom* 7 (1969) 80-1.

**19.2** *sed extractus rumoribus falsis... in forum usque processit*: cf. Plut. *G.* 26.1-3; *H.* 1.34.2-35.2; Dio 64.6.2-3. Although the story-line in each is clearly taken from the 'common source', there are slight differences of emphasis and detail. The soldier who claimed to have killed Otho was, according to Plutarch and Tacitus, a *speculator* named Julius Atticus. Galba's question may have been either *quis iussit*? or *quo auctore*? (cf. the Greek τίς σε...ἐκέλευσε ['Who gave you your orders?']). Tacitus, however, uses this as an opportunity to emphasize for the last time Galba's *severitas*, with the question *commilito, quis iussit*?

*ibi equites... incitati desertum a suis contrucidarunt*: S. brings his story to a rapid conclusion, with a few details to follow. He does not give us a picture of the aged *vir militaris* (so enfeebled that he had to be carried in a litter) tossed this way and that in a forum packed with people (cf. Plut. *G.* 26.4; *H.* 1.40.1), who watched and waited, as if at some *munus*, to see what the outcome would be.

**20.1** *sunt qui tradant, ad primum tumultum... donativum etiam pollicitum*: both S. and Tacitus (*H.* 1.41.2) give alternative versions of Galba's last words. In both cases the first alternative is less dignified – Tacitus' very much less so: *alii suppliciter interrogasse, quid mali meruisset, paucos dies exsolvendo donativo deprecatum* (cf. Dio 64.6.4).

*plures autem prodiderunt... ut hoc agerent et ferirent, quando ita videtur, hortatum*: this alternative is, of course, much more dignified; however, the two versions are not mutually exclusive. Galba clearly knew that he had not much chance if the praetorians were indeed completely suborned by Otho; cf. his remark, quoted above (19.1), about the linen corslet. He may have tried both to dissuade the soldiers from killing him by acting as a 'fellow-soldier' and, when he saw that this was useless, to die with some dignity.

*omnes qui arcesserentur sprevisse nuntium excepta Germanicianorum vexillatione*: we learn from *H.* 1.31.2-3 that the German troops in

Rome in January, 69 were bivouacked at the Atrium Libertatis (precise location unknown but perhaps somewhere on the line of the later Imperial Fora). They seem, in general, not to have shared in the disaffection of the other soldiers in the city. Tacitus also tells us that *diu nutavere*, which can hardly be harmonized with S.'s *in auxilium advolaverunt*. However, since both Tacitus and S. have the detail that Galba had shown great kindness to them, various explanations for their non-appearance must have arisen: S.'s, that after a stay near the forum of perhaps almost six months they did not know their way thither, seems rather unconvincing.

**20.2** *iugulatus est ad lacum Curti*: cf. *H*. 1.41.2-3; Plut. *G*. 27.1-2. Galba's litter was overturned when his bearers panicked and he was tumbled out on to the ground near the Lacus Curtius (almost at the centre of the *Forum Romanum*) while the people who had been watching either fled or were chased away by the soldiers.

*ac relictus ita uti erat, donec gregarius miles a frumentatione rediens abiecto onere caput ei amputavit*: this is perhaps the most horrific sentence in S.'s account of Galba's murder. We have a picture of a bloody corpse lying abandoned and of an ordinary soldier casually coming along carrying his grain ration. The juxtaposition of the awful and the mundane is highly effective. This soldier then spots a prize, throws away his ration and cuts off Galba's head. The impression of mindless insensitivity is almost overwhelming, but this account is apparently not from the common source, since both Tacitus (*H*. 1.41.3) and Plutarch (*G*. 27.2-4) indicate that Galba's head was cut off more or less at the same time as he was killed and that his attackers went on mutilating his now-headless corpse.

*et quoniam capillo arripere non poterat... ad Othonem detulit*: for Galba's extreme baldness, see below *G*. 21 and Plut. *G*. 13.6. From a conflation of Tacitus, Plutarch and S. it is clear that the common source gave four names of soldiers in its account of Galba's murder. The fourth, Fabius Fabullus (given by Plutarch at *G*. 27.3) cut off Galba's head, and this is suppressed by Tacitus because of the unseemly details (cf. Syme, *Tacitus* 189 and n. 6).

*Galba Cupido, fruaris aetate tua*: H.C. Nutting (*CP* 23 [1928] 287-8) examines the phrase *aetate frui* and, quoting Sen. *Phaed.* 447, Ovid,

*Ars Am*. 3.65 and Livy 26.50.5, concludes that in the present passage the intent is wholly crude: since Galba was thought to have boasted that he was still 'some fellow' (see next n.), this phrase should be rendered 'Go it, Galba, you Cupid!'

*quod ante paucos dies exierat in vulgus, laudanti cuidam formam suam*: obviously a flatterer; cf. below 21 for a description of Galba's rather decrepit physical appearance towards the end of his life. He was not only bald but also very wrinkled (Plut. *G.* 13.6).

*Patrobii Neroniani libertus centum aureis redemptum eo loco... abiecit*: Patrobius is mentioned by our sources as one of the most notorious of Nero's freedmen and he was executed (probably towards the end of 68) in Galba's purge of Neronian agents (see above, 15.2, n. on *quin etiam populo R. deposcente supplicium... increpuit*). As for what was done with Galba's head, Plutarch (*G.* 28.2-4) agrees with S., stating that it was thrown down in the place called Sessorium ἧ τοὺς ὑπὸ τῶν Καισάρων κολαζομένους θανατοῦσιν ['where those being punished by the emperors are put to death']. Tacitus, on the other hand, says (*H.* 1.49.1) that Galba's head was placed *ante Patrobii tumulum*.

*in privatis eius hortis Aurelia via*: their precise location is unknown, though probably they lay in the vicinity of the Janiculum (cf. Eutrop. 7.16).

### PERSONAL DETAILS ABOUT GALBA (21.1-23.1)

**21.1** *statura fuit iusta, capite praecalvo, oculis caeruleis, adunco naso*: existing portraits would not, of course, show his baldness since Romans regarded this as shameful (cf. S. *DJ* 45.2). In addition, Plutarch mentions that his face was wrinkled (*G.* 13.6), but this does not really give us much of a description. Regarding coin portraits, Ines Soncini has suggested (*RIN* 73 [1971] 63-76, esp. 74-6) that there are essentially two types, the commoner one rather conventional (cf. *BMC Imp. I* Plate 56, no. 7 for the type), the other vivacious, individualized and realistic (for the type, see *BMC Imp. I* Plate 52, nos. 6, 12, 19). Moreover, J. Charbonneaux (in M. Rénard [ed.], *Hommages à Albert Grenier I* [Bruxelles, 1962] 397-402) identifies a marble head now in the Louvre as an official portrait of Galba issued during his principate. This head is very different from the one illustrated in MW, Plate 1 (also in Paris).

*manibus pedibusque articulari morbo distortissimis:* this must refer to some general disease of the joints such as rheumatism or, more probably, arthritis (cf. OLD *s.v.* 'articularis'). Gout is also a possibility (cf. L-S, *s.v.* 'articularis').

*ut neque calceum perpeti... valeret:* this accords very ill with our earlier picture of the aged *vir militaris* on the march to Rome (above, 11) as does the account of his severe hernia immediately below. Perhaps the picture of Galba in his linen corslet being carried in a litter into the forum on 15th January, 69, accords more closely with reality.

**22.1** *tempore hiberno etiam ante lucem:* of course, since the nights in winter are much longer than in summer, this may mean simply that Galba got up and had his *ientaculum* at much the same time (by *our* clock) all the year round. However, by implication, Galba's practice was considered excessive.

*usque eo abundanti < s > :* this is the emendation of I.G. Graevius and *abundanti < s >* refers to *cibi.*

*ut congestas super manus reliquias circumferri iuberet spargique ad pedes stantibus:* this consecutive clause *ought* to illustrate the quantity of food that Galba was in the habit of tackling. The words *super manus* are particularly difficult to interpret: the commonest suggestion seems to be 'in front of him' (Baumgarten-Crusius, Hofstee, Mooney, Rolfe). Baumgarten-Crusius quotes a dissertation by D.C. Grimm (Leipzig, 1798) where the reading *circum se ferri* is adopted, which implies that Galba had *everyone else's* leavings piled up around him and then, when he was finished, what remained was distributed to the attendants (*ad pedes stantibus*). Since it certainly was customary to distribute left-overs to the attendants, Hofstee suggests, perhaps rightly, that the meaning here is that Galba tackled so many dishes at dinner that *his* leavings gathered together were sufficient for all the servants at the table.

*libidinis in mares pronior:* in spite of S.'s qualification (*et eos non nisi praeduros exoletosque*), Galba was remembered not only as a homosexual but as a pederast: cf. *Epit. de Caes.* 6.2: *in adulescentes infamis* (probably alluded to at Aur. Vict., *Caes.* 6.1: *rapere trahere vexare ac foedum in modum vastare cuncta et polluere*). For S.'s attitude towards homosexuality, see T.F. Carney, *PACA* 11 (1968) 11-12, 20-1.

*ferebant in Hispania Icelum... de Neronis exitu nuntiantem*: for Icelus' arrival in Spain, see above 11, n. on *supervenientibus ab urbe nuntiis*.

**23.1** *periit tertio et septuagesimo aetatis anno, imperii mense septimo*: for a discussion of Galba's year of birth, see above 4.1, n. on *M. Valerio Messala Cn. Lentulo cons. natus est VIIII Kal. Ian....* For the duration of his principate, see above 10.1, n. on *cum... conscendisset tribunal.*

*senatus, ut primum licitum est, statuam ei decreverat*: this will have come *after* the death of Vitellius (20th December, 69; see below, *Vit.* 16, n. on *postridie responsa opperienti*), who originally made his bid for power by rebelling against Galba. At the time of the Flavian rebellion, attempts were made to win over former supporters of Galba and these were apparently more numerous than might be imagined (see *H.* 2.55.1 for moves to honour his memory in Rome after the death of Otho). The decree described here was proposed by Antonius Primus, but was apparently in keeping with the Flavian line at the time (*H.* 3.7.2); cf. *H.* 4.40.1, for Domitian's proposal *de restituendis Galbae honoribus* (early January, 70). However, after the Flavian victory, official enthusiasm for Galba rapidly cooled (see next n.).

*sed decretum Vespasianus abolevit, percussores... opinatus*: clearly, this represents the end of a Flavian rehabilitation of Galba. This statement looks like a fabrication, but it is expressed in very general, even vague, terms and certainly no one would venture to question it or have the temerity to demand details. The ultimate Flavian line on Galba seems to have been that he rebelled against Nero, an unsatisfactory ruler but nonetheless the legitimate holder of the Principate. (Vespasian, of course, disliked Nero but acted properly towards him.) This served to explain why the saviour Vespasian was prepared to rebel only against a tyrant and usurper such as Vitellius.

# Otho

## OTHO'S BACKGROUND AND CAREER TO JANUARY, 69 (1.1-5.1)

**1.1** *Maiores Othonis orti sunt oppido Ferentio*: there is some doubt as to the correct form of the name of this town. *Ferentium*, attested perhaps by the majority of ancient sources (cf. also S. *Vesp.* 3 for a locative/genitive form *Ferenti*) is probably the correct Latin form, while *Ferentis* (or perhaps *Frentis*) was the original Etruscan form. It was a typical small town on the Etruscan plain, situated a few miles to the east of the Via Cassia and lay about 12 miles south-east of Lake Bolsena. The most important archaeological find there (1921) was the discovery of the chamber tomb of the Salvii, which contained twenty sarcophagi, dating probably from the last decades of the second century B.C. to 23 B.C. That the Emperor Otho himself was actually born at Ferentium, as Tacitus asserts (*H.* 2.50.1; cf. *Epit. de Caes.* 7.1) may be confirmed by an inscription found there, and dedicated to him as Princeps by the *municipes* (*CIL XI* 7417 = MW 78).

*familia vetere et honorata*: while this may well be true, it is not clear when the name Otho was adopted. It is not found in the tomb-inscriptions at Ferentium, but when this family appears in Rome, the name is 'Salvius Otho'; perhaps even more significant, it is the name 'Otho' alone which S. uses in this opening of the *Life*, and it is this name which is noteworthy. *Cognomina*, which originally belonged to the Etruscan name-system are, for the most part, *family* names and are so passed down from generation to generation like *gentilicia* so that 'Otho' can be called a *cognomen gentile*; cf. its use in three successive generations of this family, indicative perhaps of a desire to keep up part of the Etruscan tradition which lay in the family's background. See further W. Schulze, *Zur Gesch. lat. Eigennamen* (2nd Ed., Berlin, 1966) 315-16, n. 1.

*avus M. Salvius Otho... nec praeturae gradum excessit*: details survive of only one of the offices which this M. Salvius Otho held: he was a moneyer (*iiivir aere argento auro flando feriundo*) somewhere between 12 and 3 B.C. For the social (and political) importance of this post, usually held in one's late teens, see E. Birley, *PBA* 39 (1953) 199-205; T.P. Wiseman, *New Men in the Roman Senate 139 B.C.-14 A.D.* (Oxford, 1971) 147-53. The dates of his quaestorship and praetorship and of any other offices which he may have held are unknown.

Perhaps the most interesting feature of his career is Livia's influence. Degrassi has suggested (*RPAA* 34 [1961-2] 76) that he was born c. 26-25 B.C. and that his father, the *eques Romanus* mentioned here by S., was the husband of *Titia L.f.*, who died at the age of eighteen or nineteen on 14th September, 23 B.C. and whose sarcophagus is the latest of those deposited in the tomb of the Salvii at Ferentium. This would serve to explain the second cognomen Titianus, later found in the family – an attractive and economical hypothesis which would relegate to the category of *vituperatio* S.'s remark *matre humili incertum an ingenua*. However, if the *eques Romanus* moved from Ferentium not long after 23 and his son was 'taken up' by Livia (the connection here is quite untraceable), the absence of his mother could well have given rise to hostile gossip. His failure to advance beyond the praetorship is also inexplicable; he may have died young.

**1.2** *pater L. Otho...procreatum ex eo crederent*: the identity of the Princeps' grandmother remains a mystery. That she was a mistress of Tiberius is certainly not impossible. Her grandson was later prepared to be a complaisant husband for a subsequent princeps (or so it was alleged – see below S. *O.* 3.1-2; *H.* 1.13.3; *Ann.* 13.46) and his grandfather may perhaps have been prepared to tolerate such a situation for the sake of personal advancement. However, it is more likely that this is typical Suetonian gossip, based principally on Tiberius' affection, and *plerique* is the clue: if S. had found anything positive in his examination of the archives of Augustus' principate, we would have names and details here (cf. S. *Vesp.* 1 for an example of careful genealogical research).

Lucius Salvius Otho was born no later than A.D. 1 (from his consulship in A.D. 33) and perhaps a few years before. From the duties which were entrusted to him (see nn. immediately below), it is clear that he was a strict, conscientious and efficient administrator, enjoying the confidence of three successive emperors – Tiberius, Gaius and Claudius. By the end of his life he belonged to the inner circle of Claudius' *amici*. The date of his death is uncertain, though he was dead by A.D. 55 (cf. S. *O.* 2.2 with *Ann.* 13.12).

*urbanos honores*: only the date of his (suffect) consulship is known – A.D. 33, in succession to Galba (cf. S. *G.* 6; *H.* 2.50.1; *Ann.* 13.12.1). In addition, he was a Frater Arvalis, a *flamen* and, in A.D. 39 at least, *promagister* of the Arval Brethren (*AFA* for 39, esp. October 27th = Smallwood nos. 7, 8, 9).

*proconsulatum Africae*: the date is quite uncertain. However, since the proconsulship of Africa or Asia was normally the culmination of a public career, a date rather late in Otho's life would appear most likely. S. tells us (below, 1.3) that Otho incurred Claudius' displeasure during his governorship of Dalmatia (A.D. 42-3 – see below, n. on *in Illyrico*). This and the fact that he returned to court and subsequently regained Claudius' good-will (which may have taken some time) leave 47-8 as the most likely dates of those 'available' for his proconsulship.

*extraordinaria imperia*: S.'s addendum *ausus etiam est in Illyrico...* proves that this was not a regular governorship, but, rather, a special commission (and although S. uses the plural, we know of this one only in Otho's career) to settle affairs after the revolt of L. Arruntius Camillus Scribonianus. On the other hand, Otho clearly had command of troops and power of life and death over them: this makes it likely that, officially, he was *legatus Augusti pro praetore provinciae Dalmatiae*. The 'extraordinary' aspect of his command may have lain in the fact that he was appointed at very short notice and at a time when no new appointment had originally been planned.

*ausus etiam est in Illyrico milites quosdam... capite punire*: in general, military law was stricter than civilian law and soldiers had fewer rights than ordinary citizens (e.g., see Jos. *BJ* 3.102-103). It has recently been argued that the so-called *ius gladii* was held by *all* provincial governors not only in the first three centuries A.D., but also during the Republic and that it was not a specifically delegated power but an inherent part of their office: see P. Garnsey, *JRS* 58 (1968) 51-9. Either way, therefore, Otho was acting within his rights in executing soldiers found guilty of mutiny, although he was not in this case acting either wisely or tactfully.

*in Illyrico*: there is no doubt that this refers to the province of Dalmatia. Otho's tenure of the province was A.D. 42-3 (cf. J.J. Wilkes, *Dalmatia* [London, 1969] 83, 443; A. Jagenteufel, *Die Statthalter d. röm. Provinz Dalmatia* [Wien, 1958] 25-7, with detailed bibliography).

*motu Camilli*: L. Arruntius Camillus Scribonianus (*cos. ord.* A.D. 32) was governor of Dalmatia from about A.D. 40 until 42 when, at the urging of L. Annius Vinicianus, he made a bid for power (cf. Pliny *Ep.* 3.16.7-9; *H.* 1.89; 2.75; *S. Claud.* 13.2; 35.2; Dio 60.15.1-16.7), which quickly failed, though many senators and *equites* precipitately went over to his side, to their ultimate regret.

The background of Camillus Scribonianus is significant: he was almost certainly the son of M. Furius Camillus (*cos. ord.* A.D. 8) and was adopted by L. Arruntius (*cos. ord.* A.D. 6). He also had some connection with Cn. Pompeius Magnus, from whom his son L. Arruntius Furius Scribonianus later claimed descent (*CIL III* 7043 = *ILS* 976). Although the precise details of this connection are not clear, the link, either real or adoptive, appears to be Pompeia, a daughter of Sextus Pompeius and Scribonia. This Pompeia was at one time married to L. Scribonius Libo, and their daughter Scribonia became the wife of M. Licinius Crassus Frugi (*cos. ord.* A.D. 27) and the mother of L. Calpurnius Piso Frugi Licinianus, Galba's heir.

*quod... ex paenitentia praepositos suos quasi defectionis adversus Claudium auctores occiderant*: the *paenitentia* was very rapid: *intra quintum diem* according to *S. Claud.* 13.2; cf. Orosius 7.6.7; Dio 60.15.3 (though the detail of Scribonianus' suicide is incorrect; cf. *H.* 2.75). This incident highlights a problem of military law which has never been satisfactorily settled: the degree of responsibility of the ordinary soldier in obeying orders which appear to be 'illegal'. In returning to their loyalty to Claudius, the legions in Dalmatia found themselves forced to disobey orders from their superiors on the spot, but since their oath was to Claudius, in strict law they were correct in refusing to obey their dissident officers. However, they had no right to *kill* any officers (who should have been sent to Rome for trial as rebels), and it is here that the conflict between political expediency (Claudius' condoning of their actions and promotion of their ring-leaders) and military discipline (Otho's treatment of the matter from the point of view of a commander on the spot) becomes acute. Otho knew that troops who had killed their superiors with impunity would be impossible to control subsequently. However, with a little less *severitas* on his part and somewhat more political finesse on Claudius', the matter could perhaps have been resolved by means of a discreet transfer of the troops in question to another area or areas.

*et quidem ante principia se coram*: clearly, S. regards this as the crowning touch of Otho's *severitas*, because by having the executions carried out with full ceremony and in his own presence, Otho was demonstrating in signal fashion his decision to override Claudius' earlier act of leniency. It was an act of considerable courage, especially since Claudius, a man notoriously timid and suspicious (S. *Claud.* 35.1), had given the legions in Dalmatia (*VII* and *XI*) the titles *Claudia pia fidelis* (Dio 60.15.4).

**1.3** *quo facto sicut gloriam auxit, ita gratiam minuit*: exactly what Claudius' displeasure entailed is not made clear, but Otho's actions may possibly have made him suspect that another Scribonianus had arisen (cf. S. *Claud.* 37.1: *nulla adeo suspicio, nullus auctor tam levis exstitit, a quo non mediocri scrupulo iniecto ad cavendum ulciscendumque compelleretur*). Perhaps Otho was recalled immediately, or the term of office assigned to him was curtailed. However, Otho was no Scribonianus: he did not belong to one of the great Republican families and his political connections, which lay entirely within the Julio-Claudian family (cf. Livia's influence), in no way enabled him to sneer at the Princeps. Accordingly, as soon as the opportunity presented itself, he re-ingratiated himself with Claudius.

*quam tamen mature reciperavit detecta equitis R. fraude... compererat*: Dio dates this conspiracy to A.D. 43 (60.18.4). Nothing further is known of it, and S. does not mention it in his list of conspiracies against Claudius (*Claud.* 13, where a conspiracy of two *equites* is mentioned; but this is clearly not the same incident and S. appears to date it earlier than the revolt of Scribonianus). From this we may conclude that S. did not learn of it while doing his research into Claudius' principate, but discovered it while investigating Otho's antecedents.

*senatus honore rarissimo, statua in Palatio posita*: mention of the Senate implies that the statue was in a public place on the Palatine Hill; cf. *Ann.* 15.72.1 for statues of Tigellinus and Nerva set up after the detection of the Pisonian conspiracy and S. *Tit.* 2 for a statue of Britannicus set up by Titus; see also *G.* 23 and *Vit.* 3.1 for other statues set up by decree of the Senate.

*Claudius adlectum inter patricios conlaudans*: this was during Claudius' censorship in A.D. 47-8, on which see below, *Vit.* 2.4, n. on *mox cum Claudio principe duos insuper ordinarios consulatus censuramque gessit.*

*ex Albia Terentia splendida femina*: it seems likely that the Princeps' mother was the daughter of Q. Terentius Culleo and his wife Albia. *Splendida femina* appears to be a reference to her lineage. Tacitus, on the other hand, in his obituary notice of Otho at *H*. 2.50.1 mentions that his father had been consul and his grandfather praetor and adds: *maternum genus impar nec tamen indecorum*. This may be technically true for the two generations specified, but a Q. Terentius Culleo had been *praetor peregrinus* as long ago as 187 B.C. (*MRR I* pp. 368, 370 n. 3), and it is tempting to associate him with her family. If they were survivors of a line prominent in the period of greatest senatorial influence, they might well consider themselves socially superior to the Salvii Othones of recent (and perhaps slightly dubious) distinction: hence, possibly, S.'s cautious *splendida femina*; cf. Eutropius, 7.17.

*duos filios tulit, L. Titianum et minorem M. cognominem sibi*: S. has apparently misunderstood the effects of the Etruscan *cognomina gentilicia* (cf. above 1.1, n. on *familia vetere et honorata*), and he seems to think that the two brothers were *L. Salvius Titianus* and *M. Salvius Otho*. However, there is ample evidence that the full name of the elder brother was L. Salvius *Otho* Titianus (e.g. *CIL VI* 5512; *AFA* 30th January, A.D. 69 = MW 2, lines 46, 48).

*L. Titianum*: since L. Salvius Otho Titianus was the elder brother of the Princeps, he must have been born before A.D. 32 (cf. 2.1, below). He was *cos. ord.* in A.D. 52 (*Ann*. 12.52) and if his son L. Salvius Otho Cocceianus was born earlier than 52, as seems quite likely (cf. below, 10.2, n. on *fratris filium*), he would have been eligible for the consulship in his thirty-second year (cf. p. 40); accordingly, A.D. 20 is his latest possible year of birth.

He was *proconsul Asiae*, probably in A.D. 63-4; his quaestor was Cn. Iulius Agricola, and Tacitus comments on his corrupt government there (*Agr*. 6.2). Prior to A.D. 69, his only other activities of which any record survives concern the Arval Brethren. He first appears in the *Acta* in A.D. 57 as *promagister*, and he plays a prominent part in activities in 58, 59, 60, 63 and 66 (where fragments of the *Acta* are dateable). In 69 he served as *promagister* under both Galba and his brother.

After Otho's *coup* on 15th January, 69, L. Titianus became his brother's colleague in the consulship, in place of T. Vinius, until 28th February (*H*. 1.77.1; cf. *AFA* 28th February, 1st March 69). When Otho departed for the north on 15th March, *quietem urbis curasque imperii Salvio Titiano fratri permisit* (*H*. 1.90.3); from Tacitus' language this would seem to have been a general oversight of the remaining *praefecti* and bureaux of state exercised through the Emperor's *auctoritas* rather than through any official position. Soon afterwards the constant sniping at his generals by the troops induced Otho, already prey to all sorts of fears and uncertainties, to summon Titianus to take command of the army. This decision had disastrous consequences for Otho, but not for Titianus: after the battle near Cremona he fled to the main Othonian camp at Bedriacum, which he apparently entered under cover of darkness (*H*. 2.44.1-2). Next day, 15th April, the main Othonian army surrendered (*H*. 2.45.2: cf. Plut. *O*. 13.6 and 11-13). After his brother's suicide Titianus surrendered to the Vitellians, and along with the other Othonian commanders, accompanied Caecina and Valens to Lugdunum to await the arrival of Vitellius (*H*. 2.59.3). Titianus had little to fear from him: he had heeded his warning at the beginning of the war about the consequences if Vitellius' family in Rome were harmed (*H*. 1.75.2). He was 'forgiven' on the grounds of his *pietas* and *ignavia* (*H*. 2.60.2), and nothing more is known of him.

*tulit et filiam, quam vixdum nubilem Druso Germanici filio despondit*: very little is known about her; her name is assumed to be 'Salvia'. If betrothed to Drusus when barely of marriageable age, she would have been about 11-12 years old. According to L. Petersen (*PIR*[2] I 220, on 'Drusus Iulius Caesar') the betrothal came after his assumption of the *toga virilis* in A.D. 23 (*Ann*. 4.4.1). There is no evidence to support this, but it seems reasonable: 'Salvia' was born, then, somewhere about A.D. 12. The marriage, however, never took place, though no reason is given in our sources. Instead, to his cost, Drusus married Aemilia Lepida, daughter of M. Aemilius Lepidus (*Ann*. 6.40.4). Otho's sister is mentioned only once more: on the evening before he committed suicide (i.e., 15th April, A.D. 69) Otho wrote her a *codicillus consolatorius* (below, 10.2).

**2.1** *Otho imperator IIII Kal. Mai. natus est Camillo Arruntio Domitio Ahenobarbo cons.*: i.e., 28th April, A.D. 32. This gives to the family of

L. Salvius Otho (*cos.* A.D. 33) an extremely strung-out appearance. As we have seen, 'Salvia' appears to have been born c. A.D. 12; Lucius was born c. A.D. 19-20 and Marcus was born in A.D. 32. That Albia Terentia should have borne children over a period of twenty years is not impossible: that she should have borne *only* three during such a period may, however, appear improbable. Perhaps there were many children, the majority of whom were either still-born or died in infancy (cf. the three sons of Germanicus and Agrippina born between c. A.D. 8 and A.D. 11, all of whom died very young; cf. *PIR*² I 218, 225, and *stemma* of the Julio-Claudian family; Mommsen, *Hermes* 13 [1878] 245-65, esp. 247-8).

*a prima adulescentia... a patre*: cf. *H.* 1.13.3: *namque Otho pueritiam incuriose, adulescentiam petulanter egerat, gratus Neroni aemulatione luxus*; L. Otho's taste for order and discipline clearly extended to his own family, but equally clearly his frequent absences from Rome meant that Otho received little or no stabilising paternal influence during his formative years. The intermittent bursts of strict discipline which his father attempted to impose were probably worse than useless, and may even have served to make him the wilder.

*prodigus ac procax*: cf. Plut. *G.* 21.3: ἀκόλαστον...καὶ πολυτελῆ ['unrestrained...and spendthrift']. Otho was so extravagant that he sometimes teased Nero about his 'meanness', and even outdid the Emperor in conspicuous and reckless expenditure (Plut. *G.* 19.4-5; cf. Pliny *NH* 13.22). His family does not seem to have been particularly wealthy, and nothing is known of Otho's private means, if any; cf. *H.* 1.21.1.

*ferebatur et vagari... in sublime iactare*: S. presumably has no information about the young Otho's fellow Mohocks and although a 'gang' is perhaps implied, we are here left with a curious picture of a wild young rake tossing people in a blanket single-handed! It is noteworthy, however, that Nero too had a penchant for nocturnal adventures in the city (see S. *Ner.* 26.1-2; *Ann.* 13.25.1-3; Dio 61.9.1-4).

**2.2** *post patris deinde mortem*: the date is uncertain and could be anywhere between 47 (his adlection to the Patriciate) and 55 (cf. p. 90).

*libertinam aulicam...paene decrepitam*: her identity is unknown, though Nagl (*RE II* A 2038) suggests that she was Acte, which seems highly improbable since Acte was not in any way *gratiosa* before she became Nero's mistress. Furthermore, given Nero's passion for her, it seems most peculiar that Otho should have sought to worm his way into Nero's favour by pretending to be in love with her himself.

*facile summum inter amicos locum tenuit*: in describing Nero's passion for Acte in A.D. 55, Tacitus mentions Otho and Claudius Senecio as his confidants (*Ann.* 13.12.1). However, in spite of Otho's *summus locus*, which is proved by his remark to Nero: οὕτω με Καίσαρα ἴδοις ['Just as you will one day see me Caesar'] (Dio 61.11.2), Nero does not seem to have had much confidence in Otho's abilities (his reply to Otho's remark was: οὐδὲ ὕπατόν σε ὄψομαι ['I shall not see you even as consul']). When he was sent to Lusitania Otho had apparently held no office above the quaestorship (cf. below, 3.2: *provinciam administravit quaestorius*), and there is no record of his having performed any military service. His only other attested position in Rome prior to his departure for Lusitania is membership in the Arval Brethren in the latter part of 57 (*CIL VI* 2039 = Smallwood 19).

*congruentia morum, ut vero quidam tradunt, et consuetudine mutui stupri*: the position of *ut vero quidam tradunt* is odd. It would appear that this passage is to be understood asyndetically, with the break coming after *morum*, and *et* ( = *etiam*) used adverbially rather than as a conjunction; *vero* will mean 'but in fact'. The meaning, then, is: 'Nero and Otho became close friends because of the similarity of their characters, but in fact, as some say, because they had a sexual relationship as well'. While Nero's bisexuality is amply attested (e.g. S. *Ner.* 28-29; *Ann.* 15.37.4; Dio 62.28.3; 63.13.1-2), there is very little in the way of real evidence to prove the same of Otho: apart from this blunt statement in S., there is only an aside in Dio (64.8.3 – referring to Otho's imitation of Nero in A.D. 69) and suggestions that Otho was effeminate (cf. below, 12.1, esp. *munditiarum vero paene muliebrium*).

*ac tantum potentia valuit... ad agendas gratias introducere*: during the period 54-9 only one restitution of a consular convicted for *repetundae* is known, that of Lurius Varus in 57, recorded at *Ann.* 13.32; see further *PIR²* L 428 and E. Groag, *WS* 50 (1932) 202-5. If he is the person alluded to here by S., several interesting possibilities emerge:

in 57 Otho was in his twenty-fifth year, which under the Augustan system was the minimum age at which one could hold the quaestorship. Holding the quaestorship gave admission to the Senate and S.'s words *non dubitaret in senatum... introducere* imply that Otho was at this time a senator. Furthermore, Otho had certainly been quaestor by the time he was sent to Lusitania (cf. below 3.2: *provinciam administravit quaestorius*). Therefore we may conclude that Otho was quaestor in 57, in Rome obviously, and so, probably, a *quaestor Caesaris*. As such he would have presented to the Senate Nero's formal request for *restitutio*.

## OTHO, AGRIPPINA, NERO AND POPPAEA (3.1-2)

Chapter 3 of the *Life* of Otho raises in an acute form all the major problems of source criticism which bedevil the study not only of the Year of the Four Emperors but also of the reign of Nero. There are extant today five accounts of the Otho-Poppaea-Nero Triangle: Plutarch's (*G.* 19.2-20.2), Suetonius' (here), Tacitus' two versions (*H.* 1.13.3-4 and *Ann.* 13.45-46) and Dio's (61.11.2-4), and although no two of them are identical, they are generally regarded as reflecting the three main literary sources for the last hexad of the *Annals* and for part at least of the year of the four Emperors – Pliny the Elder, Cluvius Rufus and Fabius Rusticus, though there is no scholarly agreement today about which version comes from which source. See, for example, Syme, *Tacitus* 290; G.B. Townend, *Hermes* 89 (1961) 242-7; O. Schönberger, *Historia* 12 (1963) 500-9, esp. 500-1 and nn. 2-5.

From such studies it becomes clear that, although we may have a general idea of what the primary sources for this period were like, it is impossible to analyse every incident and ascribe each variant precisely to a particular source. Furthermore, it is probably a mistake to think exclusively in terms of Pliny the Elder, Cluvius Rufus and Fabius Rusticus as the primary sources for this period (not that we have much impression of Fabius). Plutarch, in particular, tends to be downgraded by the assumption that he merely reproduced Pliny, but we should remember that he travelled in Italy some time after the battle of Bedriacum (Plut. *O.* 14.1), that he had an influential senatorial patron who had been in Otho's suite in 69, and this could well have gained him access to many who participated in events as far back as A.D. 58-9 (see further, C.P. Jones, *Plutarch and Rome*

[Oxford, 1971] 74-8). Furthermore, if we assume that Tacitus began to collect material for the *Histories* about A.D. 98, his distance from the events leading up to Agrippina's murder was little different from that of an historian today investigating the outbreak of the Korean War.

**3.1** *omnium autem consiliorum secretorumque particeps*: by means of this adjectival phrase, which underlines the impression of Otho's influence left at the end of the preceding chapter, S. introduces the most impressive and awful illustration possible of Otho's closeness to Nero. The dramatic skill is considerable, although the logic of the argument is faulty: S. creates the impression that the 'Poppaea incident' was subsequent to Agrippina's death (since it leads straight into the story of his 'banishment' to Lusitania). This may even be true, if we reject completely Cluvius Rufus' story (*Ann.* 14.2.1) of a contest between Agrippina and Poppaea for Nero's affections (and certainly S. has no mention of it).

*die, quem necandae matri Nero destinarat*: the date of Agrippina's death can be pinpointed with reasonable accuracy, since our sources appear to place it during the Quinquatrus Minervae (19th-23rd March) of A.D. 59 (S. *Ner.* 34.2; *Ann.* 14.4.1; closer precision is hard: cf. J.D. Bishop, *CP* 55 [1960] 167-9 and R. Katzoff, *Historia* 22 [1973] 77 and n. 28). Moreover, we should at least consider the possibility that there was no *die, quem necandae matri Nero destinarat*: Tacitus' story (*Ann.* 14.1-2; cf. S. *Ner.* 34.2-4; Dio 61.12.1-14.4) is riddled with improbabilities (on this, see A. Dawson, *CJ* [1969] 252-67, esp. 252-7), and modern biographers of Nero find it difficult to explain why he should have decided to murder his mother in 59, especially since she had lost all effective power three or four years previously (e.g. M. Grant, *Nero* [London, 1970] 73-6; B.H. Warmington, *Nero: Reality and Legend* [London, 1969] 46-7). Conceivably, Nero's indictment of his mother and his allegation that her freedman Agerinus had been sent to assassinate him were no more than the literal truth, as was his statement that she committed suicide when her attempt failed (*Ann.* 14.10-11; cf. Dio 61.14.3; S. *Ner.* 34.3).

*cenam utrique exquisitissimae comitatis dedit*: this is presumably the banquet described in S. *Ner.* 34.2 and *Ann.* 14.4, and the culmination of the series described in Dio (61.13.1-2). *Exquisitissimae comitatis,* with the unnecessary and exaggerated superlative, deftly and perhaps slightly maliciously confirms the impression we have already gained of Otho's rarified, almost Wildean aestheticism.

*Poppaeam Sabinam*: the daughter of T. Ollius, who perished in connection with the fall of Seianus in A.D. 31, and of Poppaea Sabina, the greatest beauty of her day, who incurred the enmity of Messalina and was driven to suicide in 47 (*Ann*. 11.1-2), she took the name of her maternal grandfather, C. Poppaeus Sabinus, *cos. ord.* A.D. 9. Blessed with charm, beauty, fame and wit, as Tacitus says (*Ann*. 13.45.2), *huic mulieri cuncta alia fuere praeter honestum animum*, Poppaea was married first to the *eques* Rufrius Crispinus, praetorian prefect from 47 (at least; cf.*Ann*. 11.1.3) to 51 (*Ann*. 12.42.1), by whom she had a son (*Ann*. 13.45.4; S. *Ner*. 35.5), then to Otho (?), and finally to Nero, to whom she bore a daughter, Claudia Augusta (January-May, 63: *PIR*$^2$ C 1061). She was pregnant again when she died in 65 (*Ann*. 16.6.1; S. *Ner*. 35.3).

*tunc adhuc amicam eius*: the *tunc adhuc* is not helpful since the story of Poppaea, introduced with *item*, clearly begins as simply another illustration of how close Otho was to Nero: *tunc adhuc* will therefore mean no more than 'up to the time when this particular story began'. On the other hand, the reader of this chapter undoubtedly gets the *impression* that Otho's involvement with Poppaea comes *after* the murder of Agrippina since it is this involvement which leads straight to Otho's 'banishment' to Lusitania. Compare with the rather prim *amicam eius* Tacitus' blunt *principale scortum* (*H*. 1.13.3).

*abductam marito*: *sc.* Rufrius Crispinus, no doubt much older than Poppaea and since his dismissal at Agrippina's urging in A.D. 51 no longer, perhaps, of much interest to his ambitious wife. However, the dismissal of Rufrius and possible social slights which accompanied it may have engendered in Poppaea an intense dislike of Agrippina, which caught fire later on.

*demandatamque interim sibi*: the *interim* here corresponds to *donec Octaviam uxorem amoliretur* (*H*. 1.13.2).

*nuptiarum specie recepit*: S. has no doubt that there actually was a marriage ceremony; cf. 3.2 below, *diducto matrimonio* and *uxoris*. The intention, however, according to the tradition followed here, was that it should be 'a marriage in name only'. So far, then, S. has painted for us a coherent picture of Otho as Nero's most intimate friend, and there are hints that Nero believed him to be wholly homosexual and therefore 'safe' as a protector for Poppaea.

*nec corrupisse contentus adeo dilexit ut... tulerit animo*: at this point S.'s story becomes somewhat inconsistent. Not only does Otho seduce Poppaea, but he falls violently in love with her and makes no secret of it. The first part is foolish enough, but, under the circumstances, the second is tantamount to lunacy. Poppaea too seems rather different from the cold and calculating character depicted by Tacitus.

**3.2** *creditur certe... ac depositum reposcentem*: this has the appearance of being the sort of anecdote about Nero which members of the upper classes would gleefully relate; or perhaps S. himself elaborated on the basic story of the 'deposit' so that he would be able to present this grotesque parody of the traditional *paraklausithyron*. *Creditur certe* suggests that S. is sceptical about the truth of the story, which he finds too amusing to omit.

*diducto matrimonio*: this phrase tends to be translated misleadingly: cf. J.C. Rolfe (Loeb) 'Therefore Nero annulled the marriage...'; R. Graves 'Fear of scandal alone kept Nero from doing more than annul the marriage...'. The idea that an emperor could annul people's marriages at his whim is completely mistaken. In this case, it is likely that, at Nero's behest, Poppaea issued a *repudium* which unilaterally ended the marriage (done in writing and witnessed by seven adult Roman citizens; see further Buckland, *Textbook*[3] 116-18; J.A. Crook, *Law and Life of Rome* [London, 1967] 104-6).

*sepositus est per causam legationis in Lusitaniam*: according to Plutarch (*G*. 19.9-20.1), Otho was in peril of his life but Seneca, who was well-disposed towards him, advised and persuaded Nero to send him to Lusitania. This posting was, of course, highly irregular, since a *legatus Caesaris pro praetore* was normally of praetorian or consular rank. However, it seems somewhat inappropriate to regard this posting as 'a flagrant example of favouritism' (cf. next chapter *ultionis occasio*), as P.A. Brunt does (*Latomus* 18 [1959] 555 n. 4; cf. A.N. Sherwin-White, *PBSR* 15 [1939] 16-17).

*provinciam administravit...per decem annos*: this appears to come from the same tradition as that followed by Tacitus when he placed Otho's banishment within the events of A.D. 58 (*Ann.* 13.46.3). Equally, it appears to contradict S.'s own statement about Otho's presence in Campania at the time of Agrippina's murder in March, 59 (see 3.1). The only way in which S.'s statements can be made self-consistent is for us to assume that Otho was sent to Lusitania between April and June (?) of 59. He would have been governor until his departure for Rome with Galba in the late summer of 68. This means that he was governor of Lusitania for nine years plus something, which may casually have been described as ten years; cf. the conventional 'six-year' duration of the Second World War (3rd September, 1939-8th May, 1945).

*moderatione atque abstinentia singulari*: cf. *H.* 1.13.4: *comiter administrata provincia*; *Ann.* 13.46.3: *non ex priore infamia, sed integre sancteque egit*; also Plut. *G.* 20.2. This is the astonishing thing about Otho: when he had no responsibilities, his behaviour was appalling, but when he assumed a specific task, everyone was pleasantly surprised. His behaviour after he became Princeps confirms these reports of his conduct in Lusitania.

**4.1** *ut tandem occasio ultionis data est, conatibus Galbae primus accessit*: since Otho had been in Lusitania about a year longer than Galba was in Hispania Tarraconensis (assuming that he went there in 59), he probably felt that he was doomed to stay there indefinitely; no doubt he had come to know Galba fairly well in the meantime and Galba's revolt in April, 68 will have seemed the best prospect for a return to Rome. Accordingly, when Galba sought his help (cf. above *G.* 10.3), he supported him as vigorously as possible. Plutarch tells us (*G.* 20.3) that he gave him all the gold and silver that he had and sent him those of his servants best suited to wait upon an emperor's table.

*ex affirmatione Seleuci mathematici*: this appears to be a mistake on S.'s part, for Seleucus was *Vespasian's* court astrologer (*H.* 2.78.1). Both Tacitus (*H.* 1.22) and Plutarch (*G.* 23.7) state that Otho's astrologer was named Ptolemaeus, while Tacitus adds that Otho had acquired him from Poppaea Sabina; he is also thoroughly scathing about this man's influence over Otho, describing him as *sceleris instinctor, ad quod facillime ab eius modi voto transitur* (*H.* 1.22.3).

**4.2** *nullo igitur officii aut ambitionis in quemquam genere omisso*: Tacitus adds the detail (*H.* 1.23.1) that Otho made a point of ingratiating himself with all the soldiers with whom he came into contact, and this would include those members of the Praetorian Guard who came to Spain to accompany Galba to Rome.

*quotiens cena principem acciperet... demerebatur*: Plutarch (*G.* 20.7) and Tacitus (*H.* 1.24.1) give the same story, the only variants being that Tacitus gives the everyday value of the *aureus* (HS 100) and names Maevius Pudens, a close friend of Tigellinus, as Otho's agent in making these payments.

*cuidam etiam de parte finium cum vicino litiganti adhibitus arbiter... redemit emancipavitque*: Tacitus gives the story in much more general terms (*H.* 1.24.2) but adds the detail that the *quidam* was a *speculator* named Cocceius Proculus. S. is notably precise here in using correct legal terminology: an *arbiter* was essentially the same as a *iudex*, but was more usually employed in a case involving *bona fides*. Again, with the word *emancipavit* S. uses correct legal terminology: Italic land was a *res mancipi* (Gaius 2.14a-27), full title in which could be conveyed only by the ritual process known as *mancipatio* (Gaius 1.119-122) or, less commonly, by a formal procedure called *in iure cessio*.

## OTHO'S *COUP D'ÉTAT* (5.1-6.3)

This section should, of course, be read in close conjunction with the account of the fall of Galba (*G.* 18.1-20.2; pp. 80-6).

**5.1** *sed postquam Pisone praelato spe decidit, ad vim conversus est instigante super animi dolorem etiam magnitudine aeris alieni*: cf. above *G.* 17 nn. Tacitus paints for us (*H.* 1.21.1) a graphic picture of Otho's chagrin at the events of 10th January. In addition, he must have been borrowing and extorting large sums of money on the strength of his influence and expectations (see below 5.2) and his debts are said to have amounted to 50 millions (Plut. *G.* 21.3: presumably Plutarch here means drachmae; the total would therefore be HS 200 million).

**5.2** *hoc subsidium tanti coepti fuit*: compared to the size of Otho's debts, 1 million sesterces was a small sum indeed with which to finance a *coup d'état*. Plutarch mentions (*G.* 23.8-24.3) that most of the former adherents of Nymphidius Sabinus and Tigellinus supported and encouraged Otho, and that the principal agents in the organization of the Praetorian Guard for the *coup* were an *optio* named Veturius and a *tesserarius* named Barbius Proculus (both of whom would, from the nature of their jobs, know many of the men), assisted by Otho's freedman Onomastus (*H.* 1.25).

**6.1** *tulerat animus post adoptionem statim castra occupare cenantemque in Palatio Galbam adgredi*: Tacitus states (*H.* 1.26) that the planned *coup* was ready on 14th January and that the conspirators were going to seize Otho as he returned from dinner (and presumably take him to the praetorian camp where he would be proclaimed). However, they were deterred by the difficulties of carrying out such an action at night, since there were many troops scattered throughout the city and they were afraid that some drunken soldiers might grab the wrong person and proclaim him Emperor! S.'s reason for the postponement of the *coup* seems much more in keeping with what we see elsewhere of Otho's sensitivity to and appreciation of the soldiers' point of view (cf. below 8.1-2; 9.3; 10.1; 11.1; 12.2). Presumably S. has it from some military source – perhaps his father (cf. below, 10.1).

**6.2** *ergo destinata die*: if we combine this phrase with the preceding sentence (*medium... tempus religio et Seleucus exemit*), it becomes clear that the date for the *coup d'état* was actually determined by astrological considerations. This may seem wholly outlandish, but it is not unknown even today. In 1967, the then Governor of California was sworn in at one minute past midnight on 2nd January, the time allegedly being chosen for astrological reasons (*Newsweek* 69, 16th January, 1967: 30).

*in foro sub aede Saturni ad miliarium aureum*: the Golden Milestone was a marble column covered with gilt bronze and was erected by Augustus in 20 B.C. (Dio 54.8.4). It was regarded as the point at which all the great highways of the Empire converged (Plut. *G.* 24.7; cf. Pliny, *NH* 3.66).

*mane Galbam salutavit, utque consueverat osculo exceptus*: it seems to have been customary for the emperor to greet his closest friends and associates with a kiss at the morning *salutatio*. Tiberius, perhaps predictably, had no enthusiasm for this practice and banned it by edict (S. *Tib.* 34.2), though it was soon revived (cf. Pliny, *NH* 26.2-4) and had become so common by the time of Domitian that Martial devotes two poems to an attack on what he regards as a social menace (11.98; 12.59).

*etiam sacrificanti interfuit audivitque praedicta haruspicis*: we learn from Tacitus (*H.* 1.27.1) that the sacrifice took place in front of the Temple of Apollo on the Palatine and that Umbricius, the *haruspex*, *tristia exta et instantes insidias ac domesticum hostem praedicit* (cf. Plut. *G.* 24.4-5; Dio 64.5.3). Otho was standing next to Galba at the moment when the pronouncement was made.

*deinde liberto adesse architectos... ad constitutum*: the freedman was Onomastus (cf. above, 5.2, n. on *hoc subsidium tanti coepti fuit*) and from the information given here and by Tacitus (*H.* 1.27.1-2) and Plutarch (*G.* 24.6-7), Otho's route from the Temple of Apollo to the Golden Milestone can be traced in detail.

*alii febrem simulasse aiunt eamque excusationem proximis mandasse, si quaereretur*: this variant is found only in S. and we can therefore say nothing certain about its provenance; (for interesting speculation, however, see P. Noyen and G. Sanders, *AC* 28 [1959] 223-31 and G.B. Townend, *AJP* 85 [1964] 356-7.) It is possible that S.'s variant actually arose because Otho, bandy-legged and splay-footed as he was (below, *O.* 12.1), began to trip over his feet as he made his way through the *domus Tiberiana* and that, as his excitement got the better of him, Onomastus took him by the arm both to restrain him and prevent him from tripping up. This pair must have presented an odd sight to the staff of the palace and Onomastus may have explained Otho's high colour and uncertain gait to those they passed as an attack of fever.

**6.3** *tunc abditus propere muliebri sella in castra contendit*: Tacitus (*H.* 1.27.2) and Plutarch (*G.* 25.1-3) state that there were only twenty-three soldiers waiting for him at the Golden Milestone and that Otho, seeing the fewness of their number, became afraid. Plutarch even hints that he tried to call off the *coup* but was hustled away by the soldiers who would not hear of it. As Otho's group approached the camp more and more soldiers 'tagged along', as S. indicates below.

*ibi missis qui Galbam et Pisonem trucidarent*: for the death of Galba, see above *G*. 19-20 and nn. Piso was apparently with Galba when the Emperor was killed (*H*. 1.39.1) but managed to escape, though wounded, and took refuge in the Temple of Vesta, where he eluded detection for a while. Otho, on receiving the head of Galba, demanded Piso's as well and sent troops to hunt him down (*H*. 1.43; Plut. *G*. 27.5-6).

*ad conciliandos pollicitationibus... quod sibi illi reliquissent*: that Otho should have made some such vague but generally satisfactory statement of policy when he was hauled into the praetorian camp and saluted as Emperor is to be expected: he could hardly have remained mute! However, after describing for us a scene of soldiery run wild, Tacitus gives us a speech by Otho (*H*. 1.37-38), probably his own invention, which sounds like a revolutionary manifesto and consists mostly of diatribes against Galba, his ministers and his heir.

## OTHO'S PRINCIPATE IN ROME (7.1-8.2)

Of the eight and a half weeks which Otho spent as Princeps in Rome (15th January-15th March, 69) Tacitus provides the most detailed account (*H*. 1.45-47 for the first day, and *H*. 1.79-90 for the remainder), but his time indications are very vague: *interim* (*H*. 1.71.1); *per idem tempus* (*H*. 1.73); *interim* (*H*. 1.74.1). We then have reference to the coming civil war with Vitellius (*H*. 1.79.1); *interim* (*H*. 1.80.1); and *per eos dies* (*H*. 1.88.1). Suetonius' account is very brief and concentrates on a few episodes only; his time indications are extremely vague too: *dein vergente iam die* (*O*. 7.1 – 15th January); *postridie* (*O*. 7.2); *sub idem vero tempus* (*O*. 8.1); *verum haud dubio bello* (*O*. 8.1). Most of the events of Otho's principate in Rome, then, seem to have been remembered as occurring more or less simultaneously and this will reflect the principal source or sources used by our extant authors (cf. Plut. *O*. 1.1-5.4; Dio 64.7-10.1).

For this reason it is not possible to construct a detailed chronology of Otho's principate from 15th January-15th March. However, certain items can be assigned to approximate dates: an expeditionary force was sent to Gallia Narbonensis probably during the first few days of March (see below, 9.2, n. on *apud Alpes*) and apparently in conjunction with the preparations for *this* expedition the order was given to move a military unit (a cohort of Roman citizens) from Ostia to Rome, which in turn gave rise to a violent outbreak of the praetorians (see below 8.2, n. on *verum haud dubio bello iamque ducibus... appropinquantibus*). In addition the Arval Brethren give certain dates in January, February and March of A.D. 69 which enable us to pinpoint more exactly events which are somewhat blurred in our literary sources, especially the details of the formal grants of Otho's various powers (see below, 7.1, n. on *gesturusque communi omnium arbitrio*).

One of the major elements in any consideration of Otho's policies as Princeps must be his relationship with the Praetorian Guard. The praetorian officers and men were his only enthusiastic supporters, and he was compelled to tread a narrow and difficult path between retaining their favour (at the price of excessive indulgence, if necessary) on the one hand and conciliating other groups in Rome and the Empire on the other, with the aim of broadening the basis of his support. This was an almost impossible task, since the praetorians were deeply suspicious of the Senate (e.g. *H*. 1.80.2 and 82.1; cf. Plut. *O*. 3.3-10) and certainly had no respect for it (not without justification: cf. *H*. 1.35.1 with 1.45.1), while the Senate and people generally were horrified at the manner of Otho's coming to power (*H*. 1.50.1), and the members of the upper classes were especially fearful where the praetorians were concerned (*H*. 1.81). Given this basic situation, Otho knew that he could not follow Galba's policy of punishing opponents and rewarding only partisans. Galba's end had shown how dangerous such a policy could be.

Towards the Praetorian Guard and other city soldiery Otho was exceedingly indulgent: the praetorians were allowed to choose their own prefects, and Flavius Sabinus was re-instated as urban prefect by the troops (*H*. 1.46.1; he had been Nero's prefect but had been dismissed by Galba: Plut. *O*. 5.4). Time and again we see Otho flattering the soldiers and shamelessly begging favours from them (*H*. 1.36, 45-6, 80-5, esp. 84.4; Plut. *O*. 1.2; 3.11-13). This policy is characterised by Tacitus' sarcastic *omnia serviliter pro dominatione* (*H*. 1.36.3).

With regard to the upper classes, Otho knew full well how important recognition by the Senate was for his position in the Empire as a whole (cf. the words which Tacitus puts into his mouth when he calls it *caput imperii et decora omnium provinciarum*: *H.* 1.84.3). Active co-operation by members of the Senate would be even more valuable. He therefore exerted himself to the full to win them over, and with regard to his own formal powers and offices, he followed a strictly 'constitutionalist' line (see below 7.1, n. on *gesturusque communi omnium arbitrio*). Likewise, certain exiles restored by Galba were especially easy for him to win over; for Galba had, in some cases at least, failed to give them back the property which had been confiscated by the state. In general, Otho was anxious to avoid giving offence to anyone: hence in making his arrangements for the consulship he kept the designations of Nero and Galba, and made alterations only by filling in blanks and shortening terms (*H.* 1.77.2; see also G.B. Townend, *AJP* 83 [1962] 113-24).

In the provinces, in contrast to Galba, Otho was generous with his grants of citizenship, and he did not restrict himself to paying off debts. Evidence is scanty, but, with regard to Spain and Gaul, we may note that Otho apparently tried to compensate for Galba's shortcomings (cf. *H.* 1.78.1). Indeed, in Gaul, his grant of citizenship to the Lingones may have been a gambler's attempt to pry them loose from their attachment to the army of Upper Germany (*H.* 1.54.1). In addition, the designation of Otho's old friend Pompeius Vopiscus as consular colleague with Verginius Rufus was widely regarded as a compliment to the city of Vienne (*H.* 1.77.2). In the Danubian provinces, the energetic Galban partisan Cornelius Fuscus was left in office as *procurator* of Dalmatia, and the equally energetic Antonius Primus remained as *legatus* of Leg. *VII Galbiana* in Pannonia. Slightly further east, an incursion of the Rhoxolani in Moesia was repelled by Leg. *III Gallica*, and the governor M. Aponius and the three legionary legates of that province were all extravagantly rewarded (*H.* 1.79.5). The result of these and other efforts in Pannonia, Dalmatia and Moesia can be seen in the persistent loyalty shown towards Otho by the seven legions of this area. This was perhaps his most significant success as Princeps.

Overall, we may conclude that Otho accomplished a surprising amount in the eight weeks or so that he spent as Princeps in Rome. Of course, possession of the city and recognition by the Senate and the praetorians inevitably counted for much, especially with the eastern provinces (*H*. 1.76; cf. 1.84.3-4), and their recognition of him implied nothing in the way of loyalty or enthusiasm. In Rome itself, his attempts at conciliation surprised and pleased those most fearful of him, but their support was, at best, wary and transitory, and Tacitus may well reflect contemporary views in the savage attack on Otho's character with which he begins and concludes his account of his principate (*H*. 1.50; 2.31).

**7.1** *dein vergente iam die ingressus senatum*: cf. Plut. *G*. 28.1; *H*. 1.47.1. The Senate was summoned by the *praetor urbanus*, which was constitutionally correct, both consuls (Galba and Vinius) now being dead. Furthermore, since new business could not be placed before the Senate *after* the 10th hour of the day (Sen. *Tranq*. 17.7), this being mid-January, it was probably called into session no later than about 2.30 p.m.

*quasi raptus de publico et suscipere imperium vi coactus*: this probably did become the 'official' version of how Otho was proclaimed Princeps (cf. Dio 64.8.1, where Otho claims to have tried to oppose the soldiers!). Certainly to a casual bystander, the events described at *H*. 1.27.2 and Plut. *G*. 25.1-3, where a scared-looking Otho was suddenly surrounded by a gang of armed men and hustled away in a litter would have tended to confirm this 'explanation'. For the idea that early emperors undertook the burden of office 'reluctantly', see A. Jakobson and H.M. Cotton, *Historia* 34 (1985) 497-503.

*gesturusque communi omnium arbitrio*: this is probably no more than a conventional pledge to rule in a 'constitutional' manner, but there is evidence to show that Otho was scrupulous about constitutional niceties. Although Tacitus tells us (*H*. 1.47.1) that at this meeting of the Senate *decernitur Othoni tribunicia potestas et nomen Augusti et omnes principum honores* (cf. Plut. *G*. 28.1; Dio 64.8.1), what was passed by the Senate was, strictly speaking, only a recommendation: *de iure* these powers had to come from the people. Accordingly, a series of 'elections' took place (the evidence for which is the *AFA* for ?16th, 26th January, 28th February, 5th and 9th March [ = MW2]). It was, of course, the Senate's resolution which mattered, but these curious survivals were gone through to ensure public goodwill.

*ac super ceteras... nullum indicium recusantis dedit*: to the casual reader it may appear that the information about the greeting 'Nero-Otho' refers to Otho's first day as Emperor, but this sentence and the rest of the information contained in 7.1 have no precise temporal context. The narrative sequence is... *Palatium petit... dicitur ea nocte* (7.2). Apparently no specific information survived about the occasion or occasions on which the *infima plebs* hailed Otho as 'Nero'; cf. Plut. *O*. 3.1; *H*. 1.78.2.

*immo, ut quidam tradunt, etiam diplomatibus... Neronis cognomen adiecit*: the source of this particular story is revealed by Plutarch (*O*. 3.2) to have been Cluvius Rufus, governor of Spain after Galba's departure for Rome (cf. *H*. 1.8.1), and Cluvius' information is described as referring specifically to *diplomata* sent to Spain. S. does seem to have doubts about the truth of the story; (cf. *certe*, implying a contrast, with which the next sentence begins).

*diplomatibus*: originally a *diploma* was a *laissez-passer* for those using government resources or facilities while making a journey, and with the coming of the *vehiculatio* (see p. 74), especially for those using its facilities (cf. *OLD s.v. diploma*). It also came to mean a certificate outlining privileges bestowed on anyone by the government, as in the military diplomata collected in *CIL XVI* (for examples, see MW 396-403). The article *s.v.* in *OCD*² is quite misleading in its basic definition.

*ad quosdam provinciarum praesides*: it would appear that once Cluvius Rufus spread the tale of the Spanish diplomata, gossip, which S. picked up, expanded this to include *epistulae... ad quosdam provinciarum praesides*, which were rather different from 'open-ended' diplomata.

*certe et imagines statuasque eius reponi passus est*: clearly no overt action on Otho's part is involved (cf. Plut. *O*. 3.1). Tacitus (*H*. 1.78.2) makes it even less the result of any Othonian initiative: *et fuere qui imagines Neronis proponerent*.

*et procuratores atque libertos ad eadem officia revocavit*: this seems somewhat sinister, when we recall Nero's administration (cf. P.A. Brunt, *Latomus* 18 [1959] 554-9). However, Otho had almost no choice, since he probably felt unable to trust Galba's officials. Little is known of this aspect of his administration, but see *H*. 1.76.3 for a celebration of Otho's accession arranged by one of Nero's freedmen.

*quingenties sestertium ad peragendam Auream Domum*: for the amount, see above *G*. 5.2, n. on *sestertium namque quingenties, sed quia notata,... ne haec quidem accepti*. The Golden House was built in the period immediately following the great fire of A.D. 64. It covered approximately 125 acres with buildings and landscaped gardens, connecting properties already belonging to the emperor on the Palatine and Esquiline Hills and occupying also the depression which lay between these hills and the Caelian Hill (the Velia ridge, site of the *Domus Transitoria*, and the Colosseum valley): see *Ann*. 15.42-43 and S. *Nero* 31. For the revolution which the Golden House represented in design, construction techniques and interior decoration, see A. Boëthius, *The Golden House of Nero* [Ann Arbor, 1960] 94-128; W.L. MacDonald, *The Architecture of the Roman Empire* [New Haven, 1965] 31-46 and Plates 21a-34; M. Grant, *Nero* [London, 1970] 163-95 (with superb illustrations).

**7.2** *dicitur ea nocte per quietem pavefactus...* μακροῖς αὐλοῖς: the sequence is clear: *ea nocte* refers to the night of 15-16th January; *postridie* will refer to Otho's first formal sacrifice as Emperor, on the morning of 16th January (for the practice cf. 6.2, above). Plutarch (*O*. 1.1), Tacitus (*H*. 1.47.2, 71.1) and Dio (65.7.1-2) show considerable variation in the order of events. S.'s account, however, is the clearest and most straightforward. Although the phrase about 'long flutes' is given by Dio (65.7.1) in a slightly different form, what is perhaps significant is the explanation that this was a proverbial expression applied to those who were doing something for which they were not fitted. This may be a misquotation of a passage from Sophocles (fr. 768) which Cicero has applied to Pompey (*Att*. 2.16.2), where Pompey is said to be no longer playing on a small flute but a large one which produces a loud, deep blast.

**8.1** *sub idem vero tempus*: a fairly loose expression, since it refers to the events of 1st-3rd January, 69: cf. above *G*. 16.2 and nn., and below *Vit*. 8.2, n. on *consentiente deinde etiam superioris provinciae exercitu... defecerat*.

*auctor senatui fuit mittendae legationis*: for a somewhat more complicated story, see *H*. 1.19.2, 74.2. The main point here is that the envoys were to announce *electum iam principem, quietem concordiamque suaderet*. It was the *Senate* to which the legions of Upper Germany had sworn allegiance on 1st January and they had demanded that the praetorians in Rome should choose a new emperor (above, *G*. 16.2). This embassy eventually reached Vitellius and the envoys apparently defected to him immediately (*H*. 1.74.2).

*et tamen per internuntios ac litteras... Vitellio optulit*: cf. Plut. *O*. 4.4-6; *H*. 1.74.1; Dio 64.10.1. Only S. states that Otho offered to form a marriage alliance with Vitellius. Nothing came of these moves and the messages which passed back and forth degenerated into insult and name-calling.

### THE PRAETORIAN OUTBREAK (8.1-2)

At this point in his narrative, S. gives a very summary account of an unexpected and wild outbreak of violence among t ie praetorian soldiers, who suspected that a senatorial counter-*coup* against Otho was being prepared or was already underway. They burst into the Palace and not only caused a panic among the senators and their wives who were dining there with Otho, but also terrified the Princeps himself. With difficulty they were calmed. The next day they were given a substantial cash payment and only very light punishment was meted out.

All our sources note this incident: the fullest accounts are in Tacitus (*H*. 1.80-85) and Plutarch (*O*. 3.3-13), while Dio's account (64.9.2-3) is even briefer than S.'s. Tacitus sees the outbreak as caused by indiscipline and he describes it in over-emotional, highly coloured language; Plutarch allows an element of genuine concern for Otho's safety on the part of the praetorians, though he appears to have misunderstood his main Latin source and erroneously places the outbreak in Ostia! Dio is so brief that we really hear only of the boldness and lawlessness of the soldiers. S.'s brief account is rather different from Tacitus-Plutarch, but this need not imply that he is following a wholly distinct tradition; for if his account can be shown to harmonize with the fuller versions and even supplement them, we can easily conclude that he is following at least one major source in common with Tacitus-Plutarch.

**8.1** *verum haud dubio bello iamque ducibus... appropinquantibus*: S. uses this somewhat vague time indication to signify the context within which he places the praetorian outbreak. In this he is similar to Tacitus, who at *H.* 1.79.1 introduces his account of the invasion of Moesia by the Rhoxolani (see above, p. 108) with the words *conversis ad civile bellum animis* and in the following chapter begins the story of the Praetorians with *interim*. News of the success in Moesia probably reached Rome at the very end of February, 69; and the sacrifices performed by the Arval Brethren on 1st March *ob laurum positam* suggest that the praetorian outbreak took place at about the beginning of March, probably during the very first days of the month.

*iamque ducibus... appropinquantibus*: there were two invasion columns dispatched by Vitellius from Germany towards Italy. The first of these, led by Fabius Valens, left Colonia Agrippinensis about 12th January, 69, and advanced south through Gaul by way of Lugdunum to Valentia and then swung eastwards towards Vapincum and the Cottian Pass through the Alps (Mt. Genèvre) and so into N. Italy; the other was led by Caecina Alienus and advanced from Upper Germany through Helvetia to an Alpine crossing at the Pennine Summit (Great St Bernard Pass) and thence to Ticinum and Placentia.

*animum fidemque erga se praetorianorum... expertus est*: there is no reason to doubt that this is the true explanation of the praetorian upheaval. It does not, of course, square with the hostile and moralizing picture of Otho which came to be accepted, and which appears so prominently in Tacitus' account. (For a possible source for S.'s rather different picture, see below *O*. 10.1.)

*paene internecione amplissimi ordinis*: cf. below 8.2, *in Palatium cucurrerunt caedem senatus flagitantes*; S. is therefore self-consistent, but the statement is almost certainly exaggerated. From Plutarch (*O*. 3.6, 8) and Tacitus (*H*. 1.81.1) we learn that eighty senators and their wives were in the palace attending a banquet provided by Otho, which the praetorians interrupted and broke up. While these people may have been in some physical danger, the main concern of the soldiers was clearly Otho's safety; and although people in Rome expected a slaughter and/or sack to take place, in fact no senator or property was harmed. The greatest exaggeration about this incident, however, is

Tacitus' introductory remarks (*H*. 1.80.1): *parvo interim initio, unde nihil timebatur, orta seditio prope urbi excidio fuit*. Perhaps one or more of the senators present recorded the incident in historical works or memoirs, and Tacitus decided that it would constitute a suitable pretext for a sermon on discipline.

**8.2** *[et] placuerat*: *et* is meaningless here and should be excised; Bücheler's emendation *ei* has merit. The decision to move weapons was clearly Otho's, and since Otho is also the subject of the concluding words of the preceding sentence, there need be no difficulty in understanding the reference.

*ei placuerat per classiarios arma transferri remittique navibus*: this is the most valuable information which S. gives us about the praetorian outbreak. It is not wholly intelligible in itself, since the weapons are merely to be 'sent back' to somewhere unspecified, but this is, no doubt, the result of excessive compression. However, if we combine this with the accounts in Plutarch and Tacitus, we get a coherent picture. Because of the coming war with the forces of Vitellius advancing from Germany, Rome was to be stripped of much of its regular garrison (*H*. 1.87.1). Otho decided to move from Ostia to Rome a cohort of Roman citizens, which had been stationed there to guard against fires since the days of Claudius. He ordered that weapons be moved from the praetorian camp in Rome by ship to Ostia so that the garrison replacements could be properly equipped and would look as soldierly and efficient as possible when they marched into the city.

*in castris*: there can be no serious doubt that this refers to the Castra Praetoria in Rome. The previous reference in this passage has been to the *animum fidemque... praetorianorum*, and it follows that *quidam* and *omnes* in the next two clauses likewise refer to the praetorians.

*insidias quidam suspicati tumultum excitaverunt*: Plutarch (*O*. 3.4-5) and Tacitus (*H*. 1.80) give more detailed accounts of the outbreak of trouble, especially Tacitus, who starts his mutiny *topos* at this point. Both state that the praetorians immediately suspected a counter-*coup* in which the weapons would be used by the *familiae* of senators.

*ac repente omnes nullo certo duce in Palatium cucurrerunt*: S. here emphasizes the confusion of the scene as the praetorians suddenly surged from the camp, no doubt by now obsessed with the idea that the senatorial counter-*coup* against Otho was already underway and that only by dashing at top speed to the palace could they have any hope of saving him; cf. *H.* 1.80.2; Plut. *O.* 3.5-6.

*repulsisque tribunorum qui inhibere temptabant, nonnullis et occisis*: according to Plutarch (*O.* 3.5-6, 9-10) and Tacitus (*H.* 1.81-82.1), no one was actually killed at the palace. S.'s somewhat misleading account may be the result of extreme compression. However, given the detail of the other accounts it seems probable that he is simply wrong here.

*ubinam imperator esset requirentes*: S. has suppressed all direct mention of the senators and their wives who were dining with Otho when the soldiers arrived (though the words *amplissimi ordinis, caedem senatus* and *in triclinium* would remind his readers of what was no doubt a well-known story). They are purely fortuitous adjuncts to his story of praetorian devotion.

*perruperunt in triclinium usque nec nisi viso destiterunt*: by his elimination of the story of the banquet, S. creates the impression (probably not deliberately) that Otho was dining more or less alone when the soldiers burst in upon him, and he says that they stopped their rampage only when they saw for themselves that he was safe. Here too perhaps he oversimplifies his account, for we have no mention of the rather humiliating lengths to which Otho had to go to quieten the troops (Plut. *O.* 3.11; *H.* 1.82.1).

### THE OTHONIAN COUNTER-OFFENSIVE (8.3-9.2)

Otho left Rome for the north of Italy and his campaign against the Vitellian invasion probably on 15th March, 69 (see below 8.3, n. on *et die quo cultores deum Matris lamentari et plangere incipiunt*). His strategic problems had two main causes: first, his intelligence-gathering in Gaul and Germany during January and February of 69 was poor; and second, he seems to have believed for far too long that he could *negotiate* a settlement with Vitellius. It was apparently news of the approach of Vitellius' forces to the Alps (*H.* 1.87.1: *quando Poeninae Cottiaeque Alpes et ceteri Galliarum aditus Vitellianis exercitibus claudebantur*; cf. above 8.1) which finally spurred him into action. He summoned the four legions of Pannonia and Dalmatia and the three legions of Moesia to Italy. However, the movement-order to these troops was not sent off from Rome until about 3rd March: on this see the important paper by K. Wellesley, *JRS* 61 (1971) 28-51. Knowing that it would take weeks for these troops to arrive and that in the meantime communications with the north-east had to be kept open, Otho sent an 'advance guard' from Rome to hold the line of the R. Po pending the arrival of the Danubian forces (for its activities, see below 9.2, n. on *circaque Placentiam*). But even this force would have required about three weeks to take up its position and if the Vitellian invasion columns were allowed to proceed unimpeded, the enemy might well be south of the Po by then. Otho had, therefore, to do something drastic and, if possible, bring the Vitellian advance to a dead stop for a while. His solution was to send a sea-borne force (urban cohorts, praetorians and marines from the fleet, all units based in Rome or nearby: *H.* 1.87.1; cf. 8.2 *per classiarios...navibus*) to Narbonese Gaul. This expedition was purely diversionary and it succeeded (see below 9.2, n. on *apud Alpes*).

All of this activity must have come *after* Otho's decision to fight. The first action would have been the sending of the movement order to the Danubian legions (c. 3rd March); the next would have been the dispatch of the diversionary force to Narbonese Gaul (and it was probably the preparations for this which triggered the praetorian disturbance); finally and very soon thereafter, the 'advance guard' was sent to the north (cf. Otho's words *'imus ad bellum'* to the praetorians on the day after the outbreak: *H.* 1.83.3).

**8.3** *expeditionem autem inpigre atque etiam praepropere incohavit*: *inpigre* is borne out by Tacitus (*H.* 1.89.3): *aspernatus est omnem cunctationem. praepropere*, however, is qualified principally by *nulla ne religionum quidem cura*. The focus in the remainder of this chapter is on omens and portents rather than on Otho's dash and vigour.

*nulla ne religionum quidem cura*: curiously enough, S. forbears here to recount the many omens and prodigies listed by Tacitus (*H.* 1.86.1) and Plutarch (*O.* 4.7-9), with the exception of the Tiber floods and their consequences. Conversely, his references to Cybele and Dis Pater are not found in our other sources.

*sed et motis necdum conditis ancilibus*: cf. *H*. 1.89.3; this is a reference to a ritual of extreme antiquity performed in March by the Salii, the dancing priests of Mars. *ancilia movere* describes the essence of the ritual: between 1st and 24th March, the Salii took the figure-of-eight shaped shields from their resting-place (the *sacrarium Martis* or *Curia Saliorum*) and carried them through the city in procession, leaping and dancing and striking their shields with a spear or staff (Dion. Hal. 2.70-71; cf. Livy 1.20.4). On the 24th March the *ancilia* were restored to their original place (*ancilia condere*), whereby S. gives us his *terminus ante quem* for Otho's departure from Rome.

*et die, quo cultores deum Matris lamentari et plangere incipiunt*: the *Mater deum*, is, of course, Cybele, the Magna Mater, and during the Republican period her main festival in Rome was the Megalensia, which lasted from 4-10th April. There seems to have been an extensive reorganization of the cult in the time of Claudius, introduced as a supplement to, rather than a replacement for, the Megalensia and lasting from 15-27th March. It is clear from S.'s use of *lamentari et plangere* that we are here concerned with the March rituals, which centred on the death and resurrection of Attis, the beloved of Cybele; cf. *H*. 1.90.1, which suggests Otho's departure from Rome on 14th or perhaps 15th March, and also *AFA* for 14th March, 69: *pr. idus Mart. vota nu<n>cupata pro s[al]ute et reditu [Vitelli] Germanici imp.* (inscribed at a slightly later date, after Otho's death, with Vitellius' name erroneously inserted and, later still, partly erased).

*nam et victima Diti patri caesa litavit, cum tali sacrificio contraria exta potiora sint*: this is the only evidence that in sacrificing to Dis Pater one looked for *unfavourable* omens. Perhaps the idea was that, if Dis was not in favour of you, you could expect to survive your coming crisis; or possibly, in making sacrifice to Dis Pater, Otho was calling down a curse on Vitellius.

*et primo egressu inundationibus Tiberis retardatus*: from the position of the account of these floods in the narratives of Tacitus (*H*. 1.86.2-87.1) and Plutarch (*O*. 4.10), it appears that they occurred at about the end of February or the very beginning of March and that S., in implying that they hindered Otho's physical exit from the city, is guilty of a rather careless compression of events. The flooding caused widespread and serious damage: the Pons Sublicius collapsed and dammed up the river bed, causing the river to flood a large area of the city. Many shops and houses were seriously affected, and the city's food reserves were badly damaged, since the *horrea* were inundated (see further R.F. Newbold, *Historia* 22 [1972] 308-19, esp. 311-15).

*ad vicensimum etiam lapidem ruina aedificiorum praeclusam viam offendit*: Newbold suggests (*Historia* 22 [1972] 311) that an earth-tremor affected the Tiber basin at about the same time as the floods.

**9.1** *simili temeritate*: this phrase, stronger than *etiam praepropere* in 8.3 above, though linked to it by *simili*, condemns not only Otho's departure for the campaign against the Vitellians (the reference is almost certainly, as before, to the date of his leaving Rome and the portents at that time) but also, and perhaps more reasonably, his decision to fight a decisive battle before all his troops had arrived from the Danubian area.

*quamvis dubium nemini esset quin trahi bellum oporteret*: this argument could certainly be applied to the situation obtaining *after* the battle of Bedriacum (cf. below 9.3); S. therefore concludes that it applied as much., if not more, to the situation *before* the battle. Accordingly, he gives what he considers to be the main reasons in favour of postponing a battle (*quando et fame et angustiis locorum urgeretur hostis*) and then goes on to speculate about Otho's decision the other way. The analysis is superficial and unsatisfactory, but it is not S.'s, for it appears to have been in the 'common source' (cf. *H.* 2.32; Plut. *O.* 8.3-5). However, the Vitellian forces in N. Italy had ample supplies and there was simply no question of *fames* afflicting them. Likewise, they were *not* penned into a 'narrow area' between the Po and the Alps. As for S.'s account of Otho's motives for deciding to fight quickly, *impatiens longioris sollicitudinis* may have some validity, given Otho's gambler's instincts, his nervous anxiety and his general lack of stomach for warfare. Similarly, the exact whereabouts of Vitellius (*sperans ante Vitellii adventum profligari proelium posse*) may well have been unknown to the Othonian commanders. However, what is wholly lacking here is any serious attempt to discover the reasons for Otho's decision to fight, and the general strategic considerations which prompted his apparently reckless initiatives.

We should first of all note that Otho's moves up to the date of his arrival at Bedriacum for a grand strategy session with his commanders (about 10th April, 69) were perfectly sound. The one thing he had to fear was a Vitellian crossing of the Po and southward thrust before the Danubian legions could arrive, and this was what began to happen. The Vitellians were not prepared to advance eastwards against the main Othonian position at Bedriacum: instead, they decided to build a bridge and break across the Po (cf. Plut. *O.* 10.2) and so drive southwards towards the Apennines and Rome. Otho countered this by ordering a substantial part of his main force to advance from Bedriacum and establish a new base close enough to the site of the Vitellian bridge to prevent its completion (cf. *H.* 2.40). This was a risky move, since his army might be attacked on its way to its new position (as indeed it was), but had it succeeded, the Vitellians would have been finished and their invasion of Italy would probably have ended without a major battle, which may well have been Otho's ultimate aim; see further K.Wellesley, *JRS* 61 (1971) 28-51, esp. 33, 38-41, 48-51.

*nec ulli pugnae affuit substititque Brixelli*: this too is heavily criticised in our sources (*H.* 2.33.2-3; cf Plut. *O.* 10.1). Otho's return to Brixellum with a considerable force of infantry and cavalry was intended to stop any Vitellian units which managed to cross the Po. On balance, however, it looks as if the damage done to the morale of the troops at Bedriacum outweighed any advantage which might have resulted from this action.

**9.2** *apud Alpes*: *apud Alpes* refers to the fighting which followed the landings of the diversionary force sent by Otho to the coastal regions of the Maritime Alps and Narbonese Gaul (for details, see *H.* 1.87.1; 2.12-15). Its composition was such that it could be assembled and sent off rapidly, possibly within a few hours of the decision to act (see p. 116); from this we may conclude that it will have left Rome by about 4th March. If we assume, perhaps slightly optimistically, that the Othonian force arrived in S. Gaul about 8-9th March, the earliest possible date for the first clash (just to the west of Albintimilium) between this force and troops sent by Valens will be about 21st-22nd March. The second clash, in which the Vitellians attacked the Othonian camp at Albintimilium, came only after they had summoned reinforcements (presumably from Forum Iulii, 64 *mp* away): this will have occurred on about 24-25th March. In this second encounter the

Vitellians were defeated and both sides thereafter withdrew, the Vitellians to Antipolis (Antibes) and the Othonians to Albingaunum in Liguria. Although the fighting was inconclusive, this diversionary attack was highly successful: had it not occurred, Valens would probably have reached the Alpine crossing at Mt. Genèvre during the second week of March; as things turned out, he was not able to cross until about 26th March.

*circaque Placentiam*: the defence of Placentia by T. Vestricius Spurinna and part of the 'advance guard' is described in detail by Tacitus (*H.* 2.20.2-22.3;). Given the distance he had to travel from Rome to take up his position in Placentia (384 *mp*), Spurinna may have arrived c. 25-26th March. Caecina arrived some time later and, after attempting unsuccessfully to talk Spurinna's forces into surrender, launched a two-day attempt to take Placentia by storm (? 30th-31st March). When this failed, he was forced to re-cross the Po and head east towards Cremona, where he fortified a camp on the north-east side of the city.

*et ad Castoris, quod loco nomen est*: there was apparently a shrine of Castor and Pollux by the roadside on the *via Postumia* 12 *mp* east of Cremona (*H.* 2.24.2). It is unclear what happened at this battle because there are major discrepancies between the accounts of Plutarch (*O.* 7.2-7) and Tacitus (*H.* 2.24-26), which cannot easily be reconciled. Caecina appears to have set an ambush for the Othonians on the *via Postumia*; this went badly wrong and his forces were routed; they would have been completely destroyed and, possibly, the main Vitellian camp at Cremona might have been captured, but for excessive caution on the part of the Othonian general Suetonius Paulinus. This battle appears to have taken place on about 5th April, 69 and it was by far the most significant of the 'minor' victories won by Otho. Its consequences were considerable: as Valens was entering Ticinum (on about 6th April) he received word of Caecina's defeat; a forced march brought his first troops to Cremona late on 7th April. This junction of the two Vitellian columns obviously reduced considerably Otho's chances for a quick victory.

*novissimo maximoque apud Betriacum fraude superatus est, cum...*
*dimicandum fuisset*: that the Othonian forces were defeated through treachery rather than straightforwardly in a set-piece battle (cf. *H.*

2.42.1; Plut. *O*. 12.1-2) was probably an excuse widely canvassed among Otho's soldiers in the north of Italy and the Danubian provinces. They never *felt* defeated and so were all the more willing to try again and attempt to restore their *amour propre* in the latter part of 69 when the Flavian movement got under way (cf. *H*. 2.86; 3.24.1). However, the version of events given here is quite inaccurate.

As we have seen (above, 9.1, n. on *quamvis dubium... oporteret*), the Othonian forces which marched west from their main base at Bedriacum (on 13th April, 69) were not intended to fight a pitched battle with the armies of Caecina and Valens. Their purpose was on 14th April to establish a forward base near Cremona and so prevent further work on a bridge which was intended to lead to a Vitellian crossing of the Po and an advance southwards towards the Apennines and Rome. Given such a plan, the need for secrecy about the Othonian march and its goal was of supreme importance. However, there seems to have been treacherous plotting among certain Othonian officers: why, otherwise, did two praetorian tribunes visit Caecina shortly before the battle (*H*. 2.41.1; cf. also Tacitus' speculations at 2.37 about the motives of Suetonius Paulinus himself). The crucial point, however, is that the Othonian manoeuvre failed and the Vitellian attack caught the troops at a very bad moment: not only were they strung out along the *via Postumia* but they were also *impediti* and the baggage and supply trains were mixed in with the marching soldiers (*H*. 2.41.3; Plut. *O*. 12.3). All of these factors, no doubt magnified with frequent telling, gave rise to the Othonian belief in *fraus*.

*apud Betriacum*: the exact form of this name is not certain: our extant sources give *Betriacum/Bedriacum*; the difference in pronunciation between -d- and -t- is very slight and since no genuine inscription bearing the name of the place survives, the decision must be purely arbitrary. Historians writing in English have tended to follow Tacitus (cf. *H*. 2.23.2) and use *Bedriacum*. Its precise position is likewise uncertain: ancient evidence suggests that it lay between 20 and 22 *mp* east of Cremona; in a recent detailed examination of the evidence K. Wellesley has concluded that the modern village of Tornata lies on or near the site of Bedriacum and that the Othonian camp lay just west of it (*JRS* 61 [1971] 28-31, 33-4).

## THE DEATH OF OTHO (9.3-12.2)

It is clear that for the ancients nothing in Otho's life became him like the leaving it. That this 'choice luxury product of the Neronian court' (R. Syme, *Tacitus* 205) should at the end of his career reveal a nobility of spirit and a willingness to sacrifice himself for the good of the state, unequalled even by the patron saint of Roman stoicism, Cato Uticensis, was an apparent paradox which our ancient sources are at a loss to explain. As is to be expected, all our sources give, in their respective dimensions, detailed and copious accounts of Otho's death (Plut. *O.* 15-18; Tac. *H.* 2.46-50; S. *O.* 9.3-12.2; Dio 64.11-15), and this undoubtedly reflects the prominence which this episode received in the 'common source' and, probably, in first-hand accounts of the period also. We need not, however, be as surprised at Otho's noble end as were our ancient sources in general or Tacitus in particular. Certainly Otho was wild and undisciplined in his youth and corrupt and probably depraved as a young man, but his fall from imperial favour in 59 and virtual banishment to Lusitania seem to have sobered him very considerably; and it is notable that his government of that province is conceded by all to have been exemplary (he did not, apparently, indulge in any sort of self-enrichment, for he was heavily in debt when he accompanied Galba to Rome late in 68). In fact, we may assume that he possessed the same sort of administrative talents as his father. Certainly it is impossible to excuse his *coup détat* and assassination of Galba but we should at least remember that it was a relatively bloodless *coup* and that far fewer died in this seizure of power than in the accessions of either Galba or Vitellius. Further-more, as we have seen, there is little cogent criticism which can be levelled at Otho's conduct of affairs during the portion of his principate which he spent in Rome, and his counter-offensive, though late in starting, was perfectly sound. Moreover, it seems that S. gives us a more balanced and, possibly, more authentic picture of Otho than any other extant source. The reason is most readily apparent in this last section of the life: S.'s father Suetonius Laetus knew Otho personally and obviously admired him; the elder Suetonius was a military tribune in Legio *XIII Gemina*, an *eques* – not a senator, a soldier – not a civilian (below, *O.* 10.1). Undoubtedly, he saw Otho at his best but, equally, we must ask why the Emperor made so deep an impression. It is clear that he possessed a special trait of personality, that spark which an earlier generation called 'glamour' and which nowadays causes the misuse of the word 'charisma'; equally clearly it appealed more readily to soldiers than to civilians; and ultimately it produced a fanaticism which led men to kill themselves around Otho's funeral pyre (below, *O.* 12.2; cf. *H.* 2.49.4; Dio 64.15.1²; and see esp. Plut. *O.* 17.10-12).

Was everything lost and need Otho have killed himself after the defeat near Cremona? Here we can agree with the negative answer to this question which is the unanimous verdict of the ancient sources (for details, see below *O.* 9.3, n. on *quam desperatione... solae subirent*). A 'second round' for Otho would, however, have involved much more than merely re-grouping his existing troops and waiting for the arrival of the remaining Danubian legions: the Vitellian forces would meanwhile probably have thrust south towards Rome and Otho would have found himself with a prolonged and bloody civil war on his hands. He loathed the idea of civil war (see below *O.* 10.1; cf. Plut. *O.* 15.7-8; *H.* 2.47.2-3; Dio 64.13.1-2) and his whole strategy had been based on winning the struggle with Vitellius without a major battle, if possible, or, failing that, in one, sharp, decisive encounter. With the defeat near Cremona, for Otho the game was over.

**9.3** *ac statim moriendi impetum cepit*: from this point to the end of 10.1 S. gives us a general background discussion of Otho's strategic position after the defeat of his force near Cremona and an assessment of his character, culminating in the event which brought him to his decision to die. It becomes clear that *statim* here is something of an exaggeration.

*magis pudore, ne tanto rerum hominumque periculo dominationem sibi asserere perseveraret*: the remainder of this paragraph is meant to represent Otho's own calculations (cf. the *sibi* here and the *secum* in the next clause). However, the *pudor*, like the *impetus moriendi*, does not arise for some little time; cf. below 10.1 *ad fin; proclamasse eum... non amplius se in periculum talis tamque bene meritos coniecturum*; cf. Plut. *O.* 15.4-8; *H.* 2.46.

*quam desperatione ulla aut diffidentia copiarum; quippe... solae subirent*: in this passage S. mentions three groups of forces available to Otho after the defeat of the troops who were attempting to establish a forward base near Cremona: *residuis integrisque* (the substantial forces which he had with him at Brixellum; cf. Plut. *O.* 10.1); *supervenientibus aliis* (the Danubian units still advancing towards Italy and Bedriacum: all the legions of Dalmatia and Pannonia would have reached him by 26th April, though detachments from Moesia could not have arrived until about 11th May); and *victis* (a goodly number of the troops defeated on 14th April appear to have fled back to Bedriacum, while a large part of the army had remained there during the advance of the rest on 13-14th April to the new forward base to be established near Cremona; cf. *H.* 2.44).

**10.1** *angusticlavius*: this word simply means 'belonging to the equestrian order', since in status-conscious Rome with its many visible marks of class distinction, those engaged in or aiming for a career in the senatorial *cursus* wore a tunic with a broad, vertical purple stripe (*latus clavus*), while those intent on the equestrian *cursus* wore a narrow stripe (*angustus clavus*; cf. Ovid, *Trist.* 4.10.29, 35).

*Othonem... usque adeo detestatum civilia arma, ut memorante quodam inter epulas de Cassi Brutique exitu cohorruerit*: the point here is not so much that both Cassius and Brutus ultimately committed suicide, but that this was the outcome of over two years of convulsion for the Roman state. The bloodshed, the thousands of deaths, even the murder of Caesar itself must have seemed quite pointless by the middle of the first century A.D.

*nec concursurum cum Galba fuisse, nisi confideret sine bello rem transigi posse*: cf. above *G.* 16.2, where the army of Upper Germany decides to send envoys to the praetorians to state that they did not like the Emperor made in Spain: *eligerent ipsi (sc. praetoriani) quem cuncti exercitus comprobarent*, and *O.* 8.1, where Otho persuades the Senate to send a *legatio* to Germany *quae doceret electum iam principem, quietem concordiamque suaderet*. Otho still believed that once the Senate and Praetorian Guard settled on a princeps, the matter was settled; of course, every precedent pointed to this, including Galba's accession the year before.

*tunc ad despiciendam vitam exemplo manipularis militis concitatum... gladio ante pedes eius incubuerit*: the same story is told by Dio, but of a cavalryman (64.11); Plutarch has an account of a soldier's suicide (*O.* 15.3) but the reasons for his death are quite different. However, in this case we must believe S., since his father was an eye-witness to the incident. Tacitus, on the other hand, appears to transfer the entire story to the last weeks of *Vitellius* (*H.* 3.54.2-3).

**10.2** *fratrem*: this passage is the only evidence that Otho Titianus fled to Brixellum at about the time of the surrender of the Othonian forces in the camp at Bedriacum on the day following the battle (i.e. 15th April, 69; see *H.* 2.45; Plut. *O.* 13.6-13). Since S. is relying on an eye-witness account, we should accept this evidence: it also makes clear the fact that Otho died on the morning of the *second* day after the battle.

*fratrisque filium*: his full name was L. Salvius Otho Cocceianus and he was the last of the Salvii Othones, perishing at the hands of Domitian *quod Othonis imperatoris patrui sui diem natalem celebraverat* (S. *Dom.* 10.3). When he was with his uncle the Emperor at Brixellum he was apparently still quite young (cf. Plut. *O.* 16.2: ἔτι μειράκιον ὄντα ['still a lad']; *H.* 2.48: *prima iuventa, trepidum et maerentem*).

*binos codicillos exaravit*: from the verb *exaravit* it is clear that these were small tablets, probably of wood, with a slightly raised edge all round and a layer of wax on the surface which was scratched with a stylus. Such tablets usually came in pairs (cf. *binos*) with cloth or tape hinges, so that when closed the two writing surfaces were on the inside and protected.

*ad sororem*: on Salvia (?), see above *O.* 1.3, n. on *tulit et filiam, quam vixdum nubilem Druso Germanici filio despondit*. Nothing further is known of her.

*ad Messalinam Neronis, quam matrimonio destinarat*: at *Ner.* 35.1 S. tells us that Statilia Messalina was the great-great-granddaughter of T. Statilius Taurus (*cos. suff.* 37 B.C.; *cos II* 26 B.C.), perhaps the second most important of Augustus' marshals, and that she was Nero's third wife.

*commendans reliquias suas et memoriam*: this implies not only that Otho asked Messalina to make offerings to his shade (*memoriam*), but also that she was to be responsible for the disposition of his ashes and for the construction and maintenance of his tomb. In fact, he was hurriedly cremated after his suicide to prevent his body falling into the hands of the Vitellians, and his ashes were buried in a modest tomb at Brixellum (below 11.2; see also Plut. *O*. 18.1-2; *H*. 2.49.3-4; cf. *Vit*. 10.3).

*quicquid deinde epistularum erat... concremavit*: cf. *H*. 2.48.1; Dio 64.15.1a. This, of course, refers to the correspondence which Otho had with him at Brixellum. There were other, more damaging letters in Rome; cf. below, *Vit*. 10.1, n. on *centum autem atque viginti... conquiri et supplicio adfici imperavit*.

*divisit et pecunias domesticis ex copia praesenti*: according to Plutarch (*O*. 17.1-2) it was now evening and Otho distributed his money carefully, giving some larger amounts and some smaller; cf. *H*. 2.48.1; Dio 64.15.1a.

**11.1** *atque ita paratus intentusque iam morti*: it is clear from S.'s account that Otho intended to commit suicide that evening, i.e. 15th April, but did not, so that he could continue to exercise his authority over his troops long enough to enable his close friends and the senators in his suite to get well clear of Brixellum.

*tumultu inter moras exorto... vetuitque vim cuiquam fieri*: cf. Plut. *O*. 16.1 and 5-6; *H*. 2.48.1 and 49.1. The soldiers were most violent towards Verginius Rufus, who had been *cos. II* during the month of March; he appears not to have departed from Brixellum during this general evacuation, since Otho's troops turned to him the next day and begged him threateningly either to assume the imperial office himself or to negotiate on their behalf with Caecina and Valens, at which point he slipped away (*H*. 2.51; cf. Plut. *O*. 18.5-7). Clearly he was the only senior person of military standing who was still at Brixellum when Otho died, and he seems, with characteristic stubbornness, not even to have appeared to transfer his allegiance to Vitellius until after Otho's death (cf. *H*. 2.68).

**11.2** *post hoc sedata siti... artissimo somno quievit*: cf. *H*. 2.49.2; Plut. *O*. 17.1-3. S. and Tacitus and Plutarch are all using the same basic source but each has at least one 'subsidiary' version (S. has his father; Plutarch has Mestrius Florus, a senator who was in Otho's suite at Brixellum; cf. *O*. 14.2-3; Tacitus has the source concealed by *utque* *adfirmatur*). This gives rise to minor variations of detail, though there is no major disagreement.

*circa lucem demum expergefactus uno se traiecit ictu... tricensimo et octavo aetatis anno et nonagensimo et quinto imperii die*: it is important to determine the date on which Otho committed suicide, because it is by counting back from this date that the dates of the other events which occurred in April of 69 can be determined. Vitellius was formally recognized at Rome on 19th April (cf. *AFA* for 1st May, 69, when sacrifices were performed *ob diem imperi [Vitelli] German. imp., quod XIII K. Mai. statut. est...* ). The distance from Brixellum to Rome is 345 *mp,* and if we allow a maximum of 125-150 *mp* per day for dispatch riders carrying exceedingly important messages to Rome (cf. A.M. Ramsay, *JRS* 15 [1925] 60-74), the message would have reached the capital in about two and a half days. Since Otho died at dawn (perhaps about 5.30 a.m. in mid-April) the message will have arrived in Rome in the early evening – too late for senatorial action that day (cf. above 7.1, n. on *dein vergente iam die ingressus senatum*). The next day, 19th April, saw Vitellius' formal recognition; the message therefore arrived on 18th April and Otho died on 16th April (see further L. Holzapfel, *Klio* 13 [1913] 294-5).

Since Otho was born on 28th April, A.D. 32, S. is simply careless in saying that he died *tricensimo et octavo aetatis anno*. As for his remark about the ninety-fifth day of this rule, the calculation here is from 15th January, the date of his accession, to 19th April, the day on which Vitellius was recognized.

For a reconstruction of the chronology of the latter part of Otho's principate, see Appendix B (p. 175).

**12.1** *tanto Othonis animo nequaquam corpus aut habitus competit*: the implications of this remark are considerable: people who perform brave and noble deeds *should* look 'brave and noble', while, presumably, effeminate men of suspected homosexual tendencies should mince and look languid. S. does seem to have believed that physiognomy revealed character: this is especially true in his descriptions of emperors such as Gaius, Nero and Domitian (for details see the study by J. Couissin, *REL* 31 [1953] 234-56; cf. E.C. Evans, *HSCP* 46 [1935] 43-84, esp. 60-70).

*fuisse enim et modicae staturae et male pedatus scambusque traditur*: it is in a sense unfortunate that Otho did not look like a Stoic hero, for then we might have had a detailed description of him from S., with precise enumeration of his distinguishing features. This he would have been in a good position to give us, since he had access to sources who had known Otho personally.

*munditiarum vero paene muliebrum... ne barbatus numquam esset*: it is impossible to say whether these details of Otho's personal grooming are true or whether they are hearsay based on his supposed effeminacy. Juvenal, for example, mocks Otho's handmirror, his skin care and, particularly, his habit of coating his face with bread (2.99-107). As for his use of a wig, a glance at the plate in *BMC Imp. I* which illustrates Otho's coinage (Pl. 60, nos. 1-14) will reveal several coins where the rows of carefully dressed curls look highly artificial and quite different from anything found on the coinage of other emperors of this period (see esp. nos. 2, 3, 10, 11).

*sacra etiam Isidis saepe in lintea religiosaque veste propalam celebrasse*: Otho appears to have been the first emperor to participate publicly in Isiac rituals in Rome, although Gaius had earlier established an official state cult of Isis, and called part of his palace the *Aula Isiaca*. For Isis worship, see J. Marquardt, *Röm. Staatsverwaltung III* (Leipzig, 1885; repr. New York, 1975) 76-80; R.E. Witt, *Isis in the Graeco-Roman World* (London, 1971), esp. chapter 17: 'The Goddess Darling of Roman Emperors'; for the mysteries, above all, the eleventh book of Apuleius' *Metamorphoses*.

**12.2** *multi praesentium militum... vim suae vitae attulerunt*: cf. *H.* 2.49.3-4: *tulere corpus praetoriae cohortes cum laudibus et lacrimis volnus manusque eius exosculantes. quidam militum iuxta rogum interfecere se, non noxa neque ob metum, sed aemulatione decoris et caritate principis*; see also Plut. *O.* 17.7-12; Dio 64.15.12.

*multi et absentium accepto nuntio prae dolore armis inter se ad internecionem concurrerunt*: cf. *H.* 2.49.4: *ac postea promisce Bedriaci Placentiae aliisque in castris celebratum id genus mortis.*

*denique magna pars hominum incolumem gravissime detestata mortuum laudibus tulit*: cf. Plut. *O.* 19.5; *H.* 2.31.1, 50.1; Dio

64.15.2ᵃ-2². It is interesting to note that, by implication, S. excludes himself from this group.

*ut vulgo iactatum sit etiam...rei p. ac libertatis restituendae causa interemptum*: this essentially meaningless allegation (cf. *Ann*. 1.3.7, relating to A.D. 14: *quotus quisque reliquus, qui rem publicam vidisset?*) came to be associated with several of the more genial members of the Julio-Claudian house, who died young (e.g. Drusus, the brother of Tiberius: S. *Claud*. 1.4; *Ann*. 1.33.2; Germanicus Caesar: S. *Calig*. 3.2; *Ann*. 2.82.2; Dio 57.18.6-7) and represents both a sentimental hankering on the part of certain members of the upper classes in Rome and a means of indicating dissatisfaction with the government of the day.

# Vitellius

## THE RISE OF VITELLIUS (1.1-3.1)

**1.1** *adulatores obtrectatoresque imperatoris Vitelli*: nothing adulatory about Vitellius has survived, which is not surprising, since the literary tradition about him was established during the regime of the Flavians who had overthrown him. Indeed, S. *Vit.* 10.1 is the only passage in our extant sources which depicts Vitellius in a light which is at all favourable.

The official Flavian line seems to have been that Vitellius was a worthless tyrant, a corrupt military adventurer, and that Vespasian, stung by accounts of his cruel and vicious behaviour in Rome after his victory (cf. Joseph. *BJ* 4.588-600; 4.647), felt impelled to come to his country's rescue. We may note in passing that this view of Vitellius as a mere usurper also serves to explain why Vespasian did not become his country's 'saviour' in A.D. 68: Nero was the legitimate ruler; cf. Philostr. *VA* 5.29. That this explanation is either misleading or simply untrue on two counts – the planning of the Flavian attempt probably began about the time of Nero's death; and, since this attempt was actually launched on 1st July, A.D. 69, word of Vitellius' behaviour in Rome cannot by then have reached the East (see below S. *Vit.* 11.1) – need not have detracted from the effectiveness of the propaganda.

*nisi aliquanto prius de familiae condicione variatum esset*: sc. before A.D. 69, when one would expect this sort of thing in the propaganda war with Otho and the Flavians. The account which follows was presumably concocted before A.D. 14 (cf. *Divi Augusti quaestorem*) and is typical of what happens with genealogies at a time of social mobility when new classes are penetrating a traditional aristocracy.

**1.2** *extat Q. †Elogi... libellus*: the majority of mss. read *extatq elogi* (or *elogii*); the only significant variant is *elogium* (the eleventh century Codex Gudianus 268). Without resorting to emendation, one can read *extatq* as *extatque*, followed by either *elogi... libellus*, or *elogium ad Quintum Vitellium Divi Augusti quaestorem, libellus quo continetur*. But what exactly does *elogium* mean? And could it be anything like as long as a *libellus*? Laudatory *elogia* were usually short inscriptions in either prose or verse (cf. *OLD s.v.* 1: 'an elegiac distych'). If we accept the *-que* in *extatque* as epexegetic of *variatum esset*, it might also be better to take *elogium* as equivalent to a genitive plural and read *extatque elogiorum ad Quintum Vitellium Divi Augusti quaestorem libellus, quo continetur*, which would refer to a collection of short pieces comprising a history of the Vitellii in the remote past.

However, the *-que* seems very strained and since S. appears to have read the work, which, being highly laudatory, was probably not anonymous, we would expect him to mention the author's name, especially since he mentions Cassius Severus as the principal *hostile* source on the Vitellii. For this emendation is necessary and suggestions are numerous; e.g. *Q. Clodii* Muretus; *Q. Longinii* Lipsius; *Q. Eulogii* or *Eclogii* I. Casaubon. All are paleographically possible, but none is compelling because the names are otherwise unknown. I. Casaubon's suggestion that the author was a freedman of the *Divi Augusti quaestor*, named Q. Vitellius Eulogius, is perhaps most attractive.

*Fauno Aboriginum rege*: Faunus was a rustic deity with a festival celebrated on 5th December, for which the principal evidence is one of Horace's *Odes* (3.18). Very little is known about Faunus or his cult; the meaning of his name is disputed and the various theories, both ancient and modern, give rise to widely differing explanations of his origin and function; e.g., Servius (ad *Georg.* 1.10) says: *quidam Faunos putant dictos ab eo quod frugibus faveant*, implying a derivation from *favere* ('the kindly one'); but cf. Varro on Fauni (*L.L.* 7.36): ... *in silvestribus locis traditum est solitos fari futura a quo fando Faunos dictos*; i.e., the name is derived from *fari* ('the speaker, the seer'). From these quotations we may note connections with fields and woods (cf. Verg. *Georg.* 1.10 and *Aen.* 8.314) and we should also note the possibility that Faunus was originally plural.

*Vitellia*: perhaps not surprisingly, this goddess is heard of nowhere else: *quae multis locis pro numine coleretur* is really somewhat lame! The name Vitellia may be a reworking of some other name such as Vitula (cf. the similar Julian Iulus >Iulius, which may even have provided the starting-point), though Vitula, a goddess or spirit with a mysterious festival on 8th July has the first syllable long, while in Vitellius it is short. However, given the invented nature of the whole genealogy, we may well doubt the cogency of such an objection.

*horum residuam stirpem ex Sabinis transisse Romam atque inter patricios adlectam*: this story is somewhat disjointed but it appears that the main branch of the family has died out, leaving only collaterals in Sabine territory. What we have here is almost a doublet of the story of the *gens Claudia* which moved to Rome from Sabine country under the leadership of 'Attius Clausus' in 504 B.C. (Livy 2.16.4-5; D.H. 5.40; Plut. *Poplicola* 21.4-10; Appian *Reg.* 12; for a variant see S. *Tib.* 1.1).

S. gives no indication of date for this immigration of the Vitellii. He also fails to mention the appearance, in the annalistic accounts of 509 B.C., of two brothers M. and M.' Vitellius, members of the Senate (and therefore patricians), whose sister was married to M. Iunius Brutus and who, along with the Aquilii and the sons of Brutus, became involved in a conspiracy to restore the Tarquins (Livy 2.3-5; D.H. 5.6-13; Plut. *Poplicola* 3.4-7.8; cf. Gundel, *RE IX A s.v.* 'Vitellius' nos. 1 and 4. For a persuasive hypothesis concerning the 'origin' of these Vitellii, see R.M. Ogilvie, *Commentary on Livy 1-5* [Oxford, 1965] 242).

**1.3** *viam Vitelliam ab Ianiculo ad mare usque*: this name is not otherwise attested. Several roads ran from the Ianiculum (a ridge on the Etruscan bank of the Tiber, which was fortified in the reign of Ancus Marcius to guard the western end of the Pons Sublicius; cf. Livy, 1.34.6) to the sea by or near the right bank of the Tiber. It is possible that one of these later roads, the *via Ianiculensis* or the *via Aurelia* perhaps, replaced an earlier route (cf. T. Ashby, *The Roman Campagna* [London, 1927; repr. 1970] 226-7).

*item coloniam eiusdem nominis*: presumably therefore Vitellia. This was one of the fourteen *priscae coloniae Latinae*, founded, usually jointly, by Rome and the Latins in the period before the dissolution of the Latin League in 338 B.C. However, the correct form of its name, its foundation date and its location are all uncertain. Livy mentions the place twice (2.39.4 and 5.29.3): in the first passage it is simply a Latin town called Vetelia (for possible meanings of this name, see Ogilvie *ad loc.*) but in the second it is a *colonia Romana* called Vitellia, evidently founded before 393 B.C. The place does not appear to have flourished, since it had disappeared by the time of the Latin War of 340-38 and is not heard of again.

*quam gentili copia... olim depoposcissent*: this story presents us with another suspicious doublet, this time reminiscent of the famous story of the *gens Fabia* which fought alone at the Cremera against the Veientes in 478 or 477 B.C. (Livy 2.48-50; cf. 2.51.1; Diod. 11.53.6; D.H. 9.18.5-9.22.6).

*tempore deinde Samnitici belli praesidio in Apuliam misso*: the term *praesidium* implies a garrison, and this suggests the second Samnite War (328-304 B.C.), and more specifically the period immediately following the Caudine Peace of 321. In 318-17 Rome made alliances with various Apulian communities in order to threaten the Samnites with warfare on two fronts (Livy 9.20.4-9; cf. 9.13.6; Diod. 19.10.2) and in 315, soon after the resumption of war, attacked Luceria, the main Samnite base in Apulia (Livy 9.12.9). After its capture Luceria became a Latin colony (Livy 9.26.1-5; Diod. 19.72.8-9).

*quosdam ex Vitelliis subsedisse Nuceriae*: this looks like a muddle. In Apulia the major centre of Roman power was *Luceria* (see prev. n.), a place frequently referred to, apparently erroneously, as *Nuceria* (see Philipp, *RE XIII* 1565-6 for details).

*progeniem longo post intervallo repetisse urbem atque ordinem senatorium*: this completes the fantasy in a tidy manner. It is clear, however, that when they first appeared in Augustan Rome in the person of P. Vitellius of Nuceria, *procurator Augusti*, the Vitellii were not accepted as the long-lost scions of an ancient senatorial family. They had to make their way – with imperial favour, naturally – for this was the only means by which new men could gain the *latus clavus*.

**2.1** *contra plures auctorem generis libertinum prodiderunt*: after the flattering account of the origins of the Vitellii, we come to what was evidently the more generally accepted version, with variations in detail. S. sometimes uses *plures* for *complures* (cf. *DJ* 76.3; 81.4; *Aug.* 21.3; *Calig.* 57.4; *Tit.* 3.2). This passage may help to explain how the usage arises: so far we have seen the flattering version, presumably the work of a single author (?Q. Eulogius); what follows is given by *more* authorities, but they are probably not numerous.

*Cassius Severus nec minus alii*: this probably means 'Cassius Severus, with great vehemence'! We may well suspect muckraking in this section, since Cassius Severus, an orator of the Augustan age, had a very bad reputation for *vituperatio* (cf. *Ann.* 1.72.3; 4.21.3).

*sectionibus et cognituris uberius compendium nanctus*: *sectionibus* means 'by the sale of confiscated or captured goods'. Presumably this Vitellius either sold such goods on behalf of the *aerarium* or, perhaps more probably, bought them cheap in job lots, possibly at the time of the Sullan proscriptions, and sold them in the sort of operation which today is loosely called 'an army surplus store'.

*cognituris* is much more difficult. The word occurs only four times in extant literature (cf. *TLL s.v.* 'cognitura') and in each of the other three occurrences (Quint. *Inst.* 12.99; Gaius 4.124 [*bis*]; Fr. Vat. [Paul?] 324; an additional citation in Lewis and Short is wrong), it means simply 'the duty of a *cognitor*', which is what the *OLD* gives, except for the gratuitous addition of 'or attorney,' which is perhaps misleading. The reference appears to be to a 'representative' in litigation: by a kind of legal fiction a *cognitor* actually *became* the party to a lawsuit (cf. Buckland, *Textbook*³, 708-11, section *CCXXXIX*, 'Representation in Litigation'). Presumably this service was rendered for a fee.

*sed quod discrepat, sit in medio*: Suetonius here affects not to be interested in the *minutiae* of the sordid origins of the family, but only after he has given us them!

**2.2** *ceterum P. Vitellius... eques certe R. et rerum Augusti procurator*: at this point Suetonius 'cuts the Gordian knot' about the family background and, beginning with the earliest person about whom he is sure (*certe*), makes this P. Vitellius the starting-point for a detailed examination of the family. Since P. Vitellius was a *procurator rerum Augusti*, he must have been an *eques*, as S. says; presumably he is the one referred to in the preceding paragraph. For the possibility that the *rerum Augusti procurator* was really *A.* Vitellius, see below, n. on *Aulus in consulatu obiit*.

*quattuor filios... reliquit Aulum, Quintum, Publium, Lucium*: we cannot be certain that this order of names reflects the true chronological order of the four sons, because Lucius, the most successful, comes last, which gives a neat climax to the account of the family success in this generation. Furthermore, Lucius may also be placed last because he was the father of the Princeps Vitellius and so the account of his career leads naturally into that of his son.

*Aulus in consulatu obiit*: there is little that can be added to what S. tells us here. A. Vitellius was suffect in A.D. 32 to L. Arruntius Camillus Scribonianus, while Cn. Domitius Ahenobarbus, the other *cos. ord.*, remained in office for the whole year. Since the *Fasti* do not list an additional suffect for 32, we may assume that he died late in that year. However, *CIL VI* 879 mentions a *Ti. Caisaris Augusti legatus pro pr. A. Vitellius A.f.* Hanslik (RE Suppl. IX *s.v.* 'Vitellius' no. 7a) suggests a stonemason's error in the *A.f.* This will not do, since a *novus homo* setting up a short (in this case) dedicatory inscription to the Princeps is going a) to look at it, and b) to make sure that the details are correct. It would therefore appear that S. has got the name of the *procurator Augusti* wrong.

*praelautus alioqui famosusque cenarum magnificentia*: if this is true and not merely a doublet from the gourmandizing activities of the better-known A. Vitellius, the Princeps (see below *Vit.* 13 and, for example, *H.* 1.62.2; 2.62.1, 87, 95), it may perhaps suggest a family failing (see also the next n. below).

*Quintus caruit ordine, cum...placuisset*: this was in A.D. 17 when Tiberius forced the removal or obtained the resignations of five senators, among them Q. Vitellius, *prodigos et ob flagitia egentes* (*Ann.* 2.48.3). This Q. Vitellius is presumably the man mentioned above (*Vit.* 1.2) as *Divi Augusti quaestorem*: it was he who had the 'fantasy' version of the early history of the Vitellii cobbled together. As a youth he must have seemed promising, since Augustus picked him to be one of his own quaestors. We have, of course, no information as to the precise degree of notoriety which he achieved, but O. Hirschfeld's suggestion that *quetedii* in the desperate and famous crux at *Ann.* 1.10.5 conceals *Q. Vitellii* is both paleographically reasonable and highly persuasive (*Hermes* 24 [1889] 103-4).

*Publius, Germanici comes, Cn. Pisonem inimicum et interfectorem eius accusavit*: the impression we get of P. Vitellius is of a loyal, conscientious, capable, but politically not very adroit staff officer. Unlike his brother Lucius he made all the *wrong* choices at the crucial points in his career. We first hear of him during Germanicus' campaigns in Germany (*Ann.* 1.70; 2.6.1). The fact that he was a *legatus legionis* in A.D. 15 implies that he had held the praetorship: this is confirmed by his governorship of Bithynia in A.D. 17-18, which in turn suggests a date for his praetorship no later than A.D. 11 or 12. S.'s remark below *post praeturae honorem inter Seiani conscios arreptus*, therefore, while not inaccurate, is definitely misleading. After his term in Bithynia P. Vitellius seems to have joined the suite of Germanicus in the East, perhaps at Antioch as early as the winter of A.D. 18-19, and he was present when Germanicus died on 10th October, 19. With Germanicus' other devoted lieutenant, Q. Veranius, he hurried back to Rome and there (A.D. 20) led the prosecution of Cn. Calpurnius Piso (*cos. ord.* 7 B.C.), the enemy and alleged poisoner of Germanicus (*Ann.* 2.74; 3.10.1).

*inter Seiani conscios arreptus... morbo periit*: after the death of Germanicus, Sejanus became all-powerful (cf. Dio 57.19.5-8) and anyone who wished to 'get on' had to pay court to him and receive his approbation (on this see the revealing speech which Tacitus gives to the *eques* M. Terentius at *Ann.* 6.8). At the time of the fall of Sejanus (18th October, A.D. 31; cf. EJ p. 54 and *ILS* 157, 158), P. Vitellius was prefect of the *aerarium militare* and was accused of having offered its resources *rebus novis* (*Ann.* 5.8), a reference to the mysterious 'plot' allegedly fomented by Sejanus (for an account of the fall of Sejanus, see R. Seager, *Tiberius* 214-23, with a discussion of the 'plot' on 214-17; cf. R. Syme, *Tacitus* 406). There is nothing to suggest that Vitellius was guilty of anything, but in the witch-hunting hysteria prevalent in Rome at the time he obviously felt that he had no chance. What is remarkable, however, is that no 'guilt by association' affected his family: within three years of the death of P. Vitellius two of his brothers reached the consulship as *novi*.

**2.4** *Lucius ex consulatu Syriae praepositus*: L. Vitellius was perhaps the most talented of the four brothers and fundamentally he may have been, as S. says below, *innocens et industrius* (cf. *Ann.* 6.32.4: *regendis provinciis prisca virtute egit*). However, he was in many ways quite unappealing. *ex consulatu Syriae praepositus* implies that he went straight to Syria from his consulship (he was *cos. ord.* A.D. 34) and, since there were apparently two *suffecti* in that year, Magie may well be correct in suggesting that he went to Syria before the end of 34

(*Roman Rule II* 1364 n. 39). Trouble had broken out in the East, apparently in 34, and involved Parthian interference in Armenia. Tiberius acted with vigour and skill, sending Vitellius to Syria with more than usual powers (cf. *Ann*. 6.32.3: *cunctis, quae apud Orientem parabantur, L. Vitellium praefecit*). Vitellius' instructions appear to have been to preserve Roman interests in Armenia and to arrange the removal of Artabanus III from the Parthian throne, all without recourse to arms, if possible. In Armenia Vitellius was wholly successful; in Parthia, Artabanus was sufficiently humbled that he was prepared to meet Vitellius, make a formal treaty recognizing the Roman nominee as King of Armenia and surrender one of his sons as a hostage.

*Artabanum Parthorum regem... ad veneranda legionum signa pellexit*: there are numerous problems connected with this meeting: where did Artabanus meet Vitellius? what did he do at the meeting? when was it held? In his other account of this incident (*Calig.* 14.3) S. emphasizes the hatred and contempt which Artabanus had always felt for Tiberius (cf. S. *Tib.* 66) and states that he *ultro petiit* (cf. here *Lucius... regem summis artibus... pellexit*) the friendship of *Gaius* and came to a meeting at which he crossed the Euphrates and *aquilas et signa Romana Caesarumque imagines adoravit* (cf. Dio 59.27.3). Josephus, on the other hand, has *Tiberius* order Vitellius to establish friendly relations with Artabanus (*AJ* 18.101-5). These two traditions cannot be harmonized; Josephus implies a date some months at least before the death of Tiberius, presumably in the autumn of 36 at the latest. The ascription of the diplomatic triumph to the principate of Gaius may be the result of Vitellius' well-known penchant for flattery and adulation. As for the obeisance to standards and images of the Caesars, J.G.C. Anderson's comment may suffice (*CAH X* 750): '...an admission of vassalage which no Parthian king would have made save with the sword at his throat. The truth has been preserved by Josephus.'

*mox cum Claudio principe duos insuper ordinarios consulatus censuramque gessit*: after the ample successes of his career under Tiberius and his remarkable *tour de force* in gaining the friendship of the bitterly jealous and suspicious Gaius (Dio 59.29.2-6; cf. below 2.5), in the principate of Claudius Vitellius crowned his career as the most successful politician of the Julio-Claudian period by going further than anyone who was not connected with the imperial house either by blood or marriage. He was *cos. ord. II* and *III* in 43 and 47 as colleague to the Princeps, and in 47-48, as Claudius' colleague in the censorship for the traditional eighteen months, he received the most signal honour of all (on this *census* see *Ann.* 11.13; Pliny *NH* 10.5; Aur. Vict. *Caes.* 4.4; and esp. S. *Claud.* 16).

*curam quoque imperi sustinuit absente eo expeditione Britannica*: Dio (60.23.1) states that Claudius returned to Rome in 44 after an absence of six months. This gives an indication of the length of Vitellius' *cura imperii*.

Constitutionally, there was no such thing as a 'deputy' princeps or 'acting' princeps and, in theory, the emperor was supposed to do his job wherever he happened to be. In practice, however, this could be difficult when he was absent from Rome and so, on occasion, some person was left in charge. It is pointless to seek a formal legal definition of the powers of such 'deputies': they were simply acting *in loco Principis*; they had his confidence and they were among his closest friends and advisers. People therefore simply accepted the situation and did what they were told.

*sed amore libertinae perinfamis...pro remedio fovebat*: this outlandish and, to us, rather disgusting story is far from unique in ancient literature. In Latin the richest source of information on the medical, paramedical and magical uses of spittle is Pliny's *Natural History* (see, in general, 28.35-39; cf. 28.76; 28.193); for a survey of the whole question, F.W. Nicolson, *HSCP* 8 (1897) 23-40.

**2.5** *idem miri in adulando ingenii primus C. Caesarem adorare ut deum instituit...osculabundus*: cf. Dio 59.27.2-6. However, Vitellius' career as a toady and flatterer began during Tiberius' principate when he had cultivated Antonia Minor, the mother of Claudius (*Ann.* 11.3.1).

*Claudium uxoribus libertisque addictum*: on this see esp. *Claud.* 29.1 and Mottershead's useful n. (with full references to ancient sources). There is no doubt that Claudius relied heavily on those close to him both for advice and for action; his wives and freedmen exploited these opportunities to an extent that was unwisely obvious. However, the resulting picture in our sources is almost certainly exaggerated.

*a Messalina petit*: Valeria Messalina, daughter of Claudius' cousins M. Valerius Messalla Barbatus and Domitia Lepida, was married to Claudius as his third wife in A.D. 38 or 39, when she was no more than fourteen years of age; she bore him two children, Octavia (by 40) and Britannicus (in 41). A woman of exceptional cruelty and profligacy, she finally went so far as to 'marry' her current lover, C. Silius, in 48 and Claudius was stampeded by his freedmen ministers, Narcissus in particular, into agreeing to her execution (S. *Claud.* 26.2; cf. *Ann.* 11.26-38).

*Narcissi quoque et Pallantis imagines aureas inter Lares coluit*: during the principate of Claudius, Narcissus and Pallas were probably the most influential freedmen (cf. S. *Claud.* 28) and certainly the richest: Narcissus amassed a fortune of HS 400 million and Pallas one of HS 300 million (see R. Duncan-Jones, *The Economy of the Roman Empire*[2] [Cambridge, 1982] 343, App. 7, nos. 2 and 6). Narcissus seems to have been the most influential freedman in A.D. 41-8, but in that year after the fall of Messalina, when the question of a new wife for Claudius arose, Pallas urged the advantages of an alliance with Agrippina. His advice prevailed (*Ann.* 12.1-3) and with Vitellius' assistance legal and religious difficulties were smoothed over and the marriage took place. Henceforth Pallas was the most influential freedman and in A.D. 50 as ally to Agrippina he helped bring about the adoption of Nero by Claudius. After Claudius' death he remained influential for a while (Narcissus was immediately forced to commit suicide: *Ann.* 13.13; Dio 60.34.4-6), but he was pushed aside when Nero began to break free of Agrippina's domination and died in 62, allegedly poisoned by Nero. Whatever the truth about the influence (and honesty) of such freedmen, who were undoubtedly competent and talented administrators, the sort of actions attributed here by S. to Vitellius will have earned him considerable ill-repute.

*saeculares ludos edenti Claudio*: in addition to this passage the sources for the secular games of A.D. 47 are: *CIL VI* 32324-5, 32336; Pliny *NH* 7.159; 8.160; S. *Claud.* 21.1-3; *Ann.* 11.11.1-2; Censorin. *DN* 17.11; Aur. Vict. *Caes.* 4.14; Zosimus 2.4.3. The main significance of these games was probably that they came in Rome's 800th year. The games were held early in June, with the Parilia on 21st April, A.D. 47, marking the beginning of the centenary.

Details of the system used to calculate the *saeculum* or, indeed, of its length cannot be asserted with anything approaching certainty: since a new *saeculum* was said to begin when everyone who had witnessed the beginning of the previous *saeculum* had died, different bases of calculation appear to have been used at different times. During the middle to late Republic the *saeculum* was a slightly flexible 100 years, but in 17 B.C. Augustus used a *saeculum* of 110 years. Claudius would appear to have been using a 100 year cycle. However, he seems to have approved of the *basis* of Augustus' calculation, but not the actual calculation itself (S. *Claud.* 21.2). It has therefore been suggested that Claudius did use the 110 year *saeculum* but started from 504 B.C. (A.U.C. 250), when Poplicola, *cos. IV*, is said to have initiated such games (cf. Plut. *Poplicola* 21.3). This year had the added advantage of being the traditional date for the arrival in Rome of the *gens Claudia* (S. *Tib.* 1.1; Plut. *Poplicola* 21.4-10; see A. Momigliano, *Claudius* [Oxford, 1934] 89-90).

**3.1** *decessit paralysi altero die quam correptus est*: L. Vitellius is last heard of in A.D. 51, *validissima gratia, aetate extrema* (*Ann.* 12.42.3), when a senator accused him of treason and of having a desire for the imperial power. However, Agrippina now repaid her debt to Vitellius (cf. above, p. 139) and *minis magis quam precibus* brought Claudius round to exiling the *accuser*. Vitellius probably died fairly soon thereafter (before 54 at any rate: see below, n. on *statua pro rostris... PRINCIPEM*).

*duobus filiis superstitibus, quos... consules vidit*: these were Aulus (the Princeps) and Lucius. They were consuls in A.D. 48 (the year after their father's third consulship), with Aulus as *cos. ord.* (*Ann.* 11.23.1) and Lucius as his suffect. The fact that Aulus was the elder of the two sons leads to interesting, though speculative, conclusions about their birthdates (see below, *Vit.* 3.2, n. on *A. Vitellius... cons.*).

*Sestilia probatissima nec ignobili femina*: the comment on her character is confirmed by Tacitus (*H.* 2.64.2; 3.67.1), though he calls her Sextilia. She may have been the daughter of a mint official who hailed from Antium (Fluss, *RE* II A *s.v.* 'Sextilius' no. 32), which might explain S.'s cautious *nec ignobili femina*. She was in Rome early in 69, when Otho made special arrangements for her protection (Plut. *O.* 5.3; cf. *H.* 1.75.2), and she appears to have remained there throughout the year. In mid-July when Vitellius entered the city in triumph, he embraced her publicly at the Capitol and bestowed on her the title *Augusta* (*H*. 2.89.2; cf. Dio 65.4.5). According to Tacitus, she died *fessa aetate* about the middle of December, only a few days before Vitellius himself was killed (*H*. 3.67.1); cf. below *Vit*. 14.5 for a much more lurid story.

*defunctum senatus publico funere honoravit*: under the Principate the impulse for such honours usually came from the emperor; e.g. *Ann*. 3.48.1 (A.D. 21): *sub idem tempus, ut mors Sulpicii Quirini publicis exsequiis frequentaretur, petivit a senatu* (*sc*. Tiberius). For a discussion of the history of this practice, see Mommsen, Staatsr. III 1187-9; cf. also J.M.C. Toynbee, *Death and Burial in the Roman World* (London, 1971) 55-6.

*statua pro rostris... PRINCIPEM*: the setting-up of statues in this location was also a senatorial prerogative (cf. *Galba* 23). From the inscription we may presume that this was done in Claudius' lifetime; cf. his comment quoted by Josephus (*AJ* 20.12): ὁ κράτιστος καί μοι τιμιώτατος Οὐιτέλλιος ...['the excellent Vitellius, most highly regarded by me'].

## THE CAREER OF VITELLIUS TO HIS ACCESSION (3.2-9.1)

**3.2** *A. Vitellius L. filius imperator... Druso Caesare Norbano Flacco cons*: S. here gives as Vitellius' birthdate either 24th or 7th September, A.D. 15 (cf. Dio 65.22.1); however, to this information we must add from *Vit*. 18: *periit... anno vitae septimo quinquagesimo*, which implies a different year, A.D. 12, for his birth (*H*. 3.86, *septimum et quinquagensimum aetatis annum explebat* should probably read *explerat*). Since under Augustan 'rules' a patrician was eligible for the consulship in his thirty-third year (cf. above, *G*. 6.1 n. on *honoribus ante legitimum tempus initis*) and *Lucius* Vitellius was suffect consul in 48, he must have been born no later than 15 and Aulus, as the older brother, some time earlier, presumably in 12. As for the exact date, an examination of events in the campaign of the autumn of 69 and their relationship to Vitellius' birthday celebrations in that year (mentioned at *H*. 2.95.1 and Dio 65.4.3) indicates that 7th September is far more likely than the 24th for Vitellius' birthday (cf. L. Holzapfel, *Klio* 15 [1918] 105-18).

*pueritiam primamque adulescentiam Capreis egit inter Tiberiana scorta*: Tiberius left Rome, never to return, in A.D. 26 (*Ann*. 4.57) and in 27 settled on the island of Capri (S. *Tib*. 39-42; *Ann*. 4.67; Dio 58.1.1 and 5.1). Given his longing for seclusion and his loathing of public attention, it is not surprising that increasingly lurid tales began to circulate about sexual irregularities, though only from about A.D. 31 (*Ann*. 6.1; S. *Tib*. 43-45; Dio 58.22.1). If Vitellius was born in A.D. 12, he would have turned nineteen in 31: the phrase *pueritiam primamque adulescentiam... egit* is therefore meaningless, though possibly the later date for his birth represents an attempt to give this story an air of authenticity; see further C.L. Murison, *AHB 1* (1987) 97-9.

*Capreis*: S. displays a possibly unhealthy interest in the stories of Capri and of the *spintriae* (cf. T.F. Carney, *PACA* 11 [1968] 11-12). However, his one other reference to *spintriae* is odd; at *Calig*. 16.1 he says of Gaius: *spintrias monstrosarum libidinum aegre ne profundo mergeret exoratus, urbe submovit*. What were they doing in the *city*? This suggests that the tradition about them may be as bogus as the stories about Vitellius.

*existimatusque corporis gratia initium et causa incrementorum patri fuisse*: again, this story may appear superficially plausible, but it will not stand up to close examination. The career of L. Vitellius started even before Aulus was born, and that career will have been well on its way by A.D. 26, when Tiberius left Rome, so that to say that Aulus could in any way have been responsible for the *initium* of his father's career is nonsense; as for its *incrementa*, the allegation is only marginally more plausible.

**4.1** *omnibus probris contaminatus*: this suggests that later propagandists could find very little to say about Vitellius during the principates of Gaius and Claudius.

*Gaio per aurigandi... studium*: cf. S. *Calig*. 18.3; 54; Dio 59.2.5, 5.2-5, 14.6-7: with regard to his public performances Gaius seems almost to have been on a par with Nero.

*Claudio per aleae studium*: Claudius' addiction to gaming was notorious; cf. S. *Claud*. 5.33.2; Sen. *Apocol*. 12 *ad fin*; 14-15.

*cum propter eadem haec*: for Nero's addiction to chariot racing, see S. *Ner.* 22.1-2; 24.2; 53. Like Gaius (cf. S. *Calig.* 55.2), Nero was a fanatical devotee of the *factio Prasina* (the Greens); Vitellius, perhaps oddly, was, in 69, a supporter of the *factio Veneta* (the Blues; see below, *Vit.* 7.1).

*praesidens certamini Neroneo*: for the institution of the *Neronia*, the first 'Greek games' held in Rome, see S. *Ner.* 12.3; *Ann.* 14.20-21; Dio 61.21.1-2. The presidents at the various contests were, unusually, ex-consuls. The games were supposed to be quinquennial (see Tacitus' notice of their second celebration in A.D. 65: *Ann.* 16.2.2 and 16.4-5) and it is clear that it was in A.D. 65 that Nero first performed in public, which enables us to date the incident described here by S.

**5.1** *trium itaque principum indulgentia... auctus*: A. Vitellius was clearly a chip off the old block as far as flattery was concerned. Of his *honores* we know nothing except for what is here and in *Vit.* 3.1. As for the *sacerdotia*, we know that he was a member of the Arval Brethren and participated in their rituals from the autumn of A.D. 57. In addition, he was a member of the *XVviri sacris faciundis* (a college famous for its feasts), probably, though not certainly, before his elevation to the Principate.

*proconsulatum Africae*: the date of this is not known and can only be estimated approximately. The years 55-57 seem most likely; cf. Thomasson, *Die Statthalter... Nordafrikas* II 39-40.

*curamque operum publicorum*: for this job there were two *curatores* of praetorian or consular rank and, although their precise designation varies, the fullest form of their title appears to be *curatores aedium sacrarum et operum locorumque publicorum* (*CIL VI* 3702; cf. *VI* 858). This office was established during the later years of Augustus and represented a return to the *aerarium* of responsibility for the maintenance and repair of public buildings (cf. *RG* 19-21).

*in provincia singularem innocentiam praestitit*: cf. *H.* 2.97.2: *integrum illic (sc. in Africa) ac favorabilem proconsulatum Vitellius... egerat.* In Africa, perhaps, away from the corrupting influences of Rome and the temptations of a powerful army command, the best side of Vitellius' nature could appear; cf. *H.* 3.86.2: *inerat tamen simplicitas ac liberalitas...*. Certainly the officers of a squadron of auxiliary cavalry, the *ala Siliana*, remembered him with affection and rendered his cause important assistance in the spring of 69 (*H.* 1.70.1-2).

*in urbano officio... supposuisse*: his job was apparently salaried and counted as a curule office, with magisterial insignia (Mommsen, *Staatsr. II³* 1049-51). However, this story is qualified by the word *ferebatur* and we may again be dealing with Flavian propaganda, a particularly insidious specimen, based on Vitellius' lack of resources and Nero's well-known cupidity (cf. S. *Ner.* 32.4).

*aurichalcum*: the best-known Roman use for *orichalcum* (ὀρείχαλκος 'mountain-copper,' used with zinc to make brass) was in the production of coins – the *sestertius* and *dupondius* (cf. *BMC Imp. I* li; *RIC I* 27; cf. Pliny, *NH* 34.2-4).

**6.1** *uxorem habuit Petroniam consularis viri filiam*: Petronia may have been the daughter of P. Petronius P.f. (*cos. suff.* A.D. 19) and sister of P. Petronius Turpilianus (*cos. ord.* A.D. 61). Since in 69 Vitellius' wife was Galeria Fundana (see below) and he had by her a daughter of marriageable age (*H.* 1.59.2), his marriage to her must have occurred not later than 56; and it came *after* the death of his son Vitellius Petronianus (cf. below, *mox Galeriam duxit*). Since this son was of an age to be emancipated (about sixteen years old at least) in 55-6, he must have been born c. 39-40 at the latest; his mother therefore was married by the age of thirty-eight and was herself born no later than 27, and probably earlier. She subsequently married Cn. (P.?) Cornelius Dolabella (see above *G.* 12.2, n. on *Cn. Dolabellae*). If she was the mother of Ser. Dolabella Petronianus (*cos. ord.* 86), who must presumably have been born c. 53, her son by Vitellius must have died *before* then (he would not have been her sole heir if she had another son). This, then, will push his birthdate, the date of Vitellius' first marriage, and the date of Petronia's birth back even further.

*filium Petronianum... hausisset*: there is no further information about Vitellius Petronianus. Presumably the story of his mother's will and his emancipation from his father's *potestas* is true. His death soon thereafter (*brevi*) gave rise to the ugly rumours which we have here. This is, however, unlikely to be Flavian *vituperatio*, since we also have Vitellius' 'explanation' of what happened.

*Galeriam Fundanam*: the year of her birth is unknown; the date was 3rd June: *AFA* for 69 *ad loc*. reads *III*. NON. IV[..., which could be June or July, but must be June because this entry begins *[Isdem co]s.*, as does the previous one (for 29th May) and there were new consuls on 1st July (*H*. 1.77.2).

*liberos utriusque sexus tulit*: the unfortunate boy, who was six years old in May of 69 when his mother took him to Gaul, was given at Lugdunum the title *Germanicus* and an imperatorial salutation (*H*. 2.59.3; Dio 65.1.2a; Tacitus' use of *infans* is more significant than he perhaps realized). He survived his father's fall, but some months later, in A.D. 70, he was put to death on the order of Mucianus, *mansuram discordiam obtendens, ni semina belli restinxisset* (*H*. 4.80.1; cf. Dio 65.22.2 and see below *Vit*. 18).

The daughter (Vitellia?) was the elder child, since she was promised and perhaps married in 69 to D. Valerius Asiaticus, governor of Gallia Belgica (*H*. 1.59.2: whether or not the marriage actually took place will depend on the meaning assigned to *generum adscivit*). At any rate, by late 69 Vitellius was, allegedly, offering her hand to Antonius Primus (cf. *H*. 3.78.1; see further, G.B. Townend, *AJP* 83 [1962] 125-9). Later on, Vespasian *Vitelli hostis sui filiam splendidissime maritavit, dotavit etiam et instruxit* (S. *Vesp*. 14).

**7.1** *in inferiorem Germaniam*: this was, of course, as successor to Fonteius Capito (on whose tenure in Lower Germany see above, *G*. 11, n. on *in Germania Fonteio Capitone*). The appointment may have been made while Galba was still on his journey from Spain to Rome; if it was after his arrival in Rome, it must have come soon thereafter (cf. above *G*. 12.2, n. on *ut primum urbem introiit* and *H*. 1.52.1: *sub ipsas superioris anni kalendas Decembres Aulus Vitellius inferiorem Germaniam ingressus ...* ).

*contra opinionem*: this suggests that everyone was surprised, Vitellius included. He was in straitened circumstances (see below 7.2) and this would suggest that he had been 'unemployed' for some time prior to his posting to Germany.

*T. Vini suffragio*: this correction (by L. Torrentius, 1578) of the meaningless mss. reading *T. Iun(i)* is both neat and virtually certain.

For Vinius' power, see *G*. 14.2, esp. n. on *T. Vinius legatus... cupiditatis immensae*. On *suffragium* ( = political influence, patronage), see J.K. Evans, *Historia* 27 (1978) 102-28.

*per communem factionis Venetae favorem*: there were four *factiones* in Roman chariot-racing by the end of the Julio-Claudian period: the *Albata* (Whites), *Russata* (Reds), *Prasina* (Greens) and the *Veneta* (Blues). The Reds and the Whites seem to have existed during the late Republic, with the Greens and Blues appearing probably early in the first century A.D. These names refer to the colour of the tunics worn by the drivers and the term *factio* applies to the supporters in the crowd as much as to the various stables themselves. This passage in S. is the earliest mention of the Blues (cf. Dio 65.5.1) and Vitellius' passion for them was such that in June or July of 69 we actually find the Arval Brethren performing a sacrifice on their behalf: ... *Jm. faction. Venet. porcam et a[gnam*. On *factiones*, see further H.A. Harris, *Sport in Greece and Rome* (London, 1972) 151-243; and, above all, A. Cameron, *Circus Factions* (Oxford, 1976).

*nisi quod Galba... contemptu magis quam gratia electum*: with Galba's remark cf. the famous one attributed to Caesar by Shakespeare (*Julius Caesar* 1.2.191-194):

Let me have men about me that are fat;
Sleek-headed men and such as sleep o'nights.
Yond Cassius has a lean and hungry look;
He thinks too much: such men are dangerous.

**7.2** *satis constat... ut uxore et liberis... meritorio cenaculo abditis domum in reliquam partem anni ablocaret*: *satis constat* suggests that this is simply *vituperatio* and an extreme illustration of Vitellius' financial position in 68. *cenaculum* is widely mistranslated as 'garret' or 'attic' (so Graves and Rolfe *ad loc.*; cf. *OLD s.v.*), and we are apparently to assume that only garrets were let as lodgings! It seems likely that the word *cenaculum* means simply 'flat' or 'apartment': some would be wretched and small, while others no doubt approximated more nearly to Albany. Finally, *in reliquam partem anni* requires explanation: if Vitellius left Rome around 1st November, 68, it is hard to imagine why he would let his house for two months only. The *annus* in question is probably the 'renting-year', which appears to have begun on 1st July (cf. Petron. *Sat.* 38.10; Mart. 12.32.1).

*quorum publica vectigalia interverterat*: the immediate problem here is the nature of the *vectigalia* which Vitellius embezzled. There were two kinds of *vectigalia*: a) items such as *portoria*, sales taxes, inheritance duties and rents from various types of state property which were, in the first century A.D. at least, collected by *societates publicanorum* on behalf of the state treasury, which ultimately received the revenues (cf. *Ann.* 4.6.3; 13.50-51; S. *Calig.* 40); b) local revenues, most often rents from land and other property; these revenues too were farmed. Presumably it is this second group of *vectigalia*, local revenues, with which we are concerned. Vitellius must have been involved with a *societas* which was farming revenues for the towns of Sinuessa and Formiae (they are only 18 *mp* apart and may have co-operated in putting their revenue-collection out to tender).

*terrore calumniae*: *calumnia*, the corrupt institution of an action or prosecution, could exist in both civil and criminal law. In civil law, the penalty for bringing a vexatious action was one-tenth of the amount wrongfully claimed or, in the case of a false claim of liberty from slavery, one-third of the value of the slave (Gaius, *Inst.* 4.174-181). In criminal law, condemnation for *calumnia* involved *infamia*, which meant that one could not stand for public office nor bring an accusation before a *iudicium publicum*; it usually also included exile or relegation or loss of rank. Other penalties were arbitrarily introduced from time to time by various emperors (cf. *Ann.* 3.37.1; 13.23.2; 13.33.3; S. *Tit.* 9.5; *Dom.* 9.3; Pliny *Pan.* 35).

*iniuriarum formulam... intendisset*: the use of the word *formula* relates to a technicality of Roman legal procedure in the first stage of a civil action (*in iure*). The so-called 'formulary procedure' was developed through praetorian initiative as a replacement for the cumbersome and rather primitive *legis actiones*. The *formula* was a written statement of the details of the case, hammered out between the magistrate and the parties, and used in the second stage of the proceedings – *apud iudicem*; it gave instructions to the *iudex* (named in the *formula*) on how he was to settle things, depending on which side convinced him. On the *formula*, see Gaius *Inst.* 4.30-68, esp. 39-44; 4.115-137; Buckland, *Textbook*[3] 628-62, esp. 647-59; on *iniuria* ( = insult or outrage, by words or conduct), see Gaius, *Inst.* 3.220-225;

Buckland, *op. cit.* 589-92.

**7.3** *adventientem*: this participle is perhaps less precise than it may at first appear to be: arriving *where*? The next chapter begins *castra vero ingressus*, so we are left with a somewhat vague general impression of Vitellius moving north surrounded by an aura of *bonhomie* and affability, and, perhaps unwittingly, being already primed for the coming attempt (cf. *H.* 1.52.4, esp. the final sentence, and see below, 8.1, n. on *vixdum mense transacto*).

**8.1** *castra vero ingressus... supplicia dempsit*: cf. *H.* 1.52.1: *...Aulus Vitellius inferiorem Germaniam ingressus hiberna legionum cum cura adierat: redditi plerisque ordines, remissa ignominia, adlevatae notae.*

*notas* refers to lesser penalties than reduction in rank or floggings. These were more a matter of humiliation (cf. *ignominiosis*) than major punishments; (cf. S. *Aug.* 24.2; Val. Max. 2.7.9; Frontinus *Strat.* 4.1.26-7). People accused of serious offences habitually put on mourning (*sordes*). Accordingly, as Hofstee puts it, *sordes dempsit = crimina remisit.*

*vixdum mense transacto*: this agrees with what Tacitus has: cf. *sub ipsas superioris anni* (*sc.* 68) *Kalendas Decembres Aulus Vitellius inferiorem Germaniam ingressus* (*H.* 1.52.1) with *H.* 1.55 and *nocte, quae kalendas Ianuarias secuta est, in coloniam Agrippinensem aquilifer quartae legionis epulanti Vitellio nuntiat quartam et duoetvicensimam legiones proiectis Galbae imaginibus in senatus ac populi Romani verba iurasse* (*H.* 1.56.2). Cf. also Plut. *G.* 22.3-4 and above, S. *G.* 16.2 and nn.

At this point it is worth reminding ourselves of the legions of the armies of Lower and Upper Germany and their bases and probable legates in January, 69 (see also G. Alföldy, *Epigraphische Studien* 3 [1967] 7-10):

### Legions in Lower Germany

| | | |
|---|---|---|
| I (*Germanica*) | Bonna | Fabius Valens (*H*. 1.57); replaced probably in Jan. 69 by Herennius Gallus (*H*. 4.19, 62, 70). |
| V *Alaudae* | Vetera | Fabius Fabullus (*H*. 3.14 – summer of 69). |
| XV *Primigenia* | Vetera | Munius Lupercus (*H*. 4.18 and 22; cf. Ritterling, *RE XII* 1760). |
| XVI (*Gallica*) | Novaesium | Numisius Rufus (*H*. 4.22 and 70; cf. 4.62). |

### Legions in Upper Germany

| | | |
|---|---|---|
| IV *Macedonica* | Moguntiacum | A. Caecina Alienus? (cf. Ritterling *RE XII* 1554; 1801 – till Jan. 69? legate unknown thereafter). |
| XXII *Primigenia* | Moguntiacum | C. Dillius Vocula (*H*. 4.24; *CIL VI* 1402). |
| XXI *Rapax* | Vindonissa | unknown; possibly Caecina. |

*neque diei neque temporis ratione habita*: *temporis* presumably refers to the lateness of the hour. *diei* is not clear: perhaps a reference is intended to the fact that *dies postriduani* were considered ill-omened (cf. above, *G*. 10.2, n. on *cum... conscendisset tribunal, ad fin.*). More probably S. is remembering that the soldiers of Lower Germany had just renewed their oath of allegiance to Galba (*H*. 1.55.1-2).

*ac iam vespere, subito a militibus e cubiculo raptus etc.*: this is a dramatic story but it is rather different from the version in Tacitus (*H*. 1.55-57) and Plutarch (*G*. 22.3-8). For example, no mention is made of the discussion which Vitellius is said to have held with his advisers and of the decision to offer Vitellius as Emperor to the troops (*H*.

1.56.2-3), nor of Valens' arrival from Bonn the next day, nor of the rivalry among the legions of Lower Germany in proclaiming Vitellius (*H*. 1.57.1; Plut. *G*. 22.9-10). However, *vespere* corresponds to the arrival from Moguntiacum, late on the evening of 1st January, 69, of the *aquilifer* of IV *Macedonica*, who reported the revolt of the legions of Upper Germany (IV *Macedonica* and XXII *Primigenia* only at this stage, presumably). *a militibus... raptus* presumably corresponds to the arrival next day of Valens and his salutation of Vitellius as Emperor. S.'s version, then, is extremely compressed and may represent a condensation of the main points of the 'common source', quoted (badly) from memory.

**8.2** *consentiente deinde etiam superioris provinciae exercitu... defecerat*: cf. above, *G*. 16.2. According to Tacitus (*H*. 1.57.1), this happened on 3rd January, 69; initially it can only have involved the legions at Moguntiacum. Thereafter, we are told, the civilian population of areas near the military bases, including the disaffected Treveri and Lingones, joined in eagerly and there was a general and enthusiastic upsurge of support for Vitellius.

This story of 'spontaneous' actions occurring in widely separated places is probably complete fiction. The revolt seems to have been planned some time prior to 1st January, 69 (perhaps as early as October, 68), and its outbreak was carefully orchestrated; on this see C.L. Murison, *TAPA* 109 (1979) 188-94.

*cognomen Germanici... recepit, Augusti distulit, Caesaris in perpetuum recusavit*: this is essentially correct (cf. *H*. 1.62.2 and see also *H*. 2.62.2), though there may be one slight error: about 9-10th December, 69, when things were going very badly for the Vitellian cause, ... *et Caesarem se dici voluit, aspernatus antea, sed tunc superstitione nominis* (*H*. 3.58.3). However, the Suetonian version is borne out by Vitellius' coinage, since there are no issues known bearing the title *Caesar*. Furthermore, the most striking thing about this coinage is the word *Germanicus*: the legend on the issues from Tarraco and Lugdunum (e.g., A VITELLIVS IMP GERMAN) probably means 'A. Vitellius the German Imperator' or 'Imperator by the will of the Germanies' (cf. Mattingly, *BMC Imp*. I ccxxiii); the coinage from Rome (e.g., A VITELLIVS GERMANICVS IMP) probably attempts to make *Germanicus* more of a *cognomen* and, therefore, less aggressive and, in Mattingly's words (*ibid.*), 'more constitutional'. Its invariable use on Vitellius' coinage may suggest that he intended to use *Germanicus* as a permanent replacement for *Caesar* and to break away as much as possible from Julio-Claudian practice.

**9.1** *ac subinde caede Galbae adnuntiata*: S. does not concern himself with the details of the Vitellian invasion of Italy, because Vitellius himself took no part in it. The present passage, then, is simply wrong: given the detail of Tacitus' account of events in Germany (*H*. 1.51-70), we must accept his statement that the expedition was well underway before news of Galba's death arrived (*H*. 1.64.1).

*compositis Germanicis rebus*: the reference is probably to Vitellius' elimination of any opposition to himself (e.g. the killing of Pompeius Propinquus, procurator of Gallia Belgica, the sacking of Julius Burdo, prefect of the *classis Germanica*, and the execution of four centurions at Moguntiacum who had tried to check the initial outbreak of the legions there: *H*. 1.58-59) It may also refer to his arrangements for fresh troops to be levied in Gaul to supplement the depleted legions on the Rhine (*H*. 2.57.1).

*partitus est copias, quas adversus Othonem praemitteret quasque ipse perduceret*: this is misleading and S. has oversimplified the details of the division of the forces at Vitellius' disposal (cf. *H*. 1.61). To be sure, the two-fold division outlined here has a certain validity (the main invasion force – in two parts – led by Valens and Caecina, and the back-up force, led by Vitellius himself), but only the columns led by Valens and Caecina played any part in the overthrow of Otho. However, S.'s sole hint at their rôle comes at the end of this chapter in the words *confirmatum per legatos suos imperium*.

*praemisso agmine laetum evenit auspicium*: again, S. ignores the division of the invasion force. This incident occurred on the day on which Valens' column left Colonia Agrippinensis (*H*. 1.62.3); but S. is here concerned to point a contrast between the lucky omen which the invasion force received and the bad omens which befell Vitellius.

*Viennae*: Vienna (mod. Vienne) was the city in Gaul most hostile to Vitellius and the Vitellian cause (cf. *H*. 1.65-66); Vitellius himself was uneasy about its attitude even after he had arrived in Italy (*H*. 2.66.3).

*pro tribunali iura reddenti gallinaceus supra humerum ac deinde in capite astitit*: this is a strange story and its point is not immediately apparent; obviously from its context it is meant to be a bad omen, as the following sentence, beginning *quibus ostentis par respondit exitus*, makes clear. But it is not until the last sentence of this *Life* (*Vit.* 18) that we learn why. There is a pun on *gallus/gallinaceus* ( = 'Gaul' or 'cock'), and M. Antonius Primus, legate of Legio *VII Gemina* in Pannonia and leader of the Danubian legions which overthrew Vitellius late in 69, was a native of Tolosa and therefore a Gaul; also, in his youth he was nicknamed Becco, apparently a Gallic word for a cock's beak. This story is obviously a *post eventum* fabrication and it is not even very probable in itself, since no alert person is going to allow a cock to jump on his shoulder and then on to his head. Indeed, it is downright hostile to Vitellius, since there may be a suggestion that he was asleep or half-drunk while ostensibly engaged on official business.

## THE PRINCIPATE OF VITELLIUS (10.1-14.5)

Otho committed suicide on 16th April, 69, and Vitellius was officially recognized at Rome on 19th April (above, p. 127). We are very poorly informed about the general policies and administrative practices of Vitellius' principate. Our surviving accounts concentrate on the campaign to defeat Otho, the Flavian campaign to eliminate Vitellius, and Vitellius' personal orgy of self-indulgence. Very little attention is paid to other matters and all surviving accounts are basically hostile.

*Administrative policy*: in general, Vitellius seems to have aimed at making a break with the Julio-Claudian past. As we have seen (S. *Vit.* 8.2, n. on *cognomen Germanici recepit, Augusti distulit, Caesaris in perpetuum recusavit*) he was, initially at least, disinclined to accept the traditional titles of a princeps and sought something new for himself. This is perfectly understandable, for when 'Caesar' is mentioned, only one person really springs to mind, and likewise 'Augustus'; and it is arguable that the same was true in A.D. 69. However, there is one important practical change which Vitellius did put into effect: he gave posts customarily held by freedmen to *equites* (*H.* 1.58.1). There is no doubt that by the end of the Julio-Claudian period the power and influence of imperial freedmen was widely resented. However, the growth of the imperial bureaucracy was such that the sort of job that would once have been scorned by the free-born now carried with it considerable power and patronage and was therefore attractive to ambitious men. For example, the Gallic rhetor Julius Secundus, who was certainly free-born and may have been of equestrian status, served as Otho's *ab epistulis* (Plut. *O*. 9.3). Vitellius, then, exploited this attitude and those who served under him were not subsequently ashamed of what they had done (cf. *CIL XI* 5028 = MW 338, which commemorates Sex. Caesius Propertianus, a military tribune of Legio *IV Macedonica* of the army of Upper Germany in 69, who served as imperial secretary in charge of the *patrimonium Caesaris*, legacies and petitions) because after this time senior administrative positions were commonly held by *equites*; witness the career of S. himself.

In Rome Vitellius adhered to constitutional practice by assuming his various powers gradually (cf. *AFA* 30th April, 1st May). He was lenient towards Otho's family and friends (*H*. 1.75; 2.60, 62.1; *BMC Imp. I* ccxxviii, though he still acquired a possibly exaggerated reputation for cruelty; cf. below, *Vit*. 14). He attended meetings of the Senate regularly and participated in debates (*H*. 2.91.3; Dio 65.7.2), he canvassed on behalf of his friends before the consular elections in true Republican fashion (*H*. 2.91.2), and in rewarding his supporters with consulships he tried as much as possible to avoid displacing those designated by his predecessors; hence his designations for ten years (see below, *Vit*. 11.2, n. on *comitia in decem annos ordinavit*). Finally, we should remember that the games, shows and feasts, the extravagance of which is heavily censured in our sources (e.g. *Vit*. 13; *H*. 2.91.2, 95.1-2; Dio 65.2-4, 7.1), kept the general populace happy and helped to provide employment (cf. S. *Vesp*. 18 and 19.1).

*Military Policy*: The armies of Germany had revolted because they felt cheated of what they considered their natural rewards for the suppression of the revolt of Vindex. They were ill-disciplined and almost uncontrollable, and they wanted loot and good postings, especially to the Praetorian Guard. Vitellius seems to have given in to them constantly (cf. *H*. 2.94.2) and he allowed them to pillage their way across Italy even after their final victory (*H*. 2.56-57). Of course, he had played no part in the Bedriacum campaign and as Emperor he was very much the creation of the German legions. With regard to the Othonian army, Vitellius took the easy way out and began executing certain centurions who had been Otho's most active supporters (*H.* 2.60.1). Tacitus' comment on this is illuminating: *unde praecipua in Vitellium alienatio per Illyricos exercitus; simul ceterae legiones contactu et adversus Germanicos milites invidia bellum meditabantur.* He tried to 'dilute' Othonian units by scattering them about Italy and encamping them side by side with Vitellian units (*H.* 2.66). This simply caused trouble because some of the Othonian units had not been at Bedriacum and therefore did not regard themselves as having been defeated. All these legions, however, became extremely hostile to Vitellius and they infected others with their hatred for him (*H.* 2.86).

Vitellius dismissed not only the entire Othonian Praetorian Guard (see below *Vit.* 10.1, n.) but also the urban cohorts (cf. *H.* 2.93.2). Sixteen new praetorian and four new urban cohorts were enrolled from the soldiers of the German armies. It appears that in the mad scramble for these 'plum' positions the men, rather than their officers, chose the branch of the service which they preferred (cf. *H.* 2.94.1). In short, Vitellius' military policy was completely unsatisfactory but he was really in no position to do otherwise. Where he had the scope, he tried to be as conciliatory as possible: Flavius Sabinus, Vespasian's brother, was retained as *praefectus urbi* (*H.* 2.55.1, 63.1; see further below *Vit.* 15.2-3 nn.) and all other army commanders appear to have been confirmed in their appointments. Finally, news of his recognition by the armies of the East lulled Vitellius and his soldiers into a totally false sense of security (*H.* 2.73).

**10.1** *de Betriacensi victoria et Othonis exitu, cum adhuc in Gallia esset, audiit*: according to Tacitus (*H.* 2.57) he had set off with his forces but had not gone far (*paucorum dierum iter progressus*). On the battle of Bedriacum (14th April, 69) see above *O.* 9.2, n. on *novissimo maximoque apud Betriacum fraude superatus est cum spe... dimicandum fuisset*, and on Otho's suicide (16th April) see above *O.* 9.3-11.2. Vitellius probably received this news around 20th April.

*nihilque cunctatus...uno exauctoravit edicto*: Tacitus indicates (*H.* 2.67.1) that the dismissal of the praetorian cohorts was accomplished in stages: they were first separated from each other, and then were promised *honesta missio*. This process was underway when word of the Flavian revolt reached Italy, after which they became the *robur Flavianarum partium*. S.'s words *ut pessimi exempli* (referring, of course, to their betrayal both of Galba and Nero) do not appear to jibe with Tacitus' *addito honestae missionis lenimento*. S. (or his source) must be editorializing at this point.

*iussas tribunis tradere arma*: as we saw earlier, during the praetorian upheaval in Rome in early March it was a praetorian tribune, Varius Crispinus, who had opened the armoury and arranged for the removal of weapons for the re-arming of the 17th cohort (above, *O*. 8.2, n. on *in castris*). It would appear that the weapons which had been issued to the praetorians, presumably when they left Rome for the Maritime Alps and the main battle front in northern Italy, were still in their hands. This was certainly not conducive to good order and it is not surprising that, after the Othonian collapse, the defeated troops should have been ordered to turn their weapons over to the appropriate officers. This would have happened whatever the plans for the praetorian cohorts.

*centum autem atque viginti... conquiri et supplicio adfici imperavit*: cf. Plut. *G*. 27.10 and *H*. 1.44.2, though Tacitus manages to avoid the praise which S. heaps upon this act: ...*non honore Galbae, sed tradito principibus more munimentum ad praesens, in posterum ultionem*. This action certainly took place after Vitellius reached Rome, since before his suicide Otho had burned any incriminating papers which he had with him (*H*. 2.48.1; *O*. 10.2; Dio 64.15.1a).

*egregie prorsus atque magnifice et ut summi principis*: this paragraph contains almost the only words in this *Life* which give any indication of a better and more responsible side to Vitellius' nature. Though this relief from the generally hostile account is very brief, S.'s picture of Vitellius is not as bleak as that to be found in Josephus (*BJ* 4.588-596; 4.647-652) and in Philostratus (*VA* 5.29-34). Dio (65.2-4) is equally harsh but the picture is relieved at 65.6, which begins οὕτω δὲ βιοὺς οὐκ ἄμοιρος ἦν παντάπασι καὶ καλῶν ἔργων ['Though such was his manner of living, he was not completely bereft of good deeds also'], and lists several examples. Tacitus too tends to relieve the darkness somewhat from time to time; he despises Vitellius (e.g. *H*. 2.59.1, 67.2, 91.2) and constantly harps on his *torpor* and obsessive self-indulgence (cf. 1.62; 2.31, 62, 67, 71, 77, 87, 88, 95; 3.36, 56), but occasionally we learn that Vitellius did have some redeeming features, though these are usually qualified in some way (e.g. 2.62.1, 62.2 *ad fin.*; 3.86.2: *inerat tamen simplicitas ac liberalitas, quae, ni adsit modus, in exitium vertuntur).*

**10.2** *namque itinere incohato... nonnumquam necem repraesentantes adversantibus*: S. here gives us a brief but vivid impression of the general disorder and riot which accompanied Vitellius on his journey across Gaul and Italy to Rome (cf. esp. *H.* 2.62.1, 68.1, 71.1, 77-8).

**10.3** *utque campos, in quibus pugnatum est, adit... melius civem*: for a fuller account of the same horrific scene, see *H.* 2.70, where Tacitus states that Vitellius arrived at the battlefield *intra quadragensimum pugnae diem*, i.e., by 23rd May.

*lapidem memoriae Othonis inscriptum intuens dignum eo Mausoleo ait*: cf. *H.* 2.49.4; Plutarch actually visited the tomb while travelling in Italy with his patron, L. Mestrius Florus, possibly during the principate of Vespasian: εἶδον δ' ἐν Βριξίλλῳ γενόμενος καὶ μνῆμα μέτριον καὶ τὴν ἐπιγραφὴν οὕτως ἔχουσαν, εἰ μεταφρασθείη: "Δηλώσει Μάρκου Ὀθωνος." ['When I was in Brixellum I saw both his modest memorial and its inscription, which reads in translation: "To the memory of Marcus Otho".'] (*O.* 18.2; cf. MW 34). The reference to a mausoleum is, of course, heavily sarcastic.

*pugionemque, quo is se occiderat,... misit Marti dedicandum*: sc. in exchange for the *Divi Iulii gladium* which he had filched from the same temple earlier (cf. *Vit.* 8.1).

*in Agrippinensem coloniam*: the full name was Colonia Claudia Ara Augusta Agrippinensium: it was so named in A.D. 50 when the settlement previously called Ara Ubiorum (from c. 9 B.C.; cf. *Ann.* 1.57.2) became a colony of veterans (*Ann.* 12.27.1); its name honours Agrippina the Younger, who was born there.

*in Appennini quidem iugis etiam pervigilium egit*: the idea of an all-night religious observance seems to have been rare during the Republic (cf. Cic. *Leg.* 2.21 on the rites of the Bona Dea). Under the Principate with its heavier borrowings from oriental religion, *pervigilia* became more frequent: in the main, they seem to have been associated with women (cf. *Ann.* 15.44.1) and with generally licentious conduct. In this connection we should remember Tacitus' words about the general tone of the Vitellian party as it travelled across Italy (*H.* 2.68.1): *apud Vitellium omnia indisposita temulenta, pervigiliis ac bacchanalibus quam disciplinae et castris propiora.*

The site of the *pervigilium* will depend on Vitellius' route after Bononia (cf. *H.* 2.71.1). Certainty is impossible, but if he followed the *Via Flaminia*, the highest point in the Apennines is a place called Aesis, in which was the famous Temple of Juppiter Penninus.

**11.1** *urbem denique ad classicum introiit... detectis commilitonum armis*: Tacitus (*H.* 2.89.1) gives a slightly less reproachful account. There are, however, differences: *quo minus ut captam urbem ingrederetur, amicorum consilio deterritus, sumpta praetexta et composito agmine incessit.* However, the procession which entered the city was at least quasi-triumphal (see the remainder of *H.* 2.89.1, where eagles and standards and full dress uniforms are mentioned).

The date of Vitellius' entry into Rome is quite uncertain: he had assumed the position of Pontifex Maximus on or before 18th July (see next n.) and this had to be done at Rome (cf. Mommsen, *Staatsr. II*³ 1106-7). Apart from this, the only indication of date in our literary sources comes at the end of Tacitus' description of the advance of Vitellius' army across Italy: *arvaque maturis iam frugibus ut hostile solum vastabantur* (*H.* 2.87.2). This is extremely vague and could suggest anywhere from mid-June to mid-July; see further, A.J. Coale, Jr., *TAPA* 102 (1971) 49-58; C.L. Murison, *TAPA* 109 (1979) 194-7.

**11.2** *magis deinde ac magis omni divino humanoque iure neglecto Alliensi die pontificatum maximum cepit*: cf. *H.* 2.91.1: *Apud civitatem cuncta interpretantem funesti ominis loco acceptum est, quod maximum pontificatum adeptus Vitellius de caerimoniis publicis XV kalendas Augustas edixisset, antiquitus infausto die Cremerensi Alliensique cladibus: adeo omnis humani divinique iuris expers...* The phrase about Vitellius' 'disregard for/ignorance of law, human and divine' makes it clear that both S. and Tacitus are using the same source. But what did this source say about 18th July, 69 (the anniversary of Rome's defeat by the Gauls at the R. Allia in 390 B.C.)? According to S., this was the day on which Vitellius became Pontifex Maximus; Tacitus does not actually say this and his words *could* mean that Vitellius became P.M. some time before.

*comitia in decem annos ordinavit seque perpetuum consulem*: cf. *H.* 3.55.2, referring to about the middle of November: *ipse (sc.* Vitellius) *nihil e solito luxu remittens et diffidentia properus festinare comitia, quibus consules in multos annos destinabat. comitia* refers to the formal 'election' by Senate and people of the candidates selected by the emperor. It is perhaps worth noting that S. and Tacitus are here certainly not using the same source: not only do they place the incident in quite different contexts, but it is also hard to imagine the wording that gave rise both to Tacitus' *in multos annos* and S.'s *in decem annos*, especially since S. is usually thought to be the less meticulous transmitter of source material. Furthermore, Tacitus does not have the detail about a perpetual consulship; however, this is neatly confirmed by a short inscription from Rome (*CIL VI* 929 = MW 81): *A Vitellius L.f. imperator cos. perp.* For Vitellius' re-arrangement of consulships in 69, see *H.* 2.71.2 and G.B. Townend, *AJP* 83 (1962) 113-29, esp. 124.

*et ne cui dubium foret... exultans etiam plausit*: cf. *H.* 2.95.1: Tacitus adds that the *publici sacerdotes* mentioned here were the *Augustales*, the official priests of the Julio-Claudian cult (cf. *G.* 8.1, n. on *sacerdotium triplex... cooptatus*). Vitellius had been a friend of Nero and had particularly encouraged his artistic ambitions (cf. *Vit.* 4; see also *Ann.* 14.49.1; *H.* 2.71.1). Clearly, his enthusiasm was genuine.

*de dominico*: *sc.* (?) *libro*, presumably a collection either of Nero's own compositions or of his favourite musical set-pieces (or both), which may actually have been published, or whose contents may have been well-known both to courtiers and musicians. A *dominicus liber* (or a collection called simply *dominicum*) suggests that Nero was regularly addressed as *dominus*, although it is generally assumed from S.'s censure (*Dom.* 13.1-2) that Domitian was the first to indulge himself in this way. At any rate, the practice was standard by the reign of Trajan (Pliny, *Ep.* 10 *passim*).

**12.1** *magnam imperii partem non nisi consilio et arbitrio vilissimi cuiusque histrionum et aurigarum administravit*: that Vitellius should have gathered about him a crowd of people connected with the theatre and the circus is hardly surprising in view of his earlier enthusiasms (see above *Vit.* 4; 7.1 and below 17.2). No doubt he had many old friends in these circles. Tacitus paints a graphic picture of

158

the various people who came out from Rome to meet him as he advanced triumphantly towards the capital (*H.* 2.87), and among them *adgregabantur e plebe flagitiosa per obsequia Vitellio cogniti scurrae histriones aurigae, quibus ille amicitiarum dehonestamentis mire gaudebat* (cf. *H.* 2.71.1). What S. gives us here is probably no more than vituperative exaggeration, based on Vitellius' fondness for such people and their delight in his victory.

*et maxime Asiatici liberti*: this chapter gives us the bulk of our information about Asiaticus. Tacitus describes his elevation to the equestrian order in terms almost identical to those found here (*H.* 2.57.2); at *H.* 2.95.2 he speaks angrily of his corruption: *nondum quartus a victoria mensis et libertus Vitellii Asiaticus Polyclitos Patrobios et vetera odiorum nomina aequabat*. After the Flavian capture of Rome and the arrival in the city of C. Licinius Mucianus, Vespasian's principal lieutenant, late in December, 69, there were several executions, among them the crucifixion of this freedman (*H.* 4.11.3).

*poscam*: this was a combination of wine-vinegar and water, producing a cheap and refreshing drink, which also had the advantage of not causing intoxication. It was widely used in the Roman army at all periods (cf. Plut. *Cato Maior* 1.10; SHA *Hadr.* 10.2; *Avid. Cass.* 5.3; *Pesc.* 10.3; Veget. 3.3). Perhaps the most famous example of this is to be found in the accounts of the Crucifixion (Matthew 28.48; Mark 15.36; Luke 23.36).

*circumforano lanistae*: the word *lanista* seems to be related to *lanius* (butcher) and the verb *laniare*, all of these words being ultimately of Etruscan origin. The occupation was considered a particularly degraded one and the *lanista*, like his fellow flesh-peddler the *leno*, was *infamis*.

In Rome the training and keeping of gladiators became an imperial monopoly quite early in the Principate and the giving of gladiatorial displays was almost the exclusive prerogative of the princeps (cf. Dio 54.2.4). However, in other parts of Italy and throughout the Empire anyone could put on a display: the would-be *editor* could purchase gladiators specially for the occasion, use his own troop if he had one, or, more usually, rent a troop from a *lanista*. Many *lanistae* were itinerant, working the towns of an area in a sort of 'circuit': hence S.'s epithet *circumforanus*.

*muneris*: gladiatorial shows were always called *munera* because (in theory, at least) they represented some sort of 'obligation' or 'service' to the dead (cf. Serv. *Aen*. 10.519 for the term *bustuarii* applied to them). Precisely wherein this 'service' consisted is not clear: the blood of the fighters may have been an offering in honour of the dead or to appease or strengthen their shades (cf. Tert. *De Spect*. 12). However, by the Imperial era almost any anniversary or occasion could serve as an excuse for gladiatorial shows.

*aureis donavit anulis*: for the significance of this, see S.'s remarks above on Galba's freedman Icelus (*G*. 14.2 and esp. n. on *paulo ante anulis aureis et Marciani cognomine ornatus*).

**13.1** *sed vel praecipue luxuriae saevitiaeque deditus*: chapter 13 deals with *luxuria*, a term which could be taken to mean any sort of excess in one's living habits, while chapter 14 concentrates on *saevitia*. These two chapters constitute perhaps the most sustained attack on Vitellius' character to be found in our extant sources. Most of the material in chapter 13 can be paralleled in other accounts and we may assume that these stories had *some* element of truth in them, though it is, of course, impossible to separate reality from the *vituperatio* of Flavian propaganda. On the other hand, most of the material in chapter 14 is unique to S.: some of the stories are so outrageous that we may suppose that they too are anti-Vitellian propaganda which Tacitus simply rejected out of hand but which S., with his penchant for the grotesque, retained; or we may conclude that we have here a collection of anecdotes gathered by S. himself using material from both the Flavian archives and from personal (and, no doubt, exaggerated) reminiscences.

*epulas trifariam semper, interdum quadrifariam dispertiebat*: cf. Dio 65.4.3. In general, the Romans ate rather sparingly, with only one substantial meal per day. *Ientaculum* was usually a very light breakfast indeed, nothing more than a piece of bread, possibly dipped in wine, and fruit or cheese. *Cena* underwent the same change as 'dinner' in English: this was the main meal of the day, customarily taken around noon, and it was followed by a light supper (*vesperna*). However, by the early Principate *cena* had become a late afternoon/early evening meal, and in its place around mid-day a light luncheon (*prandium*) was inserted. The *comissatio* was a sort of stylized drinking-bout which sometimes followed an elaborate *cena*: it was perhaps similar to Oxford sconcing, with all present competing.

*facile omnibus sufficiens vomitandi consuetudine*: this reminds us of the scornful words of Seneca (*Cons. ad Helv.* 10.3): *vomunt ut edant, edunt ut vomant, et epulas, quas toto orbe conquirunt, nec concoquere dignantur.* Cf. also Mart. 3.82.8-9; 7.67.9-10; Juv. 6.425-433.

*indicebat autem aliud alii eadem die, nec cuiquam minus singuli apparatus quadringenis milibus nummum constiterunt*: both Tacitus (*H.* 2.95.3) and Dio (65.3.2) preserve the tradition that Vitellius himself squandered HS 900 million (presumably from the *fiscus*) on banquets during his principate; and this, of course, is how Vitellius was remembered. See, for example, John Oldham (c. 1680), *Satires upon the Jesuits* III 267-8:

> With dainties load your board, whose ev'ry dish
> May tempt cloy'd gluttons, or Vitellius wish ...

**13.2** *dedicatione patinae quam... 'clipeum Minervae* πολιούχου' *dictitabat*: this is the only indication in our sources that Vitellius had a sense of humour: the pun is on πολιοῦχος ('holder of the city', a standard epithet of Athena – hence *Minervae*) and πολυοῦχος ('holder of a lot'). By the first century A.D. both words were pronounced identically.

*in hac scarorum iocinera... commiscuit*: cf. Dio 65.3.3 and 3.1; for details of exotic food consumed by Roman gourmets and its provenance, see Friedländer-Wissowa, *Sittengeschichte*[10] 2.306-313; *RLM* 2.165-170; Carcopino, *Daily Life in Ancient Rome* (1956) 271. Of the items mentioned here by S., only *murenarum lactes* causes any difficulty: *muraena* is probably the Murry (or Moray 'eel': taxonom. *muraena helena*), a vicious eel-like fish with strong, sharp teeth, kept in fish-ponds by the Romans and considered a delicacy at the table. *lactes* is obviously connected with *lac* and the 'milk' aspect could refer either to colour or consistency: the word seems basically to mean 'small, milky-coloured fat-covered intestines' (cf. Lewis and Short and *OLD s.v.*); however, Walde-Hoffman (*Lat. etym. Wörterbuch*[4] *s.v.*) give as a second meaning 'the milt of a male fish' (cf. similarly SHA *Elag.* 23.8).

*a Parthia usque fretoque Hispanico per navarchos ac triremes petitarum*: cf. Dio 65.3.1. Not only was the entire empire scoured for delicacies for Vitellius' table, but the navy was used to transport them. This was not, however, without precedent: see Pliny *NH* 9.62 for an account of the introduction of the *scarus* (parrot-wrasse?) to the waters between Ostia and Campania by Ti. Julius Optatus Pontianus, prefect of the fleet at Misenum in the time of Claudius.

**14.1** *nobiles viros... occidit*: we know of two only: Cn. (P.?) Cornelius Dolabella, mentioned above at *G.* 12.2 (see n. on *Cn. Dolabellae*), who married Vitellius' first wife Petronia (see above *Vit.* 6, n. on *uxorem habuit Petroniam consularis viri filiam*) – this was a sordid murder (*H.* 2.63-64); and Junius Blaesus, governor of Gallia Lugdunensis early in 69, who had decked Vitellius out in princely fashion (*H.* 2.59) and had presumably accompanied him to Rome. For his death, see *H.* 3.38-39: Vitellius obviously feared and disliked him and was, apparently, worked up to murder him by his brother Lucius, who seems to have been the evil genius of his principate (cf. *H.* 2.63.1). However, there is no convincing motive for this crime and the details of a supposedly secret meeting between the Emperor and his brother (*H.* 3.38.2-4) suggest that there was, in fact, no murder.

*etiam unum veneno manu sua porrecto in aquae frigidae potione*: this may be another reference to the death of Junius Blaesus; cf. *H.* 3.39.1. The facts in this case seem to be that Vitellius hated and feared Blaesus; the latter fell ill and Vitellius went to visit him and evidently enjoyed the sight of his (imagined) rival's fatal illness – *notabili gaudio Blaesum visendo*.

**14.2** *tum faeneratorum et stipulatorum publicanorumque... vix ulli pepercit*: Dio tells a wholly different story (65.5.2-3): people were amused to see a crowd of soldiers or admirers in the Forum around a man who previously could not be seen for the mob of creditors. People who had dunned him in days gone by put on mourning and hid (when he came to Rome), but Vitellius sought them out and spared their lives in lieu of payment of his debts – and demanded back his notes. This sounds more in character: Vitellius was probably not a cruel man by nature (though he could be manipulated to commit acts of cruelty) and his 'revenge' on the creditors who had harried him probably cost them plenty.

A *stipulator* in Roman law was a creditor who made a certain type of verbal contract (*stipulatio*), which could cover all kinds of dealing; see further Buckland, *Textbook*[3] 434-43; Jolowicz-Nicholas, *Historical Introduction to Roman Law*[3] 279-81.

*velle se dicens pascere oculos*: Tacitus uses these words of Vitellius' visit to Junius Blaesus' deathbed (*H*. 3.39.1): *quin et audita est saevissima Vitellii vox, qua se (ipsa enim verba referam) pavisse oculos spectata inimici morte iactavit*. We can now see what has happened: the individual parts of the story of this one murder (if that is what it was) were each 'generalized' into a separate murder or a series of murders in anti-Vitellian propaganda.

**14.3** *quod Venetae factionis clare male dixerant*: cf. above *Vit*. 7.1, n. on *per communem factionis Venetae favorem*.

**14.4** *et mathematicis*: according to F. H. Cramer (*Astrology in Roman Law and Politics* [Philadelphia, 1954] 244), the term *mathematici* for 'astrologers' came gradually during the first century A.D. to replace the earlier geographic designation *Chaldaei*. However, Aulus Gellius suggests (*NA* 1.9.6) that the former is the colloquial term for the latter: *vulgus autem, quos gentilicio vocabulo 'Chaldaeos' dicere oportet, 'mathematicos' dicit*. (This may have arisen because astrologers attempted to reduce all the movements of the heavenly bodies to mathematical order.) This distinction will explain why S. calls them *mathematici* in his narrative but *Chaldaeos* when he quotes their mock edict. For details of the many expulsions of astrologers from Rome, see F.H. Cramer, *C&M* 12 (1951) 9-50, and esp. 36-9 for the Vitellian expulsion.

*bonum factum*: *sc. bonum factum sit*. This, or something like it, normally prefixed all edicts and formal declarations (e.g. S. *DJ* 80.2; *Aug*. 58.3; *Calig*. 15.3; cf. Cic. *Div*. 1.102: *maiores nostri... omnibus rebus agendis 'quod bonum faustum felix fortunatumque esset' praefabantur*.

*ne Vitellius Germanicus intra eundum Kalendarum diem usquam esset*: this is an erroneous prediction that Vitellius would perish by 1st October, 69. It is interesting to note how this story becomes less precise with the passage of time: Dio (65.1.4) says that the astrologers posted a counter-edict in which they bade him depart his life on the very day on which he actually did die – οὕτως ἀκριβῶς τὸ γενησόμενον προέγνωσαν ['so accurate was their foreknowledge of what was going to happen'].

**14.5** *morte matris*: on this see above *Vit*. 3.1, n. on *Sestilia probatissima nec ignobili femina*.

*vaticinante Chatta muliere, cui velut oraculo adquiescebat*: although hostile to the activities of astrologers in 69, Vitellius believed strongly in omens and did nothing of any importance without considering them (Zon. 11.16). A German prophetess looks like part of his *Imperator Germanicus* set-up, though she may have won his attention by predicting success at the beginning of his bid for power. On the powers exercised by German women, see Tac. *Germ.* 8.2. We know the names of several prophetesses: Albruna (*Germ.* 8.3), Veleda (belonging to the Bructeri and wielding great influence at the time of the revolt of Civilis: *Germ.* 8.3; *H.* 4.61.2, 65.3-4; 5.22.3, 24; Stat. *Silv.* 1.4.90) and Ganna (successor to Veleda, who visited Domitian, presumably in Germany, and was honoured by him: Dio 67.5.3).

## THE FALL OF VITELLIUS (15-18)

S. gives no coherent picture, either here or in the *Life* of Vespasian, of the beginnings of the Flavian revolt and the great campaign of the latter part of 69 which destroyed Vitellius and his party. Tacitus, on the other hand, devotes the last chapters of *H.* 2 (96-101) and the whole of *H.* 3 to this, and even the epitomes of Dio preserve a much more substantial account of these events than does S. (65.8-22). As is his usual practice, S. concentrates on the subject of his biography (cf. *Vesp.* 7, where the focus is on Vespasian's visit to Egypt, not the Flavian invasion of Italy) but, even so, he skips several months in a very few lines and resumes his narrative of Vitellius' last days at 15.2: *atque ubique aut superatus aut proditus salutem sibi et milies sestertium a Flavio Sabino Vespasiani fratre pepigit* (c. 17th December). It is therefore necessary for the sake of intelligibility to give a brief account of the background, outbreak and progress of the Flavian revolt.

Although this revolt began on 1st July, 69, when the legions of Egypt under Tiberius Julius Alexander proclaimed Vespasian (*H.* 2.79; S. *Vesp.* 6.3), it is clear that planning started much earlier. The official Flavian version as given in Josephus' *Bellum Iudaicum*, a work which bore Titus' own *imprimatur* (Joseph. *Vit.* 363), was that Vespasian was angered at reports of the conduct of Vitellius and his troops after their arrival in Rome, but that contemplating his distance from Italy he did nothing until forced by his equally outraged soldiers to make a bid for power (*BJ* 4.585-621). This is utterly tendentious, since Vitellius probably did not reach Rome until at least late June and there simply was not time for word of his behaviour *there* to reach the East before 1st July (though news of his behaviour before his arrival in Rome could conceivably have reached the East by this date). Both S. and Dio suggest Flavian thoughts of revolt early in 69 (*Vesp.* 5.1; Dio 65.8.3), while Tacitus seems to have suspected even earlier Flavian planning; cf. *H.* 2.5.2: Vespasian in Judaea and C. Licinius Mucianus in Syria had composed their differences at the time of Nero's death through the agency of Titus; *H.* 2.7: they decided to let Otho and Vitellius fight it out – *igitur arma in occasionem distulere*; cf. *H.* 2.6. Also, although we hear at *H.* 1.10.3 that neither Vespasian's wishes nor feelings were hostile to Galba, the mission of Titus described in *H.* 2.1-10 seems to have been very slow-moving: Galba was formally recognized as Emperor in June, 68, and yet by the latter part of January, 69, Titus had only reached Corinth. On this point we should also note Chilver's conclusion (*JRS* 47 [1957] 34): 'The penetration of Vespasian's agents into high circles is almost more extraordinary than that of Galba's; the ubiquity of his party was embarrassing when it came to paying off his debts.'

When the time for the actual revolt arrived, everything went smoothly and all the carefully-laid plans were put into operation: levies were organized, arrangements were made for the manufacture of weapons and the minting of coinage, and individuals were won over with promises of prefectures and procuratorial positions and adlections to the Senate, while a small donative was offered to the troops. Mucianus was to lead the main invasion force, while Titus was to finish off the war in Judaea and Vespasian himself hold Egypt. Envoys were sent to Parthia and Armenia to ensure that no attack would come while the eastern defences of the Empire were reduced. Finally, all the armies and their commanders were instructed to offer service and re-instatement to the members of the now-dismissed Praetorian

Guard of Otho (*H*. 2.80-82).

However, by the time Mucianus reached Byzantium, a great pro-Flavian movement had built up in the Danubian provinces. The leaders in this were M. Antonius Primus, legate of Legio *VII Galbiana/Gemina* (in Pannonia) and Cornelius Fuscus, the imperial procurator in Illyricum. All six legions in the provinces of Pannonia, Dalmatia and Moesia quickly joined the revolt and sent letters seeking support to other legions which had previously fought for Otho against Vitellius (Legio *XIV Gemina Martia Victrix*, then in Britain, and *I Adiutrix* in Spain) and to the Gallic provinces (*H*. 2.85-6). Vitellius learned only of the revolt of Legio *III Gallica* before the whole Danubian area went over to Vespasian (*H*. 2.96.1).

Antonius Primus and Cornelius Fuscus moved with incredible (and reckless) speed and pushed quite far into Italy with only vexillations. The legions gradually caught up with them, but at its peak the invasion force from the Danubian area consisted of five legions only (c. 30,000 men; cf. *H*. 3.6-10). Vitellius had at least twice that number in Italy; he dispatched Caecina and Valens to face the invaders but (this was the crucial thing and Antonius may have known of it beforehand) Caecina was already wavering in his loyalty, even before he left Rome for the north. He was jealous of Valens' influence with Vitellius and had apparently been 'got at' by Vespasian's elder brother Flavius Sabinus, the *praefectus urbi* (*H*. 2.99-100). By late October the Flavian forces had overrun Italy as far as the Apennines and had defeated the Vitellian army at the second battle of 'Bedriacum' (on 24/25th October; fought, like the first battle in April on or near the *Via Postumia* to the east of Cremona). After this Vitellian resistance stiffened and the Flavian advance was slow. However, Antonius still led the way (Cornelius Fuscus had been left at Ravenna in charge of the fleet: *H*. 3.12.3) and Mucianus came hurrying behind, considerably delayed by a Dacian invasion of the thinly defended province of Moesia. By 16th December Antonius' troops had reached Ocriculum, 42 *mp* from Rome and there they stopped to celebrate the Saturnalia (beginning 17th December), when the word came that launched them on their final dash for the capital (*H*. 3.78).

**15.1** *octavo imperii mense... in praesentis Vespasiani verba iurarunt*: for the correct chronology, see p. 165. At *Vesp*. 6.3 S. correctly places

Vespasian's acclamation by the legions of the East in early July, so why the apparent muddle here? The reasons probably lie in the events of April, 69: vexillations from Moesia had reached Aquileia in April and there learned of Otho's defeat and death; they had then gone on an enraged rampage and, according to S. (*Vesp.* 6.3), *at that time* actually proclaimed Vespasian Emperor. Tacitus adds that these troops then began to plan a revolt on Vespasian's behalf (*H.* 2.85). In later years, therefore, the soldiers from this army could, and probably did, claim that they were the first to support Vespasian – hence S.'s order of events in this sentence. However, his *octavo imperii mense* reflects the chronological truth about the revolt in the Danubian provinces: it came in August, 69, in the eighth month after Vitellius' proclamation in Germany.

*ad retinendum ergo ceterorum... largitus est*: perhaps it was his extravagance in his increasingly frantic attempts to retain popular support which accounted for the squandering of HS 900 million by Vitellius. It is easier to believe that such an enormous sum was used for this purpose than for banquets.

*dilectum quoque ea condicione in urbe egit ut... polliceretur*: this was about 9th December, 69. According to Tacitus (*H.* 3.58.2) the levy took place only after Vitellius' botched attempt to hold the line of the Apennines and lead his troops in person. This failed because of appalling omens and Vitellius returned to ease and inaction in Rome (*H.* 3.55-57). S.'s chronology here is very muddled; for the next sentence, which summarizes events up to about 17th December, begins *urgenti deinde...*, which suggests that the second battle of Bedriacum and the Flavian drive southwards came *after* the levy described here.

**15.2** *hinc fratrem cum classe ac tironibus et gladiatorum manu opposuit*: again this appears somewhat muddled, probably as a result of excessive compression by S.; cf. *H.* 3.57-58, where Tacitus gives much more detail. What remained of the fleet at Misenum deserted (late November). Vitellius eventually dispatched his brother Lucius with six (praetorian) cohorts and 500 cavalry towards Campania (c. 9th December): he was moderately successful and re-captured Tarracina, which the rebels had seized (*H.* 3.77). L. Vitellius remained in S. Latium with his troops and surrendered after the fall of Rome

(*H*. 4.2.2-3.2). Accordingly, S.'s next sentence (still part of his summary) beginning *ubique aut superatus aut proditus* is also misleading.

*hinc Betriacenses copias et duces*: *sc*. C. Fabius Valens and A. Caecina Alienus. Valens was seriously ill when Vitellius sent his troops towards the north of Italy to face the coming invasion of the Danubian legions (c. mid-September, 69). Caecina, therefore, whose loyalty was wavering if not completely undermined, commanded all the forces, and although Valens was urged on by Vitellius to follow Caecina as soon as possible (he appears to have left Rome about ten days after Caecina; cf. *H*. 3.36.1, but this is denied by J. Nicols, *Vespasian and the Partes Flavianae* [Wiesbaden, 1978] 80), he moved very slowly and failed to prevent the defection of Caecina. Instead of heading north from Umbria Valens turned aside into Etruria where he heard of the Vitellian disaster at Cremona. He then decided to sail for Narbonese Gaul and raise fresh forces for Vitellius in Gaul and Germany (*H*. 3.41-42). However, he was captured at the Stoechades Insulae (Isles d'Hyères, to the east of Massilia: *H*. 3.43), brought back to Italy and eventually executed at Urvinum (Hortense, near Mevania) about 10th December, 69 (*H*. 3.62). Caecina flourished until 79 when he was suddenly accused of plotting against the Flavian regime and executed (S. *Tit*. 6.2; Dio 66.16.3-4; see further, J.A. Crook, *AJP* 72 [1951] 162-75). It is clear then that S.'s words *atque ubique aut superatus aut proditus* refer mainly to the activities of Vitellius' *Betriacenses copias et duces*.

*salutem sibi et milies sestertium a Flavio Sabino Vespasiani fratre pepigit*: for the figures involved, see above *G*. 5.2 nn. According to Tacitus (*H*. 3.63.2), the Flavian commanders Arrius Varus and Antonius Primus and Mucianus all sent frequent letters to Vitellius offering him his life, money and a retreat in Campania, but it was only after several conversations with Flavius Sabinus that a deal was worked out, with Cluvius Rufus and the poet Silius Italicus the only witnesses (*H*. 3.65.2). On T. Flavius Sabinus, Vespasian's elder brother, see pp. 154, 166; on his character, see K.G. Wallace, *Historia* 36 (1987) 343-58; for his death, see below *Vit*. 15.3, n. on *succensoque templo Iovis Optimi Maximi oppressit*.

*statimque pro gradibus Palati... rem distulit*: Tacitus gives us only one attempted abdication, but this is preceded by a speech allegedly containing the arguments against abdication used by Vitellius' most devoted followers (*H.* 3.66-68). It looks as if Tacitus has eliminated the initial attempt (though something of the sort is implied by the counter arguments of Vitellius' supporters) so as to build up the emotional and rhetorical effect of the formal occasion (*H.* 3.68).

*nocte interposita*: this probably implies that the first attempted abdication came during the evening.

*primo diluculo sordidatus ad rostra... e libello testatus est*: Tacitus gives us the valuable information that this happened on 18th December (*H.* 3.67.2). The first attempt, therefore, came on 17th December. In 15.3-4 below S. describes yet another attempted abdication, *after* the burning of the Capitol on 19th December. In his very quickly changing moods (on these, see Dio 65.16.3-5) Vitellius may well have tried to abdicate once more, and it looks as if Tacitus has artistically reshaped a somewhat repetitive and untidy reality; at any rate, it is easier to imagine that three attempts were reduced to one than to explain how a single attempt came to be tripled.

**15.3** *animum resumpsit Sabinumque et reliquos Flavianos nihil iam metuentis vi subita in Capitolium compulit*: this took place on 18th December. Here more than almost anywhere else the hand of the Flavian propagandist can be seen, because the burning of the Cap-itoline Temple of Jupiter, Juno and Minerva was a most shocking event (cf. *H.* 3.72) and naturally the Flavians cast the blame for this on Vitellius and his supporters. There are, however, two main points: who was responsible for the decision of Sabinus and his friends to take refuge on the Capitol in the first place (S. has no doubts on this score), and who was to blame for the burning of the Capitol? The second point was the crucial one and Flavian propaganda was prepared to accept some blame on the first to ensure a more telling effect on the second. According to Josephus (*BJ* 4.645) the seizure of the Capitol was undertaken by Sabinus on his own initiative because Ἀνεθάρσει δὲ ἤδη καὶ...Σαβῖνος, ὡς πλησίον Ἀντώνιος ὢν ἀπηγγέλλετο ['And now Sabinus...also regained his courage when the approach of Ant-onius was reported']. With Sabinus safely dead, his somewhat botched attempt in Rome to take over from the (now theoretically) ex-Emperor could be used to delimit what little blame the Flavians felt they deserved for the disaster. Of course, this leads to a much more hostile account of the actual burning of the temple (see next n.).

*succensoque templo Iovis Optimi Maximi oppressit*: cf. Joseph. *BJ* 4.649 (*after* the capture of the Capitoline hill): Σαβῖνος ἀναχθεὶς ἐπὶ Οὐιτέλλιον ἀναιρεῖται, διαρπάσαντές τε οἱ στρατιῶται τὰ ἀναθήματα τὸν ναὸν ἐνέπρησαν ['Sabinus was led before Vitellius and killed, while the soldiers plundered the offerings in the temple and set it on fire']. Dio (65.17.3) is very similar but not quite so extreme since he has the temple plundered and burnt *during* the assault, rather than cold-bloodedly afterwards. Tacitus has his doubts about this episode: he is inclined to think that the Flavians used fire first (to block the approach of the Vitellians) and that the flames spread and so the temple was (accidentally) burned down *clausis foribus indefensum et indireptum* (*H*. 3.71.4). His account is thoughtful and, if not wholly clear, seems at least to be based on personal research and careful scrutiny of the evidence (cf. A. Briessmann, *Tacitus und das flavische Geschichtsbild* [Wiesbaden, 1955] 69-80; see also T.P. Wiseman, *AJAH* 3 [1978] 163-78; K. Wellesley, *AJAH* 6 [1981] 166-90).

It seems clear that Flavius Sabinus and his companions were taken prisoner during the assault and that Sabinus was brought before Vitellius and then killed. S's summary *oppressit* assigns the blame for this to Vitellius himself, which no other source does so explicitly. The burning of the Capitol and the deaths of Flavius Sabinus and many of his followers took place on 19th December. Only Tacitus waxes eloquent on the death of Vespasian's brother (*H*. 3.75.1-2), perhaps because he was aware that it solved a lot of problems: Mucianus is said to have been glad at his murder. Antonius Primus seems to have moved very slowly on the penultimate stage of his advance on Rome (at *H*. 3.78.1 Tacitus speaks of *pravae morae*) – perhaps wishing to have one less rival for Vespasian's favour; and Vespasian himself seems not to have been on wholly good terms with his brother (*H*. 3.65.1).

*cum et proelium et incendium e Tiberiana prospiceret domo inter epulas*: Townend may be correct in stating that this word-picture has a Neronian ring to it (*AJP* [1964] 365) but what does he mean when he says that S. here repeats 'the suggestion, made earlier about Nero, that the man who watches a fire must necessarily have kindled it'?

*non multo post... vocata contione iuravit*: this *contio*, the scene of Vitellius' third attempt at abdication, appears to have been summoned on the same day as the burning of the Capitol, i.e., 19th December.

**15.4** *tunc solutum a latere pugionem... quasi in aede Concordiae positurus abscessit*: mention of Vitellius' dagger makes this perhaps the most serious of his attempts at abdication (for its significance, see *H*. 3.68.2 *velut ius necis vitaeque civium reddebat*). According to Tacitus, Vitellius finally decided to deposit the dagger, which no one would accept, in the Temple of Concord and then go on to his brother's house. However, the people would not let him go to a private dwelling but demanded that he return to the palace.

*sed quibusdam adclamantibus ipsum esse Concordiam... verum etiam Concordiae recipere cognomen*: we could disregard this story as a weird and improbable invention were it not for the fact that *Concordia* is commonly depicted on the reverse side of Vitellian coins from the mint of Rome and the idea of concord obviously weighed heavily with him (see Mattingly, *BMC Imp. I* ccxxiii; pp. 368-9, 371, 375, 382-4).

**16.1** *suasitque senatui... ad consultandum petituros*: cf. *H*. 3.80.1-81.2; Dio 65.18.3-19.1. Tacitus indicates that there were several groups of envoys and that the Vestal Virgins were sent off last in a desperate attempt to postpone the final Flavian attack.

*postridie responsa opperienti*: the date is 20th December, the day on which Rome fell and Vitellius was killed. Flavius Sabinus had sent a message to Antonius Primus during the night (18-19th December) before the assault on the Flavian group on the Capitol (*H*. 3.69.4). The message reached Antonius at Ocriculum (42 *mp* from Rome) sufficiently early on 19th December for him to march his army the 35 *mp* to Saxa Rubra (7 *mp* from Rome) by very late on the same day (*H*. 3.79.1) – a most noteworthy and exceptional achievement.

S. does not mention the cavalry column sent ahead, probably from Interamna, under the command of Petilius Cerealis, to move cross country to join the *Via Salaria* and then advance south to stage a diversionary attack on Rome (*H*. 3.78.3). When the news of the attack on the Capitol reached Petilius he rushed in to attack the city. This misfired badly and he was repulsed (19th December: *H.* 3.79; Dio 65.18.3). However, the final Flavian assault came on 20th December with Antonius' forces dividing into three columns after they had crossed the Milvian Bridge and Petilius' cavalry re-joining the fight (*H.* 3.82-84.3; Dio 65.19.1-20).

*continuo igitur...ut inde in Campaniam fugeret*: cf. *H.* 3.84.4. Tacitus omits the number and occupations of Vitellius' companions. The *pistor* and *cocus* seem unlikely but S. cannot resist one last stab at Vitellius' gluttony. Finally, S.'s reference to Campania is not immediately clear; for this Tacitus has *ut... Tarracinam ad cohortes fratremque perfugeret*.

*ubi cum deserta omnia repperisset... confugitque in cellulam ianitoris, religato pro foribus cane lectoque et culcita obiectis*: Dio (65.20.1) says that he actually hid in a kennel. That a *ianitor* should have dogs is highly likely, and so Dio and S. are probably referring to more-or-less the same place. Tacitus (*H.* 3.84.4) suddenly becomes reticent and mentions only *pudenda latebra*.

**17.1** *irruperant iam agminis antecessores*: *sc.* into the palace.

*sciscitantes... ubi esse Vitellium sciret*: literally, 'asking repeatedly ...where he knew Vitellius to be'. The construction is somewhat odd, but the meaning at least is reasonably clear: the soldiers who broke into the palace *assumed* that this man (whoever he was) knew where Vitellius was lurking and they demanded that he tell them. Rolfe's 'they asked...if he knew where Vitellius was' and Graves' 'asked... whether he knew the Emperor's whereabouts' seem really to be translations of Madvig's emendation *ubi esset Vitellius num sciret*, which is, perhaps, unnecessary.

*deinde agnitus... ut custodiretur interim vel in carcere*: this is unique to S.

*donec religatis post terga manibus, iniecto cervicibus laqueo... per totum viae Sacrae spatium*: Dio 65.20.2-3 is almost identical; Tacitus (*H.* 3.84.5) has a similar but briefer account.

*reducto coma capite, ceu noxii solent*: cf. *H.* 3.85; Dio 65.21.1. For the practice of treating condemned criminals in this way, cf. Pliny, *Paneg.* 34.3: *nihil tamen gratius, nihil saeculo dignius, quam quod contigit desuper intueri delatorum supina ora retortasque cervices*.

**17.2** *parte vulgi etiam corporis vitia exprobrante*: at this point S., with somewhat tasteless artistry, works in the physical description of his subject which often comes just before the end of a life (cf. *Ner.* 51; *G.* 21; *O.* 12.1; *Dom.* 18).

*tandem apud Gemonias minutissimus ictibus excarnificatus atque confectus est et inde unco tractus in Tiberim*: S. does not give us the story of the German (? praetorian) who tried to kill Vitellius quickly (Dio 65.21.1; cf. *H.* 3.84.5), nor does he give us Vitellius' rather dignified reply to those who insulted him: *una vox non degeneris animi excepta cum tribuno insultanti se tamen imperatorem eius fuisse respondit* (*H.* 3.85; cf. Dio 65.21.2). The Scalae Gemoniae climbed the slope of the Arx between the Carcer and the Temple of Concord, on the east side of the Capitoline Hill.

**18.1** *periit... anno vitae septimo quinquagesimo*: for the date of Vitellius' death, calculations begin with Tacitus' statement that Vitellius attempted to abdicate on 18th December (*H.* 3.67), and it is clear both from Tacitus' account of events thereafter and from Josephus' dating of the fall of Rome to the third day of the month Apellaeus (*BJ* 4.654; this appears to be in accordance with the Tyrian version of the Macedonian calendar adapted to the Julian system; see E.J. Bickerman, *Chronology of the Ancient World*[2] [London, 1980] 48) that Vitellius was killed on 20th December, A.D. 69. For the date of Vitellius' birth, see above, 3.2 n. on *A. Vitellius... cons.*

*cum fratre et filio*: this is rather imprecise. L. Vitellius was apparently on his way to Rome from Tarracina when the city fell to the Flavians (Dio 65.22.1; *H.* 4.2.2-3) and he surrendered with his troops near Bovillae on the Via Appia, 10 *mp* from Rome. According to Dio, he had been promised his life but was killed anyway. This was probably only a day or two after his brother's death. For the death of Vitellius' son, see *H.* 4.80.1; Dio 65.22.2 and above *Vit.* 6, n. on *liberos utriusque sexus tulit*.

*Antonio Primo*: on this curious story, see above *Vit.* 9, n. on *pro tribunali iura reddenti gallinaceus supra umerum ac deinde in capite astitit*. For the idea that S. saw the fall of Vitellius as divine vengeance, see E. Cizek, *REA* 77 (1975) 125-30.

# *Appendix A*

## The Sulpicii Galbae

P. Sulpicius Ser. f. P. n. Saverrio (97)
cos. 304 B.C., cens. 300 B.C., interrex 298 B.C.

P. Sulpicius P. f. Ser. n. Saverrio (98)
cos. 279 B.C.

[Servius Sulpicius Galba]

P. Sulpicius Ser. f. P. n. Galba Maximus (64)
cos. 211, 200 B.C., dict. 203 B.C.

Ser. Sulpicius Galba (56)
aed. cur. 209 B.C., pont. 203-199 B.C.

C. Sulpicius Galba (49)
pont. 202-199 B.C.

Ser. Sulpicius Galba (57)
pr. urb. 187 B.C.

C. Sulpicius Galba (50)
pont. 174 B.C., pr. urb. 171 B.C.

Ser. Sulpicius Ser. f. P. n. Galba (58)
pr. 151 B.C. (Hisp. Ult.), cos. 144 B.C.

Ser. Sulpicius Ser. f. Ser. n. Galba (59)
pr. 111 B.C.(?), cos. 108 B.C.

C. Sulpicius Galba (51)
triumv. (agr. dand.?) 121-118(?) B.C.
pr. -, aug.(?) 109 B.C.

C. Sulpicius C. f. (Galba) (9)
triumv. mon. c. 103-102 B.C.

Ser. Sulpicius C. f. Galba (60)
pr. (by 91 B.C.), leg. 90-88, 86 B.C.

Ser. Sulpicius Galba (61)
leg. 61 B.C., pr. 54 B.C.

?                    ?

Ser. Sulpicius (Galba?) (20)
triumv. mon. c. 54 B.C.

Sulpicia (113)

C. Sulpicius Galba (52)
historian

C. Sulpicius Galba (53)
cos. suff. 5 B.C.
m. (1) Mummia Achaica (2) Livia Ocellina

?Ser. Sulpicius Galba (62)
cos. -

C. Sulpicius Galba (54)
cos. ord. A.D. 22

Ser. Sulpicius Galba (63)
*PRINCEPS*
m. Lepida

Sulpiciae Galbillae (118) Sulpicius (4)

two sons

174

# Appendix B

## Otho's Principate, March-April, 69

(Events in *italics* are less certain approximations)

MARCH
3    Summons dispatched to legions of Dalmatia and Pannonia (and Moesia). Immediate preparations for sending of 'advance guard' to N. Italy and amphibious force to Narbonese Gaul

*Praetorian outbreak*

4    *Dispatch of expedition to Narbonese Gaul*

*Advance Guard leaves Rome*

14   Otho's final *contio*

15   Otho's departure with large part of Senate

*Suetonius Paulinus and Marius Celsus depart for north with cavalry escort*

25/26 *Spurinna arrives in Placentia (384 mp from Rome)*

27/28 *Spurinna takes his troops on two-day march*

30/31 Caecina's assault on Placentia

APRIL
2/3  *Caecina in position in fortified camp at Cremona*

5    Battle *ad Castores*

7    Valens' advance units reach Cremona

8    *Otho reaches Brixellum*

9    *Otho travels to Bedriacum*

10   Strategic conference of Othonian commanders at Bedriacum

11   Otho returns to Brixellum

13   Othonian forces advance from Bedriacum towards Cremona

14   Battle of 'Bedriacum' (near Cremona)

16   Suicide of Otho

18   News of Otho's death reaches Rome

19   Senate formally recognizes Vitellius